Law and Economics

Erik Røsæg, Hans-Bernd Schäfer and Endre Stavang, Editors
Eva Dobos, Assistant editor

Law and Economics

Essays in Honour of Erling Eide

CAPPELEN
AKADEMISK FORLAG

ISBN 978-82-02-33611-0
1. utgave, 1. opplag 2010

Omslagsdesign: Christian Næss, Næss Design
Utsnitt fra 100-kroner seddel: Sverre Morken © Sverre Morken/BONO 2010
Portrett av Erling Eide, s. 7: Maren Arna Eide
Sats: Brødr. Fossum AS
Trykk og innbinding: AIT Oslo AS, 2010

www.cappelenakademisk.no
e-post: cafinfo@cappelendamm.no

Contents

Tabula Gratulatoria

Arne Alnæs
Mads Henry Andenæs
Finn Arnesen
John Asland
Anne and Hjalmar Austbø
Bjørg Bachke
Inger Lorange Backer
Bettina Banoun
Trygve Bergsåker
Jon Bing
Erik M. Boe
Roger Bowles
Thor Magnus Bronder
Herman Bruserud
Tore Bråthen
Erle Moestue Bugge and
Hans Christian Bugge
Kirsti Strøm Bull and Hans Jacob Bull
Vidar og Eva Karine Christiansen
Robert D. Cooter
Det juridiske fakultet,
Universitet i Oslo
Det juridiske fakultetsbibliotek,
Universitetet i Oslo
Det juridiske fakultet,
Universitet i Tromsø
Eva Dobos
Anders Eckhoff
Jan and Gro Eide
Marna and Kristine Eide
Åge Eide
Jon Elster
Svein Eng
Thordis Eriksen
Stein Evju
Ole Kristian Fauchald
Nils-Henrik von der Fehr
Per Racin Fosmark
Finn R. Førsund
Johan Giertsen
Ingeborg Glambak and
Nils Roll-Hansen
Hans Petter Graver
Karl-Anders Grønland
Viggo Hagstrøm
Marit Halvorsen
Jan E. Helgesen
Erik Hernæs
Christopher H. Heyerdahl
Jens P. Heyerdahl D.Y.
Michael Hoel
Torild Alnæs and Frederik Hoffmann

Marianne Jenum Hotvedt
Helge Hveem
Aanund Hylland
Westye Høegh
Institutt for kriminologi og rettsosiologi, Universitetet i Oslo
Institutt for privatrett, Universitetet i Oslo
Henning Jakhelln
Knut Kaasen
Asbjørn Kjønstad
Bente Klingenberg and Tore Bjørn-Hansen
Ellen and Olav E. Klingenberg
Kluge Advokatfirma DA
Unn Kløve
Henrik Lando
Annema and Jens J. Langballe
Kari and Sverre Lie
Kåre Lilleholt
Tore Lunde
Borghild and Knut H. Lykke
Gert-Fredrik Malt
Halvor Mehlum
Dag Michalsen
Ester Moen
Guiditta Cordero Moss
Kalle Määttä
Harald Ness
Gunnar Nordén
Nordisk institutt for sjørett
Tone Ognedal
Anthony Ogus
Leif Petter Olaussen
Øystein Ore
Hedvig Bugge Reiersen
Gunhild Ramm Reistad and Kjell Arne Reistad
Marianne Reusch
Vidar Ringstad
Ole-Andreas Rognstad
Erik Røsæg
Anders Ryssdal
Parvati and Per Sandven
Dag Wiese Schartum
Erik Schultz
Hans-Bernd Schäfer
Randi and David Scott
Hilde and Francis Sejersted
Beate Sjåfjell
Henry E. Smith
Lucy and Carsten Smith
Endre Stavang
Geir Stenseth
Halvor Stenstadvold
Are Stenvik
Katia Stieglitz
Bernt P. Stigum
Steinar Strøm
Studiegruppen Actor
Tone Sverdrup
Aslak Syse
Birthe Taraldset
Royall Tyler
Terese Smith Ulseth
Monica Viken
Grace Kennan Warnecke
Elisabeth and Nils-Petter Wedege
Hilde Westbye
Trine-Lise Wilhelmsen
Geir Woxholth
Hans-Magnus Ystgaard
Frederik Zimmer

Foreword

The purpose of this collection of essays in law and economics is to shed new light on subject matter that Erling Eide has taken an interest in during his academic career – as student, teacher and scholar. On this occasion, it is not Erling himself that presents his take. Rather, it is his colleagues. And given his broad education and range of interests, it is only fitting that this volume does not only include articles that analyze the law from the economic point of view, but also makes room for other contributions at the intersection of economics and law or of relevance to it. We are quite sure that this is in the spirit of our dear colleague now turning 70.

Hamburg/Oslo, June 2010

Erik Røsæg Hans-Bernd Schäfer Endre Stavang

Erling Eide and Economic Analysis of Law

Endre Stavang

Economic Analysis of Law Breaking Through

During the time Erling Eide has been employed as a professor of economics at the University of Oslo, Faculty of Law, economic analysis of law has flourished both inside and outside our law school, and Erling's role in all of this has been prominent. He has worked almost exclusively in this field for the past thirty years, and he was one of the founding fathers of the European Association for Law and Economics which has held yearly conferences since 1984. Since then, economic analysis has become part of the curriculum at many European universities, and there are a number of Master of Law and Economics programs, including one with *Erasmus Mundus* status. In addition to the fact that many doctoral students in law take some interest in the field and also apply its learning in a number of cases, there is now even a European doctoral program in law and economics.

> "Why did economic analysis of law have its breakthrough in your time, do you think, and why is its success nevertheless more limited in Europe than in America up until the present time?"

"It is difficult to explain history. Sometimes individuals have a decisive influence. Undoubtedly, Coase's work on transaction costs has been a great inspiration for what has been called the 'new law and economics', as distinguished from the traditional economic analysis of competition law, tax law, etc. Economists and lawyers gradually understood the importance of transaction costs in explaining the existence of various institutions and in designing efficient law. A related, but nevertheless separate, development was the Chicago inspired analyses of various regulations introduced by what was considered as overly optimistic rule-makers. Moreover, a number of law schools in the US have a tradition for multi-disciplinary activity that is less common in Europe. Their tradition includes the American Legal Realism which to some extent paved the road for law and economics in the US. It is possible that the Scandinavian Legal Realism has had a somewhat similar role in our country. To my knowledge, our university was the first in Europe to introduce law and economics as a compulsory course for law students, in 1996. South of Scandinavia, law has traditionally been more self-contained and less penetrable. In recent years, however, the strong law and economics movement has made advances in law schools in almost every country."

Supply and Demand

> "Well, it takes two to tango, as they say. So what about on the economists' side, I guess you can call it the 'supply side', is it your impression that economists have always been interested in law – what was the situation at the University of Oslo in the past and when you were a student?"

"Our great academic lawyers of the nineteenth century, in particular A.M. Schweigaard, also mastered the type of economic analysis available at the time. Schweigaard may be considered the first law and economics professor in this country. For some reason this tradition lost its strength, and as everywhere else, more specialized disciplines grew out of the old ones. From the 1930s our Nobel Laureates Ragnar Frisch and Trygve Haavelmo developed economics into a more scientific activity by constructing mathematical models of economic relationships and by testing such relationships using econometric methods. The result, which also included complex planning models, has been called the Oslo School. There was a price for this development, however. History and law, and thereby important sources for the explanation of economic phenomena, were neglected. At the end of my studies, when I was asked to give a talk on what economics could tell us about the role of private property, I realized that the question was hardly treated in the curriculum. In order not to reveal my ignorance, I did not accept the invitation. Towards the end of last century, however, applications of economic theory to institutions and to more specific problems in various parts of society have flourished, in Oslo as everywhere else. The gap between economics and law was gradually narrowed. Now, the study of institutions is rather common."

"Why was Coase maybe read but not used in Scandinavian economics prior to 1980?"

"When I studied economics in the 1960s, Coase's article *The Problem of Social Cost* was on the reading list, but I cannot remember that this article or its content was ever mentioned in lectures or in discussions among students. The main reason for this negligence probably was that neither economic history nor analyses of institutions were hot topics at the Department of Economics. A dominant topic was macroeconomics including fiscal and monetary policy, growth, etc. The standard tool in microeconomics was general equilibrium models in which transaction costs were assumed away."

"So the second and larger part of Coase's paper was seen as largely irrelevant, and the smaller part which included the Coase 'theorem' was unduly seen as a laissez faire endorsement and as merely another dangerous attack on rational state governance from the perspective of the 'Chicago School', I guess. Is that correct, and if so, is it a problem that economic analysis of law was and perhaps still is so closely linked with the University of Chicago?"

"The fact that the law and economics movement started in Chicago and that several of the early contributions revealed inefficiencies in various regulations has not been conducive to a wide and easy acceptance of the discipline. Law and economics, however, is much more than the Chicago School, wealth-maximizing economics. It is mainly a positive science investigating relationships between phenomena defined by the law. Clarifications of such relationships might then be used in normative studies, in the quest for good rules. In recent years, the discipline embraces subfields like behavioral law and economics, institutional economics and other types of analyses quite different from the early Chicago studies."

"And then on 'the demand side', as you might put it, what have you noticed as important changes in attitudes at our law school here in Oslo?"

"For a long time our students have been taught that judges and bureaucrats, when applying the law, sometimes have to consider the effects of their decisions. However, when a new curriculum was introduced in 1996, the importance of studying the purposes and effects of law was given higher priority. Then, nothing was more natural than substituting a course in law and economics for the previous introductory course in macro and micro economics. Analytical tools suitable for analyzing law then became part of the curriculum. I also have the impression that the general attitude towards economic analysis of law has changed somewhat during recent years. It is difficult to remain reluctant toward considering other disciplines as interesting, an attitude also present among academic lawyers, when that discipline is made more relevant for one's own research. I suppose, however, that the main reason for the more positive attitude is the fact that in recent years, law and economics has occupied a predominant position in the literature of the theory of law."

Inter- and multidisciplinary

"What has been your general experience, being the only professor of economics at a law school?"

"Of course it is a drawback not being able to discuss daily with fellow economists, as I did previously in the Department of Economics. Moreover, only relatively few colleagues at the Faculty of Law have shown any interest in analyzing the effect of laws and regulations by use of theories based on rational choice. On the other hand, the analytical work of a handful of younger academic lawyers, some of whom are trained in economics, has been inspiring. I must add that the Department of Private Law has provided very good working conditions."

Erling wrote his book on production functions in the 1970s for the Dr. Philos. degree. Here he shows his interest in cross-disciplinary and multidisciplinary scholarship by combining the latest in economic theory with learning from the field of engineering. Production functions are partly the foundation for the theory of supply. Later he would examine the other part – the theory of individual rationality – which is useful for predicting the supply of labor and of crime.

"How did you experience cross-disciplinary and interdisciplinary scholarship through your own first book? Do you think it is different for lawyers with ambitions in the same direction?"

"My book on production and cost functions for tankers dealt with the effect of prices of fuel and steel on the shape and construction of ship hulls. The idea was that when the price of fuel increases relative to the price of steel, the ship hull has to be constructed so as to reduce the resistance of moving a ship in water. In fact, in periods in which fuel becomes relatively expensive, ships tend to become slimmer in order to reduce resistance, and thus decrease fuel consumption. My impression was that most marine engineers were not that interested in the effect of relative input prices on hull construction. They considered ship construction a question of engineering science and not of economics.

I had to read a substantial amount of literature on marine engineering in order to carry out the necessary analysis, and I suppose that lawyers who engage in economic analyses will experience a similar challenge. Moreover, the period of the simple, early Chicago style analyses seems to be waning, at least in international journals. More refined models are required. However, not all fields of law and economics are equally demanding. It is more difficult to analyze the effects of law regulating phenomena that develop rapidly over time, such as the Internet, than it is to analyze more stable phenomena such as accidents. It is nevertheless advisable for lawyers and economists to cooperate. Co-authoring has become rather common, not only in economics but also in law and economics."

> "OK, but what does it take to cooperate, surely there is much to know: calculus, programming, statistics and econometrics, price, game and growth theory, etc., etc. In your opinion, what is required, and what can be recommended? And, can one become too inter- or multidisciplinary?"

"In my opinion constructive cooperation requires that each party understand what the other is doing. If the analysis requires the use of calculus or econometric modeling, cooperation would be difficult if one of the parties did not understand the basic ideas of such tools. Academic lawyers not trained in the use of such tools should probably concentrate on problems that can be analyzed by simpler analytical methods. Master's theses in law and economics written by our law students demonstrate that interesting results in some areas can be obtained by the use of rather simple methods.

An example of a study which is problematic for lawyers without training in econometrics to evaluate and discuss is a recent statistical test of the hypothesis that the supreme court justices in Norway vote according to the political color of the government that appointed them. Much of the discussion provoked by the test did not in fact relate to the test itself, but to other aspects of the possible relationship.

The faculties of many law schools in the US include people who have graduated both in law and in economics. There are signs that a similar development may take place in Oslo. If so, it would considerably enhance law and economics here."

In the 1980s, after becoming a professor of economics, Erling Eide published important work on the law of obligations and worked on the economics of crime. In the latter case, he took clues from Bentham and Becker, but his work is richer and more thorough, analytically as well as empirically. It is also based on Norwegian data. His monograph on crime and rational behavior is among the best in this field.

> "How has your work in criminology been received by specialists of criminal law: Have there been many heated debates and queries concerning the data and the results of your studies?"

"I would be surprised if more than a couple of Norwegian criminologists, at most, have read my main book in this field. I have only seen a lack of interest, basically. The lack of interest in the substantial international literature on the economics of crime is remarkable. I suppose the reason is that many Norwegian criminologists are only moderately interested in general deterrence and also that they confuse economic analysis of crime with a certain 'tough-on-crime' ideology."

> "Do you see any parallels between the criminologists' attitude toward the economics of crime and the attitude of the Oslo School of (Macro) Economics toward the new economic analysis of law and property rights in the 1950s and 1960s?"

"I think there are four main reasons for neglecting other disciplines. First, researchers are often so deeply involved in developing their own theories that they do not have the time or capacity to consider other points of view. Second, they might be afraid of being assailed by what could be a serious competitor. Third, they see the weaknesses of other disciplines and consider the weaknesses of their own discipline as much less serious. Fourth, it is necessary to invest your time and effort in order to understand other disciplines, and it is tempting, even advisable, to stick to what you know. I think all four reasons might have been of some importance in the criminologists' neglect of economics of crime. The Oslo School's neglect of adjacent fields of research was more related to the first reason, deep involvement in their own theories."

"We have talked about the criminologists, but what about the lawyers in the field of criminal law – my impression from being a judge and from being a part of the profession is that general deterrence is very much a 'working hypothesis' and a basic justification for punishment. Surely, the professors of criminal law must have taken a keen interest in your work?"

"It is remarkable that a profession that has such confidence in general deterrence shows so little interest in empirical studies of the effect of changes in sanctions. If you look through textbooks used by our faculty, both in criminal law or criminology, you will find them extremely brief and outdated in terms of empirical studies of general deterrence. When the Attorney General some years ago called for more severe sanctions, he failed to answer a question about the kind of empirical studies upon which he based his demand. As a whole, the economics of crime is almost a non-topic at our faculty of law. It is interesting that some economists show more interest. At the university college in Bodø where they use an introductory textbook I have written on the subject, the economics of crime has been among the more popular subjects for many years."

In 1996, Eide transformed his course in economics for lawyers to a course in economic analysis of (public) law. He had his hesitations, because the price – due to curricular constraints – was having to throw out Keynes and other macroeconomists. He did not do this lightheartedly, but he thought that it was the right decision, given the benefits of professional utility and fruitfulness for lawyers.

"How do you regard today the decision not to teach macroeconomics to lawyers?"

"It was a hard, but necessary decision. The time allocated to economics in the study of law was insufficient to allow both an introduction to microeconomics and the application of this theory to the study if law, in addition to macroeconomics. Macroeconomics had to cede in order to have time for what I consider to be the most important topics for lawyers."

"Yes, and the new course, which focuses quite a lot on private law, seems to be quite successful, and this relates back to the fact that your office has always been located in the halls of the Department of Private Law. Do you think that scholars of torts, contracts and property are more open to economic analysis than scholars of public law, and if so: Why?"

"The international literature in law and economics is dominated by questions of private law. On the other hand economic analysis has traditionally dealt with questions of public law. Examples are tax law, environmental law and constitutional law, in addition to regulations related to financial and monetary policy. Moreover, it is my impression that there is a growing literature of administrative law in journals of law and economics. I do not think scholars of public law are uninterested in such studies."

"A final question, Erling: Economics is forward-looking, and if you look forward, what are the most exciting problems and potential projects in front of us, in your personal opinion?"

"In general, the most important aspect of law is its preoccupation with the uncertainties of life. Law regulates activities in order to reduce risk and uncertainty, and it decides what should be done as a consequence of an accident or a breach of contract. Academic lawyers, as well as legislators, are not well trained in evaluating risk and uncertainty. The effects of all laws and regulations are uncertain. In order to evaluate the effect of legal norms, familiarity with theories of risk and uncertainty is necessary. So far, students do not learn anything about the required theory of risk and uncertainty.

Experiments indicate that doctors make serious mistakes when they have to combine (only) two uncertain symptoms of illness. Judges may be expected to perform just as poorly when they have to combine two pieces of uncertain evidence."

Compelling Public Interest

Bettina Banoun and Anders Ryssdal

Constitutional review in Norway

In most Western jurisdictions there are mechanisms in place to control the constitutionality of parliamentary and subordinate legislation. Under the Norwegian Constitution, and constitutional practice for more than 150 years, this authority vests with the courts, and finally the Supreme Court. The constitutionality of new legislation is not tried prior to its enactment or execution (even though the Norwegian Constitution Article 83 theoretically allows for such an advance check). Rather, after legislation is enacted and executed, affected citizens and firms may challenge the validity of the rules at issue by alleging breach of constitutional rules in ordinary court proceedings.

This means that the Norwegian system creates a *conflict* between the state represented by the government in court on behalf of Parliament as legislator, and disenchanted private parties to solve a constitutional issue. The constitutional issue may also be raised in litigation between private parties, but then the government has a right to intervene procedurally.

Checking the constitutionality of legislation is not treated as a bureaucratic or parliamentarian exercise, but as a fully fledged legal fight between the state, with all its powers and resources, and the private citizen or business concerned. Invariably, if a constitutional challenge appears to have some merit, the Norwegian Supreme Court will, in the final instance, refer the case to Grand Chamber or Plenary treatment.

This system places the Supreme Court as the guardian of the Constitution. Under the adversary and prosecutorial principles followed in civil and criminal trials, it is up to each party to prepare its case. The government has unlimited resources at its disposal when it seeks to defend legislation as being constitutional – in reality, the state representation is carried at the tax payers' expense. However, the private party may also have resources at its disposal, in particular when a group of citizens or firms is affected, and this group pools the resources at its disposal to counterbalance the government in court.

One such spectacular conflict was solved in the Norwegian Supreme Court in early 2010, and the Supreme Court upon a full plenary hearing passed judgment on 12 February 2010.[1] The conflict concerned a resourceful group – shipping companies – and the topic was whether a tax amendment passed by Parliament would have adverse, allegedly unconstitutional retroactive effects. The shipping companies asserted that earlier legislation allowed income from shipping to be tax exempt, as long as such income was kept in a closed loop, that is, only used for investments in new shipping activities. The government introduced a new shipping tax regime, which allowed for new investments to be made tax exempt, but at the same time abolished the said earlier legislation with the effect that over a 10-year period some 13 billion Norwegian kroner previously thought to be tax exempt, would have to be taxed. There has probably been no other case which has involved such high monetary values in the Norwegian court system, and the legal battle became a primary topic of discussion among lawyers, politicians and media observers.

In this article we wish to take a look at the court case, the effect of the judgment, and the application of the ban against retroactive laws in the Constitution of Norway Article 97. We advance the view that even if the monetary values were immense for the shipping companies, and even if the political connotations of the fight were obvious (pitting a Labour and Socialist Centre government against a group widely viewed as capitalists) the most important effect of the judgment is *not* its consequences for the distribution of income, but consequences that cannot easily be measured. The judgment's effect on future tax legislation, on citizens' confidence in legislation as well as the system of government and on the effectiveness of the Supreme Court's own powers of constitutional review are more important consequences than the monetary values involved. In reality, the government itself was a chief beneficiary of the Supreme Court majority's decision. To turn the decisive criterion used upside down, we conclude that the "compelling public interest" and the protection of democratic majority rule

1 Bergshav Tankers et al. v. The State.

favours upholding the constitutional principle at issue – not the other way around.

Constitutional rights

Initially it should be observed that, for a sitting government, constitutional bans can represent obstacles to the advancement of their policies. Even so, most Western constitutions allow for some constitutional protection of minorities against majority legislation. To be effective, this protection – in the form of particular "rights" – resides on a level above parliamentary enacted legislation, so that the constitution or constitutionally evolved principles trump all subordinate legislation. The stark reality is thus that the majority does *not* rule absolutely. Its authority is constrained by rights offered even to a minority of one person (or a politically indigestible group such as shipping companies) able to claim the right to constitutional protection.[2]

Against such a backdrop, it is tempting for politicians to regard constitutional rights as a wrench in the wheel of democratic government, and in the present case the political rhetoric backing the tax legislation at issue was richly steeped in needs to support deserving income redistribution policies over the alleged economic privileges of the shipping companies.

Under Norwegian law, constitutional protection is real, in the sense that it will be applied if a majority of the Supreme Court finds that the Constitution checks a particular piece of legislation. This means that we must take a brief look at the policy rationale of constitutional rights.

A striking feature of constitutionally protected rights is that they never advance *only* the interests of private parties. We do not see constitutional protection of rights as a blanket permit for individuals to do as they wish, if there is no policy justification underpinning a right which also distributes positive externalities to the citizenry at large. Take for instance freedom of speech (Article 100) – it is a right enjoyed by every individual to say what is on that person's mind, but at the

---

2 For an overview of the economics of constitutional rights, see Richard Posner, *Economic Analysis of Law,* 7th ed., pp. 684–685. Posner makes a distinction between freedom from interference, so-called "negative rights", and positive rights which require expenditure of resources such as e.g. a "right" to education. Constitutional rights are for good reasons mostly of the negative character.

same time freedom of speech is commonly acknowledged to be a precondition for informed political debate and for society to unmask all kinds of opinions, rather than drive their sponsors underground. The right as such is of even greater aggregate value than the interests of each individual to use the right.

Some of the same also applies for the ban against retroactive laws (Article 97), to which we turn in more detail below. This ban is historically underpinned by various policy considerations – one is the concern that the sovereign could otherwise enact laws ex post to provide a sheen of legitimacy for actions that were in reality only intended to punish the sovereign's enemies and take their lives, freedom or property. More important today, the ban against retroactive legislation greatly facilitates the general operation of the legal order. It is sufficient for any individual to check what laws are on the books, without having to fear that these laws – at the time that the status quo is being checked – will later be amended retroactively so that the "status quo" could be misleading. However in income and wealth tax cases it has been accepted that the law can be changed retroactively within the same tax year.

Even if easily explained from the perspective of such important public policy considerations, it is of course also true that constitutional framers, like legislators in parliament, suffer from lack of perfect foresight. Constitutional protection will not always operate to ensure the beneficial effects that a right's framers had in mind. Freedom of speech may, for example, be used to advance hate speech, encourage terrorism or defamation, discriminate against the less fortunate, etc. The ban against retroactive laws could theoretically freeze the authority of Parliament to prevent it from action as new and unforeseen crises arise.

For these reasons, the protection of rights is rarely absolute, but the exceptions, like the basic rights themselves, have to be framed in legal terminology. The technique employed is most often to carve out an exempting rule, allowing for the constitutional protection to be lifted if a narrow set of circumstances are at play. These exemption rules are normally formulated by the controlling authority – that is, the Supreme Court itself – through its continuing building of precedents.

In the shipping tax case, the clash between the constitutional protection against retroactive laws turned on the choice and application of the correct exemption rule allowing for such protection to be lifted. The government alleged that the tax amendment must be upheld unless it was "clearly unreasonable or unfair" allowing for retroactivity under a fairly wide set of test factors, while the shipping companies held that only if a narrow set of circumstances – “compelling public interests” – were met, then protection under Article 97 could be cancelled. As it turned out, the majority of six Supreme Court judges applied the law as advised by the shipping companies, while the minority of five went for the government solution.

The involvement of Parliament

An interesting phase during the preparation of the legislation at issue consisted of a thorough research and hearing of the constitutional issues in Parliament. The constitutional breach, as eventually established by the Supreme Court, was no accident but a carefully calculated political design, whereby the government, as advised by the Legal Department of the Justice Ministry and the Tax Legal Department of the Ministry of Finance, calculated that the legislation would not be cut down, even if the Article 97 issues were all the time in plain view. The government revocation of the earlier more favourable shipping tax rules in reality represented a calculated gamble.

The opposition in Parliament called on legal experts of high repute to testify in a special hearing on the constitutional issue. The shipping companies provided legal opinions from three different law firms, all of which advanced the view that the legislation was unconstitutional. Thus, the first issue is why, when Parliament was made aware of the constitutional problems, it did not take care of them itself.

Under established Norwegian principles of constitutional review, there is close to 35 years of precedent to the effect that the views of Parliament will carry weight when the Supreme Court later rules on the constitutionality of the laws.[3] However, the *impact* of Parliament’s view depends on what rules of the Constitution are in contention. When it comes to rights protecting private individuals (such as the freedom of speech, freedom against arbitrary detentions, the ban against punishment without trial), the courts will pay scant attention to Parliament’s views, while in the case of constitutional rules turning on major economic matters important to both the state and the individual, such as Article 97, the Court will traditionally pay more attention to Parliament’s own view.

3 Kløfta (Rt. 1976 p. 1).

In the present case, however, the Supreme Court majority did not pay any attention to Parliament's view, since it held that Parliament had applied the wrong legal test when specifying the constitutionality prism to be used to review the tax legislation under Article 97. This is interesting, since it provided the Supreme Court with an escape hatch from a possible criticism to the effect that Parliament's own opinion should have carried weight.[4]

In some countries constitutional reviews are conducted either in constitutional courts, often consisting of judges sitting with elected parliamentarians, and/or by review panels in Parliament. The Norwegian Parliament has no such structured mechanism for constitutional review of its own legislation. As noted, the task is ultimately left to the courts. Of course, it is obvious that the Norwegian Parliament does not feel free to pass legislation contravening the Constitution, but there is no standardized, organized procedure in Parliament to deal *only* with this issue. This means that the issue of constitutionality presents itself to the parliamentarians *together with* the legislation and policy choice at issue.

If the legislation is proposed by a government backed by a parliamentary majority, the forced consideration of the appropriateness and political expediency of the legislation *together with* its constitutionality means that the majority cannot find the legislation unconstitutional without also inflicting serious political harm on its own government. In the case of minority governments, the position would be different, but the shipping tax case was presented by a government backed by an absolute majority. Moreover, the pressure applied on each parliamentarian was so intense that one central politician of a government party took the stand in Parliament and revealed that he thought the bill was unconstitutional, but explained that this parliamentary party group accepted the legislation at issue only because of the position they were in.[5]

As a general consideration, it goes without saying that constitutionality review in Parliament that is closely tied to the fulfilment of political objectives sought by the same representatives who are conducting the constitutional review, will be at least ad hoc and politically influenced and, probably, largely ineffective. One cannot expect Parliament to conduct the same form of constitutional review as courts do when judges check the constitutionality of the legislation separate from its public policy appropriateness.

---

4 A corresponding solution was chosen in the ground lease case (Rt. 2007 p. 1308).

5 Per Olaf Lundteigen (The Centre Party), meeting in Parliament on 27.11.2007.

In this aspect, the shipping case was similar to the Kløfta case,[6] where the majority government had enacted legislation on the calculation of compensation in cases of unilateral takings, and with the Bank Democracy case[7] where the government brought forward legislation that extended political control over commercial banks. In all three cases, the policy reform issue was politically important to the government, and reforms were carried in Parliament through the government's majority support.

The main features of the shipping legislation

From 1996 shipping companies in Norway could elect to be subject to special taxation rules for shipping companies.[8] The purpose of this tax regime was to ensure competitive framework conditions for the shipping industry, as well as the preservation of Norway's maritime traditions. Shipping income became tax-exempt, whereas the distribution of dividends or voluntary exit from the regime elicited taxation of untaxed capital. In addition, the shipping companies had to pay tonnage tax.

On 14 December 2007 the Norwegian Parliament elected to amend the tonnage tax regime, removing the obligation of shipping companies to pay tax on the distribution of capital in respect of future income (European tonnage model). At the same time, it was decided to implement an income settlement of untaxed capital accumulated in the period 1996-2006, the so-called transition rule of the amendment act, part X.

Section X entailed that tax-exempt income earned in the period 1996-2006 would be taxed without the taxpayer having performed any actions triggering taxation. Up to 1/3 of the calculated amount could be used for environmental measures, whereas the remaining 2/3 were subject to linear taxation over a period of ten years.

6 Rt. 1976 p. 1.

7 Rt. 1979 p. 572.

8 Introduced by tax law amendment 20 December 1996 no. 110.

The constitutional debate

The Norwegian Shipowners' Association obtained three legal opinions from the law firms Hjort, Wiersholm and BA-HR, all of which concluded that the proposed parliamentary bill was unconstitutional.[9]

The opposition parties proposed that Parliament should obtain an independent legal opinion on the bill's constitutionality. However, the government parties rejected this proposal.

Instead the Parliament's Finance Committee held a hearing on 8 November 2007 calling statements by, among others, Professor Frederik Zimmer, Professor Eivind Smith and former Supreme Court Judge Gunnar Aasland, all of whom raised constitutional objections to the proposal.

One chief objection to the bill concerned the fact that there is a legal difference between providing rules on future taxation and providing rules on taxation of income from 1996. Parliament does not normally hold legal power to regulate taxation 11 years backwards in time. The longest period of retroactive taxation that had been accepted by the Supreme Court was the one-off tax after World War II (involving five years of retroactivity). The conditions surrounding the one-off tax in WW II were very different from the conditions associated with the tonnage tax bill. The effects of retroactivity are especially harsh when income is taxed after so many years. It was emphasized that there had been a form of tax settlement annually from 1996 to 2006, which now would be reversed.

Another objection was that the proposed bill did not pay sufficient attention to the need for predictability. Predictability is important to preserve citizens' confidence in the state. The need for long-term planning and predictability is given great weight when applying Article 97. The proposal concerning retroactivity in the shipping case was far-reaching and it came as a surprise.

A third objection was that the proposal for retroactive taxation appeared to lack legislative justification. Typically in terms of retroactive rules, the retroactivity is necessary to ensure future effect. In this case the situation was the reverse. A continuation of the distribution model for income already earned would preserve the position of the shipping companies and the state. The reason for the retroactivity was only a desire to increase government proceeds. Given this fact, a more detailed explanation as to why retroactivity still was considered necessary

9 Banoun was the author of the legal opinion from the law firm Wiersholm.

was called for. It was argued that comprehensive retroactivity poses more stringent requirements to the justification for the legal measure.

A fourth objection to the bill was that Parliament's own assessment of the constitutionality issue had been given too great importance. The purpose of the Constitution is to protect citizens against a parliamentary majority. A two-thirds majority is required to amend the Constitution, whereas ordinary acts may be amended through simple majority. There probably would not be a two-thirds majority in Parliament in favour of amending the Constitution to allow for retroactive tax legislation 11 years back in time. There should therefore be limits to the weight given to the assessment of the parliamentary majority itself.

Although the Legal Department of the Ministry of Justice had made the assumption that the parliamentary bill could pass muster under the Constitution, the department did, however, acknowledge that the Supreme Court had never decided a similar case. The Legal Department emphasized that it appears *"as somewhat uncertain on which conditions the courts will accept an intervention such as the one present"*.[10] Further, the Legal Department stated that the present transitional arrangements are *"undeniably of an extraordinary character in that they link the tax liability to income earned over a number of years"*.[11] It emphasized that it was *"not necessarily the case that the taxpayers must here be prepared for changes in the tonnage tax regime to also affect old income, especially when the income was earned a number of years back in time"*.[12]

Despite objections, the bill was adopted by Parliament with the support of the government parties. The political opposition voted against the bill, and referred inter alia to the constitutional objections that had emerged during the hearing.

The Court proceedings

After the hearing of two cases in the lower courts, where Aust-Agder Lower Court voted in favour of upholding the legislation, while Oslo Lower Court voted to invalidate it under Article 97, the scene was set for high drama when the Supreme

10 Odelsting Proposition (white paper) no. 1 (2007–2008) p. 246.

11 Odelsting Proposition no. 1 (2007–2008) p. 244.

12 Odelsting Proposition no. 1 (2007–2008) p. 245.

Court heard the challenge against the legislation at issue over a full week in early January 2010.

The majority found that there must be compelling reasons in the public interest in order for such retroactivity to pass muster under the Constitution. The shipping companies had a *"justified expectation"* that the tax issue had been settled until the adoption of new rules, and that new rules would apply for the future in the customary manner. The State's "package argument" that emphasis must be given to the fact that the tonnage tax regime of 2007 entailed other rules which were advantageous to the shipping companies, was rejected. The parliamentary majority had applied the wrong standard as its basis in taking the view that retroactivity was acceptable provided it was not *"clearly unreasonable or unfair"*. The act having been found unconstitutional, it was not necessary for the majority to decide on the submission that the regime conflicted with the European Convention on Human Rights, Protocol 1, Article 1.

There was strong dissent (6–5), with the minority holding the opinion that the State should be acquitted and the legislation upheld. The minority felt that the retroactivity could be accepted provided it was not *"clearly unreasonable or unfair"*. Emphasis was given to the fact that the tonnage tax regime of 2007 contained rules which were advantageous to the shipping companies. The minority was of the opinion that Parliament was not guilty of any significant misunderstandings or that Parliament had overlooked any "considerable consequences" of the act, and found that Parliament's assessment would have to play an "important role" in the Supreme Court's own assessment of the issue of constitutionality. The minority also did not consider the regime to be conflicting with the European Convention on Human Rights.

Policy implications

When turning to the effects of the judgment, it is useful to sort the impact into different categories. We look at (i) the monetary effect of the judgment on the shipping industry and the legislation at issue, which is not crystal clear even at the time of this writing; (ii) the effect on future tax legislation as such; (iii) the effect on citizens' confidence in the State and in the validity of its legislation; (iv) the effects on the vitality of constitutional review of Norwegian legislation and;

not often emphasized but most important, (v) the effectiveness of Article 97 on the system of government.[13]

1) The first issue is the financial effects for the shipping companies.

In 2007 when the retroactive tax was enacted, the shipping companies' equity was immediately converted into debt as per the legal amendment itself. Some companies lost all their equity. Some companies breached their loan conditions. The shipping companies issued stock exchange reports with information relating to what part of their equity had to be reclassified. The market prices of the shares dropped immediately. Over a 10-year period tax was to be paid in the amount of 13 billion Norwegian kroner. One company alone was handed a tax bill of 3.9 billion Norwegian kroner.

One effect of the Supreme Court judgment was that the companies regained their equity. Only three days after the announcement of the judgment, there was another due date for a new instalment of the back tax. The judgment implied that the shipping companies did not have to pay the instalment. The tax authorities further performed an automatic correction of the assessments for the income years 2007 and 2008.[14] The shipping companies will subsequently be reimbursed in respect of the excess amount of paid tax with interest.

If the shipping companies later exit the tonnage tax regime or distribute untaxed capital from the time before 2007 as dividend, this will trigger taxation. In total the shipping companies have untaxed capital from that period amounting to 21 billion Norwegian kroner (so-called "latent tax"). The Ministry of Finance has given notice that effective 26 March 2010 all new dividend will be taxed as long as the company still has untaxed capital (the first in, first out principle). The Ministry of Finance has presented a proposal for a one-off settlement in which the shipping companies may in the years 2011–2013 pay 6.7 per cent of the "latent tax", amounting to approx. 4 billion Norwegian kroner, to avoid future tax on exit from the tonnage tax regime or on dividend. This proposal is currently under discussion.

2) The second implication of the judgment is its effect on future legislation in Norwegian tax law.

---

13 For a general comment, see Eivind Smith, *Rederiskatt og rettsstat, Lov og Rett* 2010 p. 177.

14 Statement of 19 February 2010 from the Central Tax Office for Large Enterprises.

Traditionally, there has been a distinction between transaction taxes (VAT, import duties, stamp duty, inheritance tax) on the one hand and ordinary income and wealth tax on the other. As far as the former is concerned, the doctrine has been that any retroactivity is prohibited.[15] The doctrine has been different for income and wealth tax, where retroactivity within the income year has normally been permitted.[16]

However, legal developments have now taken place in both areas, reducing the distance between the two doctrines. In the Supreme Court judgment Arves Trafikkskole (Rt. 2006 p. 293) it was established that in respect of transaction taxes (VAT), retroactivity was prohibited absent compelling public interests. It was emphasized that when linking new burdens to older actions, the legislator approached the core of Article 97 of the Constitution, where the prohibition against retroactivity is strict. In the shipping tax case, the same standard was taken as the doctrine for the evaluation of retroactivity over several years.

Within the tax year there is still a significant difference between transaction taxes and income and wealth tax. In respect of the former, the legal standard "compelling public interest" will be used even for legislation causing only a few days of retroactivity. In respect of income and wealth tax, retroactivity within the income year will be accepted unless it is "clearly unreasonable or unfair".

The legal test "compelling public interest" constitutes an important guarantee for the legal protection of citizens. A requirement for compelling public interest implies that retroactive taxation over a number of years will only be accepted under extraordinary circumstances. Government proceed requirements and arguments to the effect that the tax income will be used for important welfare measures will not be sufficient. The legislature will generally be expected to attend to fiscal considerations through ordinary taxation, not by unilateral and retroactive taxation of certain groups of taxpayers.

In this context, a contrast could be made with an earlier Supreme Court judgment regarding the one-off tax imposed after World War II.[17] In 1946 it was established by law that the wealth increase of the war years 1940–1945 would be taxed as income. It appeared from the preparatory works that the tax was moti-

15 Rt. 1910 p. 174.

16 Rt. 1925 p. 588. Wealth tax is calculated on the wealth of the taxpayer at year end; as long as the changed wealth tax rules are enacted before year end, there will be no legal retroactivity.

17 Rt. 1952 p. 31.

vated by the fairness requirement that no one should emerge from the war richer while others had sacrificed their lives, health and property in the fight against the enemy.[18] The Supreme Court emphasized that the war had resulted in an exceptional need for tax revenues and that this need should be assisted also by those whose wealth had increased during the war years. Five years of retroactivity was therefore accepted.

A different example of a "compelling public interest" is the Supreme Court judgment on the obligation to pay debts in gold, which was abolished because of the dire economic situation in the 1920s and 1930s. The abolishment also cancelled historic debt holders' right to obtain their payment in gold for older debts. The legislation was upheld under Article 97 because the reform was considered as advancing a compelling public interest.[19]

In the present economic climate, the Norwegian government, sitting on the world's largest per capita sovereign fund, could marshal no similar arguments. Even if the transfer of payment was enormous by any ordinary standard, it still represented a small fraction of the Norwegian government's budget and financial fortune.

With subsequent events in less fortunate European countries such as Greece in mind, it could theoretically be queried whether a different economic climate would allow for a different outcome. In times of crisis, war, etc., tax measures not normally tolerated will be allowed in most countries because of the national need for survival.

3) The third effect of the judgment is the legal protection of confidence in legislation.

The issue of confidence in the government and the legal order was a hotly debated topic before, during and after the judgment. The government asserted that sufficient warning had been given through the fact that the tax privileges at issue were conditional, while the shipping companies pointed to the fact that the condition under the original legislation left it up to them to decide whether to exit the shipping tax regime, while the new legislation made such exit mandatory and taxable. They claimed that this represented a violation of any reasonable precon-

18 (Odelsting Proposition no. II 1945 p. 2–3).

19 Rt. 1962 p. 369.

dition for the investments undertaken in the Norwegian shipping industry over the last ten years.

Obviously, business firms have to live with legal uncertainty. Such uncertainty derives, among other things, from the possibility of legislation being changed in the future, but may also exist because unclear rules are only later clarified through court procedures that take several years, and where the final judgment will thus have a retroactive effect. On the other hand, the case at issue involved a fairly transparent precondition that had been intentionally designed by Parliament 11 years before, with a particular policy purpose, and on which the shipping companies could credibly claim to have relied. It is fair to say that the retroactivity at issue was not a trifling matter. Heavy investments in ships require predictable framework conditions for the shipping industry.

The effects of the new legislation's mandatory income settlement were those of a "trap" for shipping companies which had made dispositions for 11 years which presumably would be tax-free, unless the shipping companies themselves opted to exit the regime or chose to distribute untaxed capital. Lack of confidence in the framework caused the Oslo Stock Exchange to publicly criticize the proposal for retroactive taxation. The case also drew international interest in the financial press.

The basic message of the business representatives voicing opinions on the legislation was that it represented a galling example of retroactivity that would undermine the confidence of business interests to invest in Norwegian shipping, and in Norwegian business generally, for the future.

The citizenry's and the business community's confidence in the state, and their confidence that the existing laws actually applying in the period in which they are passed, turned out in the end to be important considerations for the majority in the Supreme Court. The evocation of the "compelling public interest" test ensures that the citizens and firms in the future can have confidence in the legislation as enacted. Only in a very narrow set of circumstances will Parliament be allowed to amend legislation retroactively.

4) A fourth issue of general interest is what would have happened to the Supreme Court's own powers of constitutional review, had the minority prevailed.

The retroactive shipping taxation was the end result of a compromise by the government parties. The Labour Party and the Centre Party wanted a more favourable taxation of the shipping companies ("the European model") for the future, whereas the Socialist Party did not. The Socialist Party was initially the only party which supported the retroactive taxation eventually adopted. By the time the legislation came to Parliament the amendment prepared by the government and parliamentarians belonging to the majority was a pre-cooked deal, where the parliamentary groups of the government parties had to swallow the government proposal based on the political situation they were in. The constitutional protection was in reality eliminated through negotiations inside the government.

The Supreme Court minority's combination of the use of the test "clearly unreasonable or unfair" even for 11 years of retroactive taxation and its strong emphasis on Parliament's own assessment on the constitutionality issue, would have rendered the constitutional review toothless and would have left the public only insignificant protection against retroactive acts.

Further, if Parliament could dictate its own view on constitutional issues through the majority's opinion, the supermajority requirements to amend the Constitution would be effectively cancelled. The importance of the Supreme Court's own powers of constitutional review is also made evident through a new Supreme Court plenary judgment dated 12 May 2010, in which the Court found that a regulation was unconstitutional even though Parliament had taken the opposite view:

> I take as my basis that Parliament clearly has concluded and assumed that the regulation does not conflict with the Constitution. This being the case, the courts must in cases of doubt comply with the view of the legislator. My view of the case is that the instruction clearly produces results which conflict with Section 106 of the Norwegian Constitution. There is no such qualified doubt concerning the interpretation of the Constitution as to cause Parliament's view to be given decisive importance. If the right of a review is to be perceived as real, then the courts must use it in such a case as this.

As stressed by the Supreme Court, Parliament's own view cannot be decisive unless there is a qualified doubt as regards the interpretation of the Constitution.

5) A final issue is what would have been the result for the Norwegian system of government, and its ability to enact legislation and design taxation schemes, had

the supreme minority's position prevailed. This is an effect that strikes at the heart of one of the public policy considerations behind Article 97 of the Constitution.

Obviously, at the time of the trade-off in Parliament, and at the time of the Supreme Court's decision, the sitting government claimed that major policy considerations favoured *allowing* the legislation at issue. However, this amounted to a rather superficial and ad hoc flavoured assessment. Any attempt to present the case as a conflict between, on the one hand, the government and the parliamentary majority and, on the other hand, the minority and the shipping companies, simply overlooks the fact that the most important effect of this particular judgment is to protect *any* democratic majority's right to rule for the term of its election. The real beneficiary of the outcome of the shipping case is the government itself.

If the retroactive shipping tax legislation had been allowed, it would have been very difficult to measure the effect of the judgment on any government's ability to enact legislation to pursue its policy goals.

Most certainly, if the lower threshold of the minority had prevailed, all kinds of relative arguments would have been brought into play to determine the scope of Article 97. In subsequent battles the outcome under such a test would have been difficult to calculate in advance. If Article 97 had not been effectively applied, the end result would have been a legal state which would have consisted of little more than a freedom to strike deals based on political expediency and convenience.

Of course, business firms such as shipping companies could still be in a position to halt negative legislation. It is indeed the normal state in democracies that lobbyists pursue such endeavours constantly. However, it is always difficult to calculate the odds of lobbying success in advance, because the calculations among and dealings with and among political authorities are less than transparent.

The effect of allowing retroactive legislation would thus have meant that a more transparent legal state would have been traded for less transparent lobbying, rent seeking and political dealings with political authorities. Established legal positions could constantly have been revisited, and acquired rights and duties subjected to renewed bargaining. This would have raised the information costs and future risks for business firms and individuals, and would have caused a retroactivity "charge" to have to be applied to any legislation conferring obligations and benefits on any particular group of legal subjects.

In 1996 a majority in Parliament consisting of the Conservative Party, Centre Party, Progress Party and Christian Democratic Party enacted the 1996 shipping tax rules. The majority in that parliament wanted the shipping income to be tax-exempt, unless the shipping companies voluntarily exited the regime or distributed untaxed capital to its owners. The Socialist Party and the Labour party were against the shipping tax regime at the time, but they were in minority.

The 2007 change could be looked upon as an attempt at achieving a replay of the 1996 decision. It is interesting to note that most of the parties behind the original shipping tax rules from 1996 were of the opinion that the change in 2007 raised constitutional concerns, and therefore voted against it.[20]

The outcome of the Supreme Court case makes it impossible for future governments and majorities in Parliament to abolish with retroactive effect what has been decided by the parliamentary majority and government at the earlier time of enactment. The government of 1996 was protected against the acts of the government of 2007, and the government of 2007 is protected against future parliaments.

After the Supreme Court's decision, an existing government, as well as its citizens, can now rest assured that a future government is not able to reverse laws with retroactive effect. The voters at any given time will be able to elect the parliament that they think is best suited to govern the country in the next parliamentary term, and a new parliament will only hold legal power to legislate for the future. The Supreme Court became the enforcer of the political authority of the ruling government at any given time. The Supreme Court's majority view was thus supported by compelling public interest!

---

20 The only party behind the original 1996 rules that voted for the change in 2007 was Centre Party. However, the only parliamentary member of the Centre Party that was also in Parliament when the shipping tax rules were enacted in 1996 was of the opinion that the change in 2007 was unconstitutional; see footnote 5.

Towards a Criminal Justice Economics?

Roger Bowles

1. Introduction

In a review of the economics of criminal behaviour Erling Eide (2000) concluded with the following challenge to improve our understanding of human behaviour, especially in relation to offending and crime:

> The formidable task for the future may be found in a proposition for social science research by the Nobel Prize Winner Niko Tinbergen (who should not be confused with J. Tinbergen who has won the Nobel Memorial Prize in economics) that four levels of analysis should be put together: the biological (genetical), the developmental (how an individual is socialized), the situational (how the environment influences behavior), and the adaptive (how a person responds to the benefits and costs of alternative courses of action).

Although there have been significant developments in the economic modelling of offending behaviour over the decade since this was written, the challenge remains unmet. Partly as a result, there remains a significant lack of complementarity between these models and the mainstream debate about criminal justice policy. The purpose of this paper is to argue that there is a lot about the economic analysis of offending that provides material for engaging in the wider criminal justice policy debate but that this has not been fully exploited because of the traditionally narrow focus of economists on sentencing and enforcement policy. The newer wave of dynamic offending models developed by Emons (2003, 2004) and others, for example, can support a richer analysis of offending than the traditional one-shot models that rely on a lottery approach in which rational agents are less likely to offend if confronted with harsher penalties. These dynamic models also offer a means of mobilizing some of the empirical findings in related social science disciplines such as criminology and psychology. They can also be used to generate wider policy implications than the menu of maximal fines and low detection probabilities that has left the economics of crime somewhat isolated and overlooked in policy debate.

This distancing from the wider discussion is probably attributable in part to criminal justice policy analysts typically using approaches of which economists are instinctively apprehensive. Cognitive Behaviour Therapy, for example, is based on the idea of "correcting deficits" assessed in individuals in relation to areas such as planning skills, anticipating the future and impulsivity. Much of this material is normative and goes beyond the framework more familiar in economics in which individuals have exogenously fixed endowments, characteristics and preferences. Some of this wider agenda is legitimate from a policy perspective since it involves policy interventions (such as rebalancing endowments or encouraging investment in human capital) that change the terms on which individuals are making decisions that potentially impose social costs on others but do not stray into efforts to manipulate preference structures.

The argument proposed here is that there is scope for economics to contribute to the "Tinbergen challenge" agenda and thus the wider criminal justice debate. This will require a willingness to use the newer dynamic models of offending in ways which exploit the building blocks of the model more and rely less on the implications for enforcement and sentencing policy. In particular we argue that there is scope for greater focus on the transition from childhood to adolescence and adulthood. A high proportion of adolescents offend, but many desist as they grow older and as their appreciation grows of the future consequences of offending and anti-social behaviour. A better understanding of the evolution of "rationality" in young people may contribute to the policy debate about how to encourage investment in human capital and how to discourage involvement in activities such anti-social behaviour and offending with their high external costs.

The objective of this short paper is to review the scope for meeting Eide's challenge by bringing together a wider set of perspectives without straying far from standard economic models. Such an agenda is likely to include a focus on: the structure of anticipation by means of dynamic models with two or more periods; the evolution of subjective discount rates and planning skills through adolescence and the role of human capital formation and reputational effects. We approach the objective by setting out a simple dynamic offending model and spelling out the key assumptions it makes. In particular we look critically at the skills required to specify the possible outcomes associated with alternative actions and to estimate probabilities to attach to each outcome and at the formulation of a subjective discount rate and attitude to risk. We then review how "deficiencies" or characteristics of various kinds may result in decisions to offend and contrast this with the approach taken in the static, full information model of offending.

An important part of the agenda is to look for ways of making use of the extensive empirical findings about offending and offenders accumulated in other disciplines. We seek to use evidence from a variety of sources to motivate discussion of the shape of discount rate schedules, the interaction between offending and substance misuse and the role of home environment and peer pressure. This includes evidence from descriptive studies of offending careers, from the psychology literature on impulsivity, which might shed light on discount rates, and on the link between offending, substance misuse and mental ill health.

2. Economic models of offending

One-shot model

The standard approach to the economics of crime is the Becker (1968) model in which offending is characterized as a lottery, with a net gain to the offender if she remains undetected and a net loss if she gets caught. The probability of being caught depends on the volume of resources put into detection by the police and the consequences for all those involved play out in a single time period. The sanction can take many forms but can be represented as a financial sum (a willingness to pay to avoid a sanction) even where imprisonment or a community punishment is imposed. A simple formulation can be expressed in terms of an offending rule:

Offend iff:

$$\pi\, U(W_0 - F_0) + (1 - \pi)\, U(W_0 + G) > U(W_0) \qquad \ldots(1)$$

Where:

π: probability of detection and conviction if offending

W_0: initial wealth at the start of period t, (t=0,1)

F_0: financial equivalent of sanction imposed for a first conviction (includes compensation H to victim)

G: gain to offender from an offence in the event of non-detection
Y: real wage (assumed to be time-invariant)

This rule makes offending decisions rely critically on three parameters, namely the individual's attitude to risk (which determines the shape of the utility function U(.)), the probability of conviction (which depends on spending on crime detection in the CJS) and the size of the sanction F_0: (a product of the legislation specifying criminal sanctions plus any "sentencing guidelines" followed by courts). The formulation is sometimes simplified further by assuming risk neutrality, in which case the decision rule can be written as:

Offend iff:

$$\pi (W_0 - F_0) + (1 - \pi) (W_0 + G) > W_0 \qquad ..(2)$$

$$G > \pi F_0/(1 - \pi)$$

Optimal enforcement policy is derived by choosing a level of expenditure on enforcement (X) in conjunction with a fine (F_0) that takes account of the total social costs of crime comprising the victim costs of crime (H), the enforcement costs (X) and the social costs (S) of imposing the sanctions to be imposed. The solution entails use of a maximal fine (that just absorbs offender wealth) along with a low level of enforcement expenditure. Fines are preferred to imprisonment because they have lower opportunity costs. In this formulation, which requires that fines be tailored to offender wealth rather than to the harm caused by the offence, the wider social cost of crime is ignored as are future consequences for the offender or the victim.

Dynamic formulation

This standard one-shot model has been challenged in recent years by dynamic formulations in which offending decisions reflect the future consequences of detection and conviction beyond the immediate impact on wealth of the imposition of a monetary sanction. The essence of these models is that they take account of the likelihood that a conviction will change the environment in which all subsequent decisions are taken by a prospective offender. A simple illustration of the more general proposition can be found in the rationale for "three strikes" legislation. Under the latter a person with two convictions faces very different terms when making offending decisions at "round 3" since one stroke of bad luck (getting caught again) can have the catastrophic consequence of life imprisonment. Although these models have been devised principally to explore the implications of punishment structures they do provide a natural starting point also for exploring the incentive and information structures of the decisions themselves. This can open up the way to using findings from a wider range of empirical data on offending and to linking economic models of offending more successfully with everyday discussion of criminal justice policy in general and sentencing policy in particular.

The one-shot model leaves the offender with no hangover effects from a conviction. The dynamic model recognizes that the environment in which the second period decisions are being made will itself be a product of the decisions and outcomes in the first period. Time consistent decisions during the first period thus need to recognize the possibility that these decisions will themselves influence the options available in the second period and the terms on which they are available (Emons 2003, 2004). This formulation is thus much richer than the one-shot model. It is also much more demanding of the capacity of the individual to formulate options and make well-informed decisions.

Consider a simple variant of the dynamic model in which we begin with a risk neutrality assumption and model the principal carry-over effect as a discount in the wage rate offered to a person with a criminal conviction.

The components needed for the model are as follows:

π, W_0, F_0, G defined as in one-shot model
F_1: financial equivalent of sanction imposed for a second conviction (includes victim compensation, H)
μ: proportional reduction in the wage (w) in the event of having a previous conviction
r: subjective discount rate at which returns in the second period are valued

The individual this time has to consider offending decisions across both periods[1]. Since nature will determine whether they are convicted in the event of offending, there are nine possible pathways in all that the individual can follow. The decision to offend in the first period may result in a conviction, so that possible outcomes are {offend: convicted}, {offend: not convicted}. Alternatively the per-

1 For a fuller account of the model see Bowles and Florackis (2009).

son can decide not to offend. It is assumed that courts make no errors, so the innocent are never falsely convicted, and so the third possible pathway in the first period is {not offend: not convicted}. In period two, corresponding with each of the three pathways from the first period are three further pathways. In each of the three the individual decides whether or not to offend, there being two possible outcomes in the event of offending and taking the associated risk of conviction. The difference is that the payoffs associated with the offending decision are different in the second period and depend on a person's conviction history. If they were convicted in period one their initial wealth at the start of period two is lower not only because of the fine and compensation they paid in period one but also because their earning power has diminished by .w as a result of loss of reputation. The strength of this wage loss effect will depend both on the degree to which employers are deterred by a criminal record and on the extent to which an offender in period one discounts future earnings. If, as seems likely, employers discriminate significantly against those with convictions, then the consequences may be serious. But if the individual is not good at anticipating the future or decides to assign little weight to future outcomes then she will be more likely to offend in the first period.

Planning skill requirements

Without ploughing through an explicit account of the various (3X3) combinations of actions and states of nature to which the two-period offending model gives rise, it is plain that some serious thought may be needed to identify the various possible outcomes and to do the backward induction needed to end up with an optimal programme of actions (a pair of decisions about whether to offend in each period). The calculation requires significant capacity to make projections into the future, and to assign reliable probability estimates to the various possible outcomes. The capacity to make well-informed decisions that take due account of one's own future varies across individuals. The ability to appreciate the future consequences of actions, and how random elements may influence outcomes, will vary systematically with a person's characteristics. It is in recognition of this that young children in many countries are treated as not criminally responsible until they reach a certain age. It is also why some adults may be regarded as mentally incapable of forming criminal intent. Economists, quite rightly for many purposes, incline to ignore the possibility that there may be limitations on the capacity of individuals to formulate coherent plans for the future. Bounds on rationality are awkward analytically and can seem rather arbitrary and difficult to capture.

But there are many policy fields that are characterized by measures that only make sense if it is accepted that citizens sometimes fail to appreciate the consequences of their actions. A tightening of the regulation of mortgage markets, for example, is under way in many countries because free market forces resulted in a proportion of households taking on levels of debt that were ultimately recognized as being unsustainable[2]. Well-informed consumers would be assumed capable of assessing such risks and limiting themselves to taking out loans that they could afford to repay. A strengthening of "consumer protection" legislation in such areas seems to imply that individuals do not trust themselves to make good choices for the longer term.

Role of discount rate

A somewhat similar argument applies in relation to the discount rate individuals apply when making offending decisions. The relative weight given to gains and losses anticipated in the future relative to gains and losses expected immediately will reflect many influences. As with the structure of the utility function economists instinctively avoid making judgments about what is an appropriate subjective discount rate. It is well established however that individuals differ in the rates they apply, and there is evidence (infra) that offenders as a group are more "impulsive" than others.

This may be of particular significance when dealing with young and adolescent offenders. When humans are first born they have very little capacity to anticipate the future: their behaviour is dominated by expressing immediate wants such as warmth or food. As adults most will have developed substantial powers of anticipation and understand the link between today's actions and tomorrow's consequences. During the transition from being a baby to becoming a thinking adult, individuals go through phases of childhood and adolescence during which they have to learn to give greater weight to the future. The possibility that they may make mistakes during this period of transition is probably what prompts legislation that enables most kinds of crime to be expunged or extinguished as young people reach adulthood.

---

2 Evidence of this can be readily established from the websites of regulators of financial services: see for example the website of the British Financial Services Authority: www.fsa.gov.uk.

Although some of the same sorts of argument seem to apply to planning skills requirements and the subjective discount rate, it is well to keep in mind that they enter the offending model in different ways. Planning skills are required to list states of the world and to assign reasonable probability estimates to each. The discount rate defines the terms on which outcomes in one period are traded against outcomes in subsequent periods. Individuals may vary in relation to both their planning skills and the rate at which they discount the future. As we will see below there appears to be some empirical evidence that offenders are distinguished from others at least to some degree by differences in their degree of impatience and their capacity to anticipate consequences reliably. The difficulty arises in particular where individuals behave as though they have very high discount rates. Reputational effects are greatly weakened if there are groups who consistently ignore future consequences. Likewise the incentive to invest in human capital will be weaker for these groups, thereby intensifying the possibility of their social exclusion.

Attitudes to risk

In the standard economic models of offending, a critical role is played by differences in attitudes to risk. Risk lovers may offend when their risk-averse counterparts do not, simply because of differences in the relative weights they assign to outcomes involving gains and losses. To express the point slightly differently it is variation in attitudes to risk that might cause problems. Criminal sanctions calibrated for the risk averse may lead to offending by risk lovers. Re-calibrating sanctions to cater for risk lovers may do harm, but in a different way, by over-deterring the risk averse.

Interpersonal utilities

The standard "selfishness" assumption models an individual's well-being as dependent exclusively on their own consumption level. In some circumstances this is relaxed to allow the well-being of family members to be taken into account.

Analysis of altruism goes further and allows the utility level of others, or the consumption bundles of others, to be taken into account (Collard 1978).

For purposes of the analysis of offending it is possible to incorporate opposite kinds of effects. In particular there may be offenders who get positive enjoyment or "gratification" from the suffering of their victims, for example in the context of damage to the property of others or certain kinds of assault and sexual attacks. In everyday discussion of criminal behaviour there may be discomfort even with the notion of "selfishness" which is fundamental to most economic models. Behaviour which is blind to the interests of others can, after all, be described less sympathetically as showing a "lack of empathy", a characteristic sometimes ascribed to "psychopaths". The obvious challenge this poses is that a reluctance to make judgments about the contents of utility functions of individuals who are genuinely indifferent to others can make economists look uncaring or amoral.

Non-economic models of offending

A key challenge is reconciling the economic approach to offending with the approach taken in other social science disciplines such as criminology and psychology. Economists have not for the most part been much interested in this agenda, as Eide's remarks (op. cit.) highlight. The assertion we make here is that the dialogue of the deaf which characterizes this field arises in part because of the reluctance of economists to consider more seriously the empirical reliability of the assumptions they make about planning skills, discount rates and attitudes to risk.

Psychologists are much less restrained in terms of the moral judgments they import, identifying "cognitive deficits" and devising programmes aimed at "correcting" these deficiencies (Barratt and Patton 1983). Cognitive Behaviour Treatment programmes to reduce impulsivity, for example, are delivered in large number to prisoners in England and elsewhere (McDougall et al. 2009). At a further stage some psychiatrists at least are prepared to recognize some individuals as having a "dangerous and severe personality disorder" and have devised therapeutic programmes for dealing with such individuals, although this remains a matter of controversy[3].

In fields such as criminology and psychology it is difficult to discern a universally-agreed approach to offending. There are overlapping theories and a good deal of empirical analysis. There are some strands with similarities with the economic approach. For example there are theories based on "personality" in which everyone faces opportunities to gain from offending but those with certain kinds of personality traits resist temptation more effectively.[4] There are models based on impulsivity

3 The Royal College of Psychiatrists, for example, concludes that there is no "entirely satisfactory" diagnosis of antisocial traits that threaten public safety.

4 These mostly refer back to the work of Eysenck: see Eysenck and Eysenck (1970).

in which individuals with greater lack of self-control, possibly related to neuropsychological deficits, are more likely to end up offending[5]. Yet another strand sees differences in parental child-rearing styles and individual differences as influencing the capacity of an individual to think through the consequences and resist the lure of offending opportunities[6]. Other models of offending are more pragmatic and focus on identifying factors associated with offending. These are often expressed in terms of the "criminogenic risk factors" likely to have the greatest impact on the risk of recidivism. Low levels of basic education and vocational skills, criminal history, egocentrism, deficiencies in problem-solving skills, substance abuse and poor work histories are recurrent components in the factors reported which have counterparts in the dynamic economic model outlined above[7].

3. Empirical issues

This very brief review of non-economic models suggests that there are parallels between the economic and other approaches that can potentially serve to allow more sharing of findings and questions between disciplines. The following paragraphs refer briefly to just a few of these areas. They focus not so much on the empirical work by economists on deterrence effects as on studies with a bearing on the kinds of issue that are prompted by the dynamic analysis of offending.

Reputation

It is well established empirically that individuals with criminal convictions tend to have higher probabilities of unemployment and that they are also likely to experience discrimination in credit, housing and other markets as well as the labour market[8]. A critical problem with this observation is that the chain of causation may be very difficult to unravel without good quality longitudinal data. Low levels of human capital may prompt both a higher probability of unemploy-

5 Farrington (1992).

6 Gottfredson and Hirschi (1990).

7 There are also some other factors which do not fit very neatly with the economics approach including negative family functioning, antisocial peer associations and attitudes to offending.

8 It is known also that they tend to have poor basic skills, poor educational qualifications, poor work histories, a high probability of substance misuse and a comparatively high probability of mental health issues (Harper et al. 2005).

ment and a greater propensity to offend. Equally, however, it may be that there are some individual characteristics and/or family circumstances that pre-dispose young people both to involve themselves in offending and to underinvest in education and training. It is likely therefore to be difficult to identify the marginal contribution of being convicted to an expected wage discount. The discount will likely reflect in part low human capital and in part the loss attributable to having a criminal conviction. In any event it is likely that a concerted offender resettlement programme will need to address both aspects by providing both additional training and finding ways to offset negative reputation effects.

Substance misuse

The role of substance abuse raises the same issue of identifying causation. It may be a consequence of having poor prospects because of a history of convictions, it may have contributed directly to past offending (through bar room fights or property offences committed to fund a drug habit) or it might pre-date offending and be a joint product of some individual personality trait or family characteristic. The economic analysis of addictive behaviour (Becker and Murphy 1988; Becker and Mulligan 1997) which emphasizes the possibility that addiction itself may contribute to an increase in the search for immediate gratification (and thus an increase in the subjective discount rate) provides another possible pathway through which substance abuse and offending may be linked. An important implication of the severely rationalist economic approach is that setting out for an evening with a view to drinking heavily in public is plainly a decision that puts an individual at significant risk of offending. Fighting opportunities should thus be treated as endogenous and not events that occur purely by chance.

Subjective discount rates and impulsivity

One issue that does not seem to have been covered in the empirical literature is the age-trajectory of subjective discount rates. It is well-established that the early onset of offending seems to be related to a higher risk that a young person will go on to become a prolific or persistent offender. This might be an indicator that as young people approach adolescence some experience a quicker or larger decline in their subjective discount rate than others. For those experiencing a decline that is delayed or shallower (whether for reasons to do with personality, upbringing or whatever) the inhibitions to offending and the capacity to anticipate consequences may take longer to develop.

The idea that the trajectory of the subjective discount rate may be playing a significant role can be pursued into adulthood. The evidence is that the propensity to offend decreases with age after reaching a peak in the mid to late teens. There are many possible explanations for an age-related decay in the propensity to offend. One possibility is that those who desist from a criminal pathway in their later teens demonstrate an improving capacity to anticipate the future that overtakes the offending urges of adolescence, while persistent adult offenders do not.

Another piece of empirical evidence points to many convicted offenders having low levels of human capital and poor planning skills allied with unusually high levels of impulsivity. Bowles and Florackis (2009) report findings from comparisons of offenders and the wider non-convicted population which show prisoners typically displaying higher scores on psychometric measures of impulsivity. This might be evidence that discount rates remain unusually high for those continuing to offend into adulthood. A natural question here would be whether in economics-based experiments prisoners would display higher degrees of impatience than non-convicted subjects.

In relation to petty crime it is possible for offenders to get stuck in a hole from which it is difficult to escape. For a person with few educational qualifications picking up a criminal conviction will depress further their prospect of employment and their capacity to borrow money from financial institutions. This leaves them restricted to a modest standard of life if not offending. They will be unable to pay any significant fine courts might try to impose and their standard of living might not fall too far in the event that they are imprisoned. The losses associated with conviction might not be very great for this person in the short term making them, in effect, enforcement-proof.

Probability of detection

In the economics-inspired literature, the role of the probability of detection has been a primary focus. In the criminal justice literature the emphasis has been more on the effectiveness of various kinds of intervention programmes. In the CCTV area for example there have been efforts to establish that car theft in car parks protected by cameras has fallen relative to thefts in unprotected parks (Welsh and Farrington 2002). One finding from these studies is that thefts may at least get displaced into other locations or other types of offence, even if the aggregate level of offending cannot be shown to have fallen significantly. This kind of evidence, insofar as it is gathered in properly controlled settings, can potentially be used as confirmation that the probability of detection is playing a significant role in the offender's calculus. Of course it also demonstrates that moving detection resources around will induce countervailing moves by offenders. It is in part this kind of responsiveness that makes criminal justice policy more difficult to model than certain other areas of policy such as some kinds of health intervention.

Offender "types"

Another piece of evidence is that there are distinct sub-groups of offenders. For example Hales et al. (2009) found from their analysis of self-reported offending in the OCJS survey[9] two groups of particular interest. One was a large group (82 % of 10 to 25-year-olds) with a low propensity to offend who accounted for around one-third (36 %) of all offences. This was about the same proportion of all offending as that admitted by the small group (4 % of 10 to 25-year-olds) described as "prolific offenders" who committed 32 % of all offences. The "prolific offenders" stood out as having a relatively younger age of onset of offending compared with other groups. This evidence is broadly consistent with findings from work on the statistical features of offending careers and reconvictions: see for example Soothill et al. (2009), Bowles and Florackis (2007).

4. Policy implications

The implications of the standard one-shot Becker model of crime are well-rehearsed. Minimization of the social costs of crime entails a mix of a comparatively small police force in conjunction with a regime of heavy financial sanctions designed to exhaust offender wealth. This does not completely eliminate crime, since it leaves "judgment-proof" defendants for whom the expected gain from crime exceeds seizable assets. But in other respects it does deter crime by adjusting the terms of the "offending lottery" to ensure that crime does not pay. Dynamic offending models produce broadly comparable results.

Our argument here is that both the one-shot and dynamic variants can be used

9 Annual sweeps of the Offending, Crime and Justice Survey were conducted in England and Wales in each of the four years 2003–6. It is a nationally representative, longitudinal survey asking children and young people in the 10–25 year age range about their offending and alcohol and drug use. For further details see: www.homeoffice.gov.uk/rds/offending_survey.html

rather differently and thereby contribute to more mainstream debate about criminal justice policy. Evidence from surveys is that a high proportion of the population of younger people offend at least occasionally. Almost paradoxically it seems that the reputational costs of a conviction may be very high and increasing, not because of the sanctions imposed but because of the way markets use convictions as signals that result in adverse outcomes for offenders.

This seems to suggest that many individuals are behaving in ways that are potentially irrational and inconsistent. Institutions such as the use of warnings by police rather than immediate sanctions and the extinguishing of convictions after a certain number of years indicate a degree of tolerance of occasional mistakes and lapses.

Another way of looking at the debate is to use the empirical evidence to isolate different kinds of offender. Economic models may help focus on why offending seems to be more prevalent amongst certain groups. Two groups of particular interest are "the young" and those labelled "prolific" or "persistent" offenders. Life-cycle models can illuminate the analysis of both these groups.

As we argued above, adolescence is a time when people are still accumulating experience that helps them understand the wider and longer term consequences of their actions. It is also a time when physiological and psychological factors may result in high levels of aggression and risk taking. Support to young people in learning how to deal with these pressures may be at least as effective in preventing offending as using punitive sanctions.

Persistent offenders may represent a more deep-seated challenge. A small proportion of offenders is typically responsible for a high proportion of the crimes committed. Many of these individuals belong to marginalized groups for whom mainstream middle class life seems distant and alien. Co-morbidity of low educational achievement, limited labour market experience and readiness, high incidence of mental illness, high likelihood of substance misuse, poor accommodation, fractured family relationships and so on mean often that these individuals have little to lose from further convictions. Escape from these unpromising situations is rarely easy since many of the factors are self-reinforcing. The high economic and social cost of crime itself may be sufficient to justify significant spending on diversionary programmes, particularly for high risk youth groups, designed to prevent access to "criminal career" pathways (Cohen and Piquero 2007).

5. Conclusion

So, we have revisited but not resolved the "Tinbergen challenge" as reiterated by Erling Eide (Eide 2000). In the decade that has elapsed since publication of the latter there has been a substantial increase in the empirical evidence available from offender databases, longitudinal studies and self-report surveys of offending. This has opened wide the scope for panel dataset analysis. There have also been theoretical advances that have resulted in a greatly improved capacity to think about the dynamic effects of offending. But there has been less sign of economists trying to draw lessons from other disciplines tackling offending issues and less sign of them looking critically at the bounds of rationality when it comes to the economic analysis of offending.

Combining the elements of improved empirical data, dynamic modelling of offending decisions and parallels from other disciplines such as psychology and criminology could potentially give rise to something like a "criminal justice economics". This would not be sufficient to meet Tinbergen's goal but it might be a useful step along the path.

References

Barratt, E.S. and J.H. Patton. 1983. Impulsivity: Cognitive, behavioral, and psychophysiological correlates, in M. Zuckerman (ed.), *Biological Bases of Sensation Seeking, Impulsivity, and Anxiety.* Hillsdale, NJ: Lawrence Erlbaum Associates, pp. 77–122.

Becker, Gary S. 1968. Crime and Punishment: An Economic Approach. *Journal of Political Economy 76*, 169–217.

Becker, G.S. and C.B. Mulligan. 1997. The endogenous determination of time preference. *Quarterly Journal of Economics*, 112, 729–758.

Becker, G.S. and K.M. Murthy. 1988. A theory of rational addiction. *Journal of Political Economy* 76, 675–700.

Bowles, R. and C. Florackis. 2007. Duration of the time to reconviction: Evidence from UK prisoner discharge data. *Journal of Criminal Justice.*

Bowles, R. and C. Florackis. 2009. Impatience, Reputation and Offending, University of York, *mimeo.*

Cohen, M.A. and A. Piquero. 2007. New Evidence on the Monetary Value of Saving a High Risk Youth, Vanderbilt Law and Economics Research Paper No. 08–07.

Collard, D. 1978. *Altruism and Economy: A Study in Non-selfish Economics.* Oxford: Martin Robertson & Co.

Eide, E. 2000. Economics of Criminal Behaviour, Section 8100 in Bouckaert, B. and De Geest, G. (eds.), *Encyclopedia of Law and Economics, Volume I. The History and Methodology of Law and Economics.* Cheltenham: Edward Elgar.

Emons, W. 2003. A note on the optimal punishment for repeat offenders. *International Review of Law and Economics*, 23, 253–259.

Emons, W. 2004. Subgame perfect punishment for repeat offenders. *Economic Inquiry*, 42, 496–502.

Eysenck, H.J. and S.B.G. Eysenck. 1970. Crime and personality: an empirical study of the three-factor theory. *Brit. J. Criminol.*, 10, 225–239.

Farrington, D.P. 1992. Criminal Career Research in the UK. *Brit. J. Criminol*, 32(4).

Gottfredson, M. and T. Hirschi. 1990. *A General Theory of Crime.* Stanford, CA: Stanford University Press.

Hales, J., C. Nevill, S. Pudney and S. Tipping. 2009. *Longitudinal Analysis of the Offending, Crime and Justice Survey 2003–06,* Research Report 19. http://www.homeoffice.gov.uk/rds/pdfs09/horr19c.pdf

Harper, G., L.-H. Man, S. Taylor, and S. Niven. 2005. Factors associated with offending. In G. Harper and C. Chitty (eds.). The impact of corrections on re-offending: a review of "what works", 3rd ed. *Home Office Research Study* 291. London: Home Office.

McDougall, C., A.E. Perry, J. Clarbour, R.A. Bowles, and G. Worthy. 2009. Evaluation of HM Prison Service Enhanced Thinking Skills Programme: Report on the outcomes from a randomised controlled trial. London: Ministry of Justice, Research Report.

Soothill, K., C. Fitzpatrick, and B. Francis. 2009. *Understanding Criminal Careers.* Willan Publishing.

Welsh, B.C. and D.P. Farrington. 2002. Crime prevention effects of closed circuit television: a systematic review. *Home Office Research Study* 252: London: Home Office.

Environmental Law's Fragmentation and Discretionary Decision-making

A Critical Reflection on the Case of Norway

Hans Chr. Bugge

1. Introduction

This year, 2010, we can celebrate the 40th anniversary of environmental legislation, properly speaking, in Norway. In 1970 three major acts were adopted: the Nature Protection Act,[1] the Water Pollution Control Act,[2] and the Oil Pollution Prevention Act.[3] Some years earlier a general permit system for air pollution emissions had been introduced.[4] And a Ministry of the Environment was established in May 1972, a few weeks before the UN Conference on the Human Environment in Stockholm.

Since then there have been important environmental achievements. Major clean-up programmes in polluting industry and polluted watercourses and fjords were carried out in the 1970s and 1980s. The level of acidity in many lakes and rivers in southern Norway has decreased, and the fish are back. The number of protected areas – national parks, protected landscapes and nature reserves – have tripled, and some 15 % of mainland Norway is now protected.[5] Since 1972 legislation aiming at protecting the environment has been considerably strength-

1 Act of 19 June 1970 no. 63.

2 Act of 26 June 1970 no. 75.

3 Act of 6 March 1970 no. 6.

4 In the Neighbour Act of 16 June 1961 no. 15.

5 In addition, major parts of the islands of Svalbard (internationally better known as Spitzbergen) are protected as national parks and nature reserves.

ened. In 1976 a framework act for control of products which are hazardous to the environment was adopted.[6] In 1981 the earlier separate acts on air pollution, water and marine pollution and waste were brought together in an integrated Pollution Control Act.[7] A new Planning and Building Act was adopted in 1985[8] with the aim of ensuring comprehensive spatial and land use planning throughout the entire country. In 1992 a general right to a healthy environment was included in Norway's written constitution *(Grunnloven)*. An act on genetically modified organisms was introduced in 1993,[9] and an act on environmental information and participation was adopted in 2003.[10]

Still, many trends lead in the wrong direction. The pollution levels of hazardous substances in many rivers, lakes and fjords have not been reduced significantly and have even increased in some instances. Biodiversity has been reduced through development, and only small parts of the country are now considered as "wilderness".[11] [12] Two recent reports from the Auditor General of Norway showed

---

6 Act of 11 June 1976 no. 79 on the control of products and consumer services *(lov om kontroll med produkter og forbrukertjenester (produktkontrolloven))*.

7 Act of 13 March 1981 no. 6 on protection against pollution and on waste *(lov om vern mot forurensninger og om avfall (forurensningsloven))*. Thus, Norway had an integrated pollution legislation long before the Directive on Integrated Pollution Prevention and Control (originally directive EC/96/61, now directive 2008/1– IPPC-directive) was adopted by the European Community.

8 Act of 14 June 1985 no. 77 planning and building act *(plan- og bygningslov)*. A new planning and building act was adopted in 2008 (Act of 27 June 2008 no. 71).

9 Act of 2 April 1993 no. 38 on the production and use of genetically modified organisms *(lov om framstilling og bruk av genmodifiserte organismer m.m. (genteknologiloven))*.

10 Act of 9 May 2003 no. 31 on the right to environmental information and participation in public procedures in environmental cases *(lov om rett til miljøinformasjon og deltakelse i offentlige beslutningsprosesser av betydning for miljøet (miljøinformasjonsloven))*.

11 In Norway's environmental policy "wilderness" is defined as areas further away than 5 kms from infrastructure and other installations.

12 Among many sources, see *St.meld. nr. 14 (2006-2007) Sammen for et giftfritt miljø – forutsetninger for en tryggere fremtid* (White paper no. 14 (2006-2007) Together for an environment without toxic substances – a basis for a safer future) and *St.meld. nr.26 (2006-2007) Regjeringens miljøpolitikk og rikets miljøtilstand* (White paper no. 26 (2006-2007) The Government's Environmental Policy and the State of the Environment).

that Norway's most valuable natural areas and biodiversity had been reduced through a "piecemeal" development all over the country.[13]

This development in itself is not the main issue of this article. The point – and the problem – is that these trends clearly differ from the objectives of environmental policy adopted over the years by the parliament *(Stortinget)* and shifting governments. Norway's seemingly ambitious and well-developed environmental legislation has not been as effective as one might have expected.

Against this background, I shall take a critical look at Norway's environmental law. I use the term "environmental law" in a broad sense, meaning all major legislation regulating activities that may have effects on the natural environment, and not only legislation with environmental protection as its main purpose. Nearly all major economic activities in society contribute to environmental problems, so that legal protection of the environment depends on principles, rules and regulations in many sectors and parts of law, and of how these are interpreted and applied.

I maintain that environmental protection in Norway suffers from three major problems related to law:

First, the legislation governing the environment is *sector-based and highly fragmented.* It is fragmented horizontally between sectors as well as vertically between levels of government, and without the necessary mechanisms for coordination.

Second, the legislation is marked by *broadly formulated rules.* They provide the responsible sector authorities with wide discretion in balancing environmental concerns against sector objectives when laying down regulations and deciding individual cases. This is particularly important because the sector authorities are those primarily responsible for controlling the environmental effects of their activities, according to the principle of integration.

Third, *the principles of environmental law* laid down in important public documents on environmental policy *are interpreted and applied most inconsistently*, or not at all.

---

13 *Riksrevisjonens undersøkelse av myndighetenes arbeid med kartlegging og overvåking av biologisk mangfold og forvaltning av verneområder, Dokument nr. 3:12 (2005-2006)* (Report from the Auditor General on the authorities work to monitor biodiversity and manage protected areas). *Riksrevisjonens undersøkelse av bærekraftig arealplanlegging og arealdisponering i Norge, Dokument nr. 3:11 (2006-2007)* (Report from the Auditor General on sustainable land use planning and land management in Norway).

These problems are certainly not unique to Norway's environmental law and are probably to some extent observed in most countries. They represent general challenges to good environmental governance and must be seen in the light of some fundamental problems in environmental law.

2. Some fundamental problems in environmental law

When we want to analyze environmental law in order to better understand how it works – or why it does not work as expected – we must be conscious of some deep-rooted problems in dealing with the environment through legal means. These are grounded in the very nature of environmental problems and in the special types of interests and conflicts we are faced with in this area of law. They may be described and categorized in several different ways. Here, I want in particular to highlight eight fundamental problems.

a) *Many environmental problems are invisible.* They are neither seen nor felt by human beings and are not perceived until their effects become evident. By that time it may be too late to stop the harmful developments. Many cannot be identified and understood without advanced science. In his book *The Risk Society*[14] the German sociologist Ulrich Beck describes these "hidden risks" as a fundamental problem and challenge to modern society.

b) *Many environmental problems are marked by uncertainties.* Environmental problems are complex and there are often uncertainties and scientific controversies about cause-effect relationships. There is still a great lack of knowledge about how various organisms, including human beings, react to environmental change and stress, and in particular to the sum of many types of stress, in both the short term and the long term. Environmental policy and law must often address uncertainties and "moving targets".

c) *Many environmental goods and services are public goods in the economic sense.* They are not the property of certain persons, but can be enjoyed by everybody.

---

14 Ulrich Beck, *Risikogesellschaft: Auf dem Weg in eine andere Moderne,* Suhrkamp Verlag, Frankfurt 1986. English edition: *Risk Society. Towards a New Modernity,* Sage Publications, London 1992 (last ed. 2004).

For example, ecological services do not "belong" to anybody, but they are fundamental for the functioning of nature and thus essential for human welfare and even survival. Since they are not subject to property right and do not have a real price in the market, they have at the outset a weaker legal status than property rights and easily identified economic interests.

d) Most environmental goods and services have an economic value both for individuals and for society. This is evident when pollution causes health problems or kills fish in a river, and when high noise levels reduce the value of houses along a major road. However, since most environmental goods and services are not valued in the market, *it is difficult to price them correctly* in decision-making. This is clearly a problem when applying legal rules that prescribe some sort of cost-benefit analysis as a basis for decision-making. It remains a problem in spite of the many efforts that are made to quantify environmental values in economic terms in a meaningful way.

e) *Many environmental problems are the unacceptable cumulative effect* of numerous actions and decisions that – individually – are rationally and economically efficient. At the same time, decision-making most often deals with individual cases. It is a fundamental challenge in environmental governance to take cumulative effects properly into account when decisions are taken on a case-by-case basis. The fact that many problems are the cumulative effect of numerous activities and products, which individually may be almost insignificant, generally makes it difficult to draw the line between legal and illegal acts and to establish clear responsibilities for environmental harm.

f) This problem is worsened by the fact that *many environmental problems are cross-sectoral both in their causes and their effects.* Activities in many different sectors work together to create the effects, and the effects in turn may affect different parts of society. At the same time institutional organization and legislation are to a large extent developed along the lines of economic sectors, and are thus too fragmented and specialized to deal consistently with the problem. Climate change and reduction of biological diversity are clear examples of this.

g) The most serious *environmental problems cross administrative borders*: boundaries between local communities, between counties and regions, and not least between states. The environmental effects of a certain activity may appear far away from their source. Completely different constituents may, on the one hand, get the benefits and, on the other hand, incur the costs of environmental degradation. Institutions are needed that can ensure comprehensive management of the environment regardless of administrative borders.

h) *Many environmental problems are long term*, and future generations will be the victims. Again, climate change serves as a clear example. But future generations do not have a defined legal status either. Generally speaking, the role of law is to regulate present conflicts – between persons and interests of today. Law and legal institutions are not well developed and only marginally equipped to regulate intergenerational conflicts and secure intergenerational justice.

Both individually and together, these factors represent profound challenges for environmental policy and law. They are particularly important when legislation is fragmented and offers the authorities broad discretionary power to balance environmental concerns and other social goals and considerations. Agreed objectives of environmental policy often become illusory when they are weighed against objectives of economic growth, employment, increased production of food, energy and goods, improved transport, and against such principles as cost-effectiveness and "local self rule". It may, of course, be argued that this is simply the result of conscious political choices and political priorities. However, I will maintain that it is partly a result of the way environmental law – the framework for the execution of policy – is construed.

3. The problem of discretionary legislation

When I lecture on Norway's environmental law, I say in fact very little about the actual protection of Norway's environment. I talk about principles of environmental law, institutions, what *can* be decided and regulated, the conditions that *may* be laid down in a pollution permit, the *procedures* that are to be followed in land use planning, and so on. "On paper" it all looks well developed and adequate. However, I say little about "the real thing": To what extent is the environment actually protected, both legally and in fact? To answer this question, I have to explain *how the authorities apply the legislation* and hence the environmental *policy*.

This is mainly due to the fact that many of the key *substantive* provisions and rules are quite general or formed in an open style; they leave much discretion to the executive in the application of the provision. They either explicitly or implicitly prescribe a general balancing between the various interests when decisions are taken. This is the case, for example, for control of pollution from major stationary sources. The key section in the Pollution Control Act states that when deciding on an application for a pollution permit, the authority must "consider the effects of the pollution together with other inconveniences and benefits of the activity".[15] The key provision in the Energy Act[16] simply states that production or transmission of energy requires a permit,[17] and the objective of the act is to ensure energy production that is "rational" for society. According to the Aquaculture Act, an installation for aquaculture requires a permit, which may be granted if it is environmentally "justifiable".[18] Also, the legal framework for spatial and land use planning in the Planning and Building Act, which i.a. is decisive for major infrastructure developments, provides the planning authority with very broad discretionary power.

The legislation establishes institutions, systems, and procedural rules, and it lays down certain general objectives and principles to be observed. But when it comes to the actual protection of the environment, *the legal core* is neither very precise nor very "hard".

There are similar problems also with legislation that at first sight may seem quite precise in terms of content and substance. For example, Norway has a quite progressive Act on Right to Environmental Information. It implements the "Aarhus Convention"[19] and goes even further in some respects. It goes quite far in providing the public with the right of insight into environmental effects of both public and private activities. But a close look reveals that the rules nevertheless leave important areas to the discretion of the authority or the private firm in

---

15 Section 11 in the Pollution Control Act.

16 Act of 29 June 1990 no. 50 on the production, transmission, sale, distribution and use of energy *(lov om produksjon, omforming, overføring, omsetning, fordeling og bruk av energi m.m. (energiloven)).*

17 Section 3-1.

18 Act of 17 June 2005 no. 79 on aquaculture *(lov om akvakultur (akvakulturloven))*, section 4 and section 6 first para.

19 The UNECE Convention on Access to Information, Public Participation in Decision-making and Access to Justice in Environmental Matters of 25 June 1998.

question to decide whether information has to be given or not. This at least creates the basis for *pretending* in the individual case that the public does not have a right to get the information it asks for. This in itself makes it difficult for the public to avail themselves of their rights. A recent evaluation showed that after four years in force the act is scarcely known even by the public authorities and industry, and it is hardly applied.

This leads to the issue of *procedural rules*. We find quite precise procedural rules in Norwegian environmental law. This is particularly important since the substantial rules are vague. They ensure transparency, public participation, and environmental impact assessments (EIA).[20] But the final outcome, how an EIA is used and to what extent its results are actually taken into account when the substantial decision is made, depends on the formulation of the substantial rule and is thus left to the discretion of the responsible authority.

Rules on information and participation also have two sides, and here is a dilemma: Who participates? Do these types of rules in reality tend to favour the resourceful segment of the concerned public? This is at the core of the NIMBY – "not in my back yard" – syndrome. The result of transparent and participatory procedures is often that environmentally hazardous activities are located in poor neighbourhoods and thus cause "environmental injustice", or they are placed in undeveloped areas in order to avoid neighbourhood nuisance and protests altogether. Social scientists discuss "the legitimacy/effectiveness dilemma". Openness and participation may give legitimacy to a decision, but it does not necessarily lead to an optimal result from an environmental point of view.

These very general observations apply both to national and international environmental law. The soft character of many international environmental treaties is well known. But it is also true that an important development has been going on in this field for some time both at the international and the European level, with the objective of making both public and private obligations and rights more precise and to strengthen enforcement mechanisms. Gradually, this development seems to reduce "the discretionary space" of the authorities. This trend is relevant also for Norway being a party to all of the most important international conventions as well as the Treaty of the European Economic Area EEA.

---

20 The EIA rules are laid down in the Act of 27 June 2008 no. 71 on Planning and Building Regulation *(lov om planlegging og byggesaksbehandling (plan- og bygningsloven))* chapters 4 and 14, and Regulation of 26 June 2009 no. 855 on Environmental Impact Assessment.

4. Must environmental law be so open?

A question is whether key elements of environmental law have to be so open and "political" in their form. In my view, the answer is partly yes. This has to do with the nature of the problem that environmental law relates to, in particular the *complexity* of the problems and of the many interests – often many conflicting interests – involved.

This complexity means that environmental law is often not a question of solving a conflict between A and B: As between a buyer and a seller, between a landowner and a tenant, or between a tortfeasor and the injured party in classical private law, or between the state and the taxpayer, between the state and the social security client, or between the prosecuting agency and the accused in public law. In these areas it is possible to lay down rather precise mutual rights and obligations on the parties (even if a certain widening of relevant interests can be observed in the development of some of these areas of law as well).

Such a bilateral relationship is often at the core of an environmental case, for example between the authority and the private actor applying for a building permit or a pollution licence for a new factory. But usually there are a number of third party interests involved in environmental cases. These are of various types and strengths; both multiple and conflicting *public* interests, and several contradictory *private* interests, and interests at different levels – local, national and international. The interests range from clear and short term economic profit on the one hand, to uncertain, vague, long term effects on ideal, "soft" and disputed values such as environmental values and future concerns at the other end of the spectrum. It is difficult to see how these complex types of conflicts can be regulated in a just and reasonable way through simple, clear-cut legal rules. Therefore it is difficult to make conflict-solving here a legal exercise alone, in the sense of applying a given rule to a given fact and getting the answer. If one does this, the risk is that the decisions are neither environmentally acceptable, nor socially just, nor efficient in the economic sense of the word.[21]

It may also be argued that discretionary rules contribute to decisions that are efficient in the economic sense. They require, explicitly or implicitly, a cost-

---

21 My book *Forurensningsansvaret (Pollution Responsibility)*, Oslo, 1999, is in part an attempt to analyze Norway's legal rules in the field of pollution control from three perspectives: environmental effectiveness, fairness and economic efficiency.

benefit analysis in each individual case and the final balance may reflect the strength and the "value" of the various interests involved. For example, a cost-benefit analysis will identify positive and negative effects of a planned project and compare possible gains and losses. A further transparent and participatory procedure will ensure that the deciding authority is provided with additional information. In theory, this should ensure an optimal – and economically efficient – solution.

However, these arguments are challenged by the fundamental problems of environmental law described above. Of particular importance in the perspective of economic efficiency is the problem of putting the right price, in terms of money, on environmental values, and the problem of cumulative effects. The balancing of values and interests is carried out in innumerable individual cases, and not by a single or a few well-coordinated public bodies, but by numerous sector authorities at the state, county and municipal levels, working rather independently and putting different values on the environment. Here we are faced with the second major problem: the fragmentation of environmental law.

5. The problem of fragmentation and the principle of integration

What is usually defined and discussed as "environmental law" are the parts of law which have environmental protection as their main objective. However, this is only a limited part of all the law which is relevant for the status of the environment – what may be called environmental law in a broad sense. The way and the extent to which environmental considerations are taken into account when these acts are applied is equally important or may be even more important than the environmental legislation in the narrow sense of the concept.

The problem of discretionary rules must be seen in the context of this fragmentation of environmental law. The fragmentation is both "horizontal" and "vertical". Most of the economic and social sectors and activities that harm the environment are regulated by special acts. Within each sector the decision-making authority is distributed between state, regional and local authorities. In total, the system is very complex.

This problem of fragmentation must be seen together with the *"principle of inte-*

gration".[22] Norway's environmental law and administration is to a large extent based on this principle. Environmental considerations are to be "integrated" into the various sector policies. Each sector authority has the main responsibility for preventing and controlling the environmental hazardous effects of its activities. For some sectors this responsibility is found in the legislation itself. For example, the Aquaculture Act[23] states that the sector ministry[24] takes the necessary decisions to ensure an "environmentally sound" aquaculture in the country. The objective of the Forestry Act[25] is both to promote forestry as an industry and "ensure biological diversity, and landscape, recreational and cultural values" in the forest. The responsible authorities are the ministry responsible for forestry[26] and local forest authorities. For other sectors the principle of integration may be merely implicit. In sector policy formulation and in individual cases environmental authorities usually have a say in the preparatory procedure, and may influence the outcome. But the final balancing between the objectives of the sector and environmental considerations is made by the sector authority itself on the basis of discretionary rules.

As a matter of fact, the principle of integration may increase the fragmentation of environmental management and weaken environmental protection. This may seem to be a paradox, since the concept of "integration" suggests the opposite. The reason is that the different authorities weigh and balance their sector objectives against the related environmental effects differently. Thus environmental values are not treated consistently across sectors. A certain part of the environment such as an ecosystem is not treated as a whole either, which it should be. The environment becomes a "consideration" which is given different weight by different authorities, on a case-by-case basis. The fundamental problems described above come fully into play.

---

22 The "principle of integration" has a "narrow" and a "wide" meaning in international environmental law. The EU directive 2008/1/EC of Integrated pollution prevention and control (the "IPPC directive") reflects the "narrow" meaning: treat all environmental effects together ("integrated") when considering a permit application for a polluting activity. The "broad" understanding is the integration of environmental objectives into the development process, and thus into the policy definition and implementation of various economic and social sectors. This is the meaning of the principle in this article.

23 Act of 17 June 2005 no. 79 on aquaculture *(lov om akvakultur (akvakulturloven))*, section 10.

24 Ministry for Fisheries and Coastal Affairs.

25 Act of 27 May 2005 no. 31 on forestry *(lov om skogbruk (skogbruksloven))*.

26 Ministry of Agriculture and Food.

Let us take a closer look at this principle and its *raison d'être*.

One "root" of the principle of integration is found in the 1987 report from the World Commission on Environment and Development, known as the "Brundtland report". The report launched sustainable development as a key objective for the international community, by which it meant "a development that meets the needs of today without compromising the ability of future generations to meet their own needs".

"Merging environment and economics in decision making" is one of the seven "strategic imperatives" recommended by the Commission to achieve sustainable development. This reflects the fundamental message in the report: "development" and "environmental protection" should no longer be seen as separate and often conflicting objectives, but as "two sides of the same coin". As the commission expressed it:

> ... But the "environment" is where we all live; and "development" is what we all do in attempting to improve our lot within that abode. The two are inseparable. .... Ecology and economy are becoming ever more intervowen – locally, regionally, nationally, and globally – into a seamless net of causes and effects.[27]

However, a fragmented legislation and administration makes it very difficult to treat ecology and economy in combination. The report states:

> The integrated and interdependent nature of the new challenges and issues contrasts sharply with the nature of the institutions that exist today. These institutions tend to be independent, fragmented, and working to relatively narrow mandates with closed decision processes. Those responsible for managing natural resources and protecting the environment are institutionally separated from those responsible for managing the economy. The real world of interlocked economic and ecological systems will not change; the policies and institutions concerned must.
>
> This new awareness requires major shifts in the way governments and individuals approach issues of environment, development, and international cooperation. Approaches to environmental policy can be broadly characterized in two ways. One, characterized as the "standard agenda", reflects an approach to environmental policy, laws, and institutions that focuses on environmental effects. The second reflects an approach concentrating on the policies that are the sources of those effects. These

27 "Our Common Future", Chairman's foreword p. xi.

> two approaches represent distinctively different ways of looking both at the issues and at the institutions to manage them.[28]

The solution, the Commission said, is to move away from the first approach, and adopt the second approach; this means to integrate environmental protection objectives into the policies of important sectors that cause environmental problems. The main challenge for institutional and legal change is expressed in the title of a key section of the report: "Shifting the Focus to the Policy Sources".[29] The Commission further develops its reasoning as follows:

> Sustainable development objectives should be incorporated in the terms of reference of those cabinet and legislative committees dealing with national economic policy and planning as well as those dealing with key sectoral and international policies. As an extension of this the major central economic and sectoral agencies of governments should now be made *directly responsible and fully accountable* for ensuring that their policies, programmes, and budgets support development that is ecologically as well as economically sustainable.[30]

It should be added that the idea of "integration" is supplemented by another key aspect in the Brundtland report: the notion of "ultimate limits". Although the commission did not want the report to be perceived as "another 'Limits to Growth' report", it states clearly that integration cannot mean just including and balancing the various interests in decision-making. The commission recognizes that, in reality, there are limits to growth:

> At a minimum, sustainable development must not endanger the natural systems that support life on Earth, the atmosphere, the waters, the soils, and the living beings.
>
> ......
>
> But ultimate limits there are, and sustainability requires that long before these are reached, the world must ensure equitable access to the constrained resource and reorient technological efforts to relieve the pressure.[31]

---

28 Op. cit. p. 310.

29 Op. cit. p. 310.

30 Op. cit. p. 314, italics added.

31 Op. cit. pp. 44-45.

In the process of follow-up of the Brundtland report the "principle of integration" was recognized as a core of the objective of sustainable development. For example, it is expressed – in the widest possible way – in the Rio declaration,[32] and it is the very basis for the international action plan Agenda 21, which describes what must be done in the various economic sectors in order to achieve sustainable development.

The Treaty of the European Community laid down the principle of integration. Its article 6 read:

> Environmental protection requirements must be integrated into the definition and implementation of the Community policies and activities (referred to in Article 3), in particular with a view to promoting sustainable development.

This is now included as article 11 in the (Lisbon) Treaty on the Functioning of the European Union.[33]

To "integrate" environmental concerns into sector policy means not only that environmental issues and effects must be *assessed and taken into account when decisions are made* but also that the objective and content of important sector policies in reality *are modified* in order to ensure long-term environmental protection. It means giving environmental concerns more weight in such areas as finance policy, consumer policy, industry policy, transport policy, energy policy, agricultural and fisheries policy, and general land use policy – just to mention some of the most important policy areas.

---

32 Principle 4 of the Rio Declaration states: "In order to achieve sustainable development, environmental protection shall constitute an integral part of the development process and cannot be considered in isolation from it."

33 With the formal modification that "Community policies and activities (referred to in Article 3)" has been replaced by "the Union's policies and activities". It should be added, however, that while environmental protection was the only main task that was to be "integrated" into other policies and activities in the EC Treaty, several objectives have been given similar status in the Lisbon Treaty, such as: high level of employment, the guarantee of adequate social protection, the fight against social exclusion, a high level of education, training and protection of human health (article 9), and "discrimination based on sex, racial or ethnic origin religion or belief, disability, age or sexual orientation" (article 10). So, since more or less "everything must be integrated into everything", the environmental integration principle has not quite the same strong meaning any longer as before.

6. The dilemma of the integration principle

Empirical studies show that real environmental policy integration is difficult, in spite of strong, ambitious and well formulated policy objectives to this effect.

Integration of environmental protection requires changes in the "paradigm", objective and priorities of important sectors and authorities at different levels. There certainly are possibilities for "win-win" situations: the "environmental solution" can be in accordance with and even improve the sector performance on its own criteria. But too often, and in the short term, it is perceived as a "problem" working against the success criteria of a sector authority and the people working there. It requires that sector authorities work with objectives, issues and problems about which they know little, with which they frequently do not identify and which they perceive as contrary to what they regard as their primary task and "mission".[34]

So, we are faced with a dilemma: environmental protection and sustainable development require that each economic sector is "directly responsible and fully accountable" for ensuring ecological sustainability of its policy and measures. But how can this be achieved if and when:

- Environmental values and economic interests are difficult to compare, even "incommensurable"?
- Environmental protection goes contrary to the objective and "paradigm" of the sector?
- Responsibility for the environment becomes a question of decisions in numerous different, fragmented sector institutions and authorities, all valuing and weighing environmental issues differently?
- Authority is divided between various levels of government, including local government with considerable independence and self-determination?

These problems require thorough consideration and cannot be solved without a number of legal and institutional measures and reforms.

34 William M. Lafferty, From environmental protection to sustainable development: the challenge of decoupling through sectoral integration, in William M. Lafferty (ed.), *Governance for Sustainable Development. The Challenge of Adapting Form to Function,* Edward Elgar Publishing Ltd, UK and USA, 2004.

7. The role of principles of environmental law

Recent developments in international and national environmental law have been influenced by several "principles" of environmental law. These may serve to overcome the problems of fragmentation and broad discretionary power, provided that they are understood and applied consistently by the various authorities. Unfortunately, this is only to a limited extent the case in Norway.

The principle of *sustainable development* has been laid down as an important overall political goal in Norway, and it has been explicitly included in several major acts.[35] But there is no agreed and consistent meaning of "sustainable development" as a concept in Norwegian law. A recent analysis indicates that the meaning differs from one act to another. It also shows that the inclusion of sustainable development or "sustainability" as an objective, in various forms, in reality does not mean anything very different from "business as usual".[36]

Likewise, the *precautionary principle* is defined as an important principle in Norway's environmental policy. However, any application of the principle in other important policy areas such as petroleum policy, energy policy, transport policy, fish farming policy and agricultural policy has been difficult to identify. The principle is now explicitly laid down in the new Nature Diversity Act,[37] and it is intended to have an effect across sectors and thus influence the application of sector legislation. To what extent this will be the case remains to be seen.[38]

In 1992 an environmental section was included as section 110 b in Norway's constitution *(Grunnloven)*. In general terms it states that everybody has the right to a healthy environment and to a natural environment in which diversity is protected. This right should also extend to future generations. In its third paragraph, however, it states that it is up to the state's authorities to define the content of this right more precisely, and thus decide how environmental and other social and economic objectives shall be balanced. So far

35 The most recent example is the 2008 Planning and Building Act.

36 Markus Jerkø, Det norske formålet "bærekraftig utvikling" (The Norwegian objective of "sustainable development"), *Tidsskrift for Rettsvitenskap* no. 3/2009 pp. 354-388.

37 Act of 19 June 2009 no. 100 Relating to the Management of Biological, Geological and Landscape Diversity (Nature Management Act).

38 For a more thorough analysis see Hans Chr. Bugge's chapter on Norway in Nicolas de Sadeleer, *Implementing the Precautionary Principle*, London, 2007.

section 110 b has only played a marginal role in strengthening Norway's environmental law.[39]

8. The combined effects of the fundamental problems, discretionary rules, fragmentation and sector responsibility. Can they be overcome?

The combination of discretionary rules, fragmented legislation, the application of the principle of integration, and the feeble application of principles of environmental law may easily give environmental values and concerns a weak legal position in decision-making. Consistent management of the environment based on certain environmental objectives becomes very difficult. The fundamental problems of environmental law, as described in the introduction to this article, are an essential factor here. When the environmental effects of an individual case are uncertain and difficult to assess, and if some of the effects in addition are long-term and distant, they will easily appear as marginal and quite unimportant compared to short-term economic benefits of, for example, a new factory, a power plant, a motorway, an aquaculture plant, a ski station or even a single recreational house. And when the law leaves much discretion to the authority, there are limited legal means to ensure that the environmental values are taken properly into account.

As already pointed out, it can of course be argued that the way environmental goals and values are treated by sector authorities and at different levels of government is simply a reflection of political priorities. The decision-makers – and ultimately the public – favour economic development, jobs, improved transport, supermarkets closer to home, etc. before environmental protection. I maintain that political priorities – as a matter of course – are part of the explanation, but not the only explanation. Law has a very important role to play as a frame for decisions, and in particular as an instrument for adopting good environmental alternatives and solutions. It becomes a legal issue when the legislation demands that environmental effects are properly assessed and ensures a fair balance.

39 See Ole Kristian Fauchald, Forfatning og miljøvern – en analyse av Grunnlovens § 110 b. (Constitution and environmenta protection – an analysis of Grunnloven section 110 b), *Tidsskrift for Rettsvitenskap* no. 1-2/2007 pp. 1-84.

The legal challenges relate to both procedural and substantial rules, and may be described as follows:

- How to ensure through legal means and instruments that environmental objectives are both fully integrated in sector policies and on an equal footing with sector objectives?
- How can law be developed to ensure that environmental values and interests are treated more consistently across sectors and levels of authority?
- How can legislation work in such a way that the objectives of environmental protection and sustainable development are naturally internalized in sector objectives and in the application of sector policies instead of being seen and treated as contrary to their primary objective, which need to be avoided?
- How can law contribute to ensure "accountability" of the various sector authorities in this respect?

It would be naïve to recommend doing away with sector legislation, the integration principle and discretionary rules altogether. The principle of integration has come to stay. Administrative fragmentation is also a fact which is very difficult to change, and there is a long tradition in Norway of flexible legislation in the field of land use, management of natural resources and protection of the environment.

Instead, the answer should be to clarify and apply recognized environmental law principles, improve sector coordination *i.a.* through strengthened land use planning, and develop substantive environmental legislation which can apply equally across sectors and at various levels of government. One necessary element seems to be a more *consistent valuing of environmental goods and services*, which are accepted and applied by the various authorities in policy formulation and in individual cases. Another important instrument is *environmental quality objectives* as a basis and framework for all decisions affecting a certain part of nature or a given geographical area. This is the core of the concept of an *"ecosystem approach"* in environmental governance. This concept has now been introduced in the new Nature Diversity Act although it is not clearly defined.

Such an ecosystem approach would ensure that the ecological system is governed in its entirety. It enables the observance of its performance in relation to decisions taken, and entails several other advantages as well. Most importantly, consistent valuing of environmental goods and services is much more feasible when carried out for a fixed ecosystem. As an illustration, environmental governance based on the performance of one river basin could clearly reveal the value of this river basin at a very early stage. In any weighing and balancing assessment, this value could be incorporated systematically, instead of carrying out a single valuation assessment for the particular environmental goods and services affected by the individual decision. In this manner, decision-making incorporates predetermined environmental values, which significantly increases accountability, transparency and consistency in environmental policy.

Another advantage of the ecosystem approach is that certain environmental objectives such as sustainability may more easily be made operational and assessed, if and when policy-makers agree in advance on what sustainability means for the particular ecosystem affected by their decision. What is the resilience of that particular ecosystem? What are the limits of its performance? What kind of trade-offs are desirable? Disclosing these questions at an early stage could make environmental policy much more consistent and sustainable. In this respect, interconnection between the fields of science, policy and law are of utmost importance.

Recent trends in Norwegian legislation point in this direction. The *2008 Planning and Building Act* has sustainable development as its overall objective. It strengthens spatial and land use planning as an instrument for cross-sector coordination in particular at the regional and municipal levels. It makes it possible for the planning authorities to lay down environmental quality objectives in municipal master plans and local development plans, and provides new zoning instruments to this effect. New principles for sustainable management of biodiversity, including the precautionary principle, are – as mentioned – laid down in the *2009 Nature Diversity Act*. It is the intention of the legislator that these principles shall be applied by all sector authorities when exercising discretionary authority in individual cases. To what extent this will be followed up, and what the results will be, remains to be seen. In addition, environmental quality norms, aiming particularly at the protection of biodiversity, may also be laid down pursuant to this new act. They may serve as guidelines when decisions are taken pursuant to sector legislation.

However, Norway's implementation of the major EU directives in this field will be even more important, and in particular the Water Framework Directive ("WFD").[40] It is one of the most ambitious and innovative pieces of environmen-

40 Directive 2000/60/EC.

tal legislation from the EU. It implies an ecosystem approach to the management of the rivers, lakes and coastal waters, by requiring binding water quality objectives. Thus it seeks to achieve a more consistent approach to water management by framing the decisions related to the environment by sectors and planning authorities at all levels.

The implementation and application of the directive appears to be a challenge for Norway due to our legal and administrative system in the field of environmental management. It is not based on natural geographical and hydrological units. Instead, it focuses on regulating activities related to water within the different sectors (not on the quality of the water recourse itself) through widely formulated, discretionary rules. The implementation of the directive raises the question of how environmental objectives in the WFD may limit various sector authorities' policy formulation as well as the exercise of discretion in individual cases.

9. Concluding remarks: A challenge to environmental law research

It must be recognized that the content and implementation of sector legislation are crucial for environmental management and protection. More consistent valuing of environmental goods and services, and implementation of environmental law principles across sectors in the balancing of environmental concerns and sector objective, appear as essential, as do legal solutions to the problem of cumulative effects.

This is a challenge for research in environmental law. It cannot be limited to environmental legislation in the strict sense but must study how the environment is considered and treated within economic sectors that directly and indirectly influence the quality of the environment. How are principles of environmental law, and environmental considerations, taken into account and valued within the "development sectors" of law? It is an important task to identify the "margin of appreciation", or the "hard core" of environmental law. We need more projects in this field, and we may need to develop methods, a more systematic approach, and knowledge concerning the relationship between environmental law and other parts of law.

The Research Group in Natural Resources Law at the Faculty of Law, University of Oslo, of which Erling Eide is an active member, has taken up these issues in one of its projects called "Consistency in Environmental Law". The basic hypothesis is that the problems we face when trying to protect the environment through law are partly due to lack of consistency in Norway's system of environmental law. The objective of the project is to identify relevant "inconsistencies" and other weaknesses in the law and/or its application and on this basis – hopefully – suggest improvements.

Crime, Corruption and Political Favoritism in Developing Countries

Robert D. Cooter and Hans-Bernd Schäfer

In 1995 I had the great privilege of working for eight months at the Norwegian Academy of Science in Oslo in an international group of law and economics scholars. Erling Eide was head and host of our group, which also included Endre Stavang. And though each of us worked on different projects we were engaged every day in discussions about our subjects, methods and papers. The atmosphere in the wonderful villa in Drammensveien was somewhat like a cross between that of a monastery and a luxury hotel. Erling was working on crime deterrence and some of the most important works in Europe on this subject are from him. After my stay, we never lost contact and he visited our Ph.D. program in Hamburg for talks with doctoral students several times. Erling was also a frequent and helpful referee for econometric submissions to the International Review of Law and Economics. I always admired his dedication, his mastery of formal methods, his crystal-clear writings, his hospitality and his fine sense of humor. *Hoch soll er leben, drei mal hoch.* It is therefore a great honor to have the opportunity to contribute to this *Festschrift* for his 70th birthday. The following article is a shortened version of a book chapter co-authored with Robert D. Cooter from Berkeley School of Law, under the title "Solomon's Knot, How Law Can End the Poverty of Nations", which Princeton University Press will publish later.[1]

1 Introduction by Hans-Bernd Schäfer.

Some facts about corruption

In the Georgian Soviet Socialist Republic of the 1970s, patients bribed medical doctors for better treatment in state hospitals, high school students bribed teachers for higher grades, farmers bribed policemen to sell in town markets and builders bribed inspectors to overlook inferior construction. Citizens generally expected to bribe state officials for permits, licences, services, exemptions and favorable decisions. Many corrupt results were sinister: low quality goods, high prices, uneven public services, unsafe buildings, environmental degradation and slow growth.[2] Some corrupt results were comical, such as when officials put a sign on a synagogue reading, "A meeting hall where prayer is forbidden."[3]

We described Georgia in the 1970s because, having passed into history, its corruption is documented. Many contemporary countries resemble it, but documentation is difficult because corruption hides from view, like termites in the foundation. State officials serve the public and themselves. When offered a bribe, conscience points one way and selfishness points the other. Some officials in every country, and most officials in some countries, succumb to bribes. Although hidden, pervasive corruption weakens the legal, physical and social foundation of economic development as surely as termites endanger a house.

The World Bank originally did not discuss the bribery that afflicted many of its biggest aid projects. Such a discussion was thought to violate its prohibition from interfering in the politics of recipient countries. In 1996, James Wolfensohn violated this taboo by referring to the "cancer of corruption" in developing countries. Two years later, the bank published an influential paper, "Assessing Aid", which argued that aid is ineffective unless given to countries with honest governments.[4] As this story suggests, the world's toleration of corruption has diminished as its appreciation of the hidden threat increased. This article explains how corruption slows economic growth and suggests strategies to deal with it.

"Corruption" often refers to improper influence of state officials. Improper influence is often illegal, but not always. Thus bribing a procurement officer is

---

2 These facts are vividly detailed in D. Levy (2007), Price adjustment under the table: Evidence on efficiency-enhancing corruption, *European Journal of Political Economy*, Volume 23, Issue 2, June 2007, pp. 423–447.

3 A famous American comedian, Will Rogers, said, "It's easy being a humorist when you've got the whole government working for you."

4 Cassidy, J. (2007). The Next Crusade. *The New Yorker*, pp. 36–51.

illegal everywhere, and contributing to the political party controlling the procurement office is legal in many countries. Similarly, bribing members of parliament to enact a bill is illegal everywhere, whereas contributing to the re-election campaign of the parliament's speaker is legal in many countries. Politicians build loyalty by rewarding it, legally or illegally. Bribes are the illegitimate cousins of pork-barrel politics.

This article focuses on illegal corruption, which must remain hidden. To measure hidden corruption, the organization Transparency International surveys the opinions of experienced people. Using these surveys, it publishes an index of the extent of corruption that observers perceive in their country's public sector. In 2009 the index ranked 180 countries by perceived public sector corruption. The following figure gives a sample of countries ranked from low to high. According to the figure, New Zealand is perceived as the least corrupt country in the survey (ranked 1), and Somalia is perceived as the most corrupt country (ranked 180).

1. New Zealand	55. Namibia	106. Argentina
2. Denmark	25. Chile	89. Mexico
3. Singapore	37. Taiwan	111. Indonesia
3. Sweden	63. Italy	146. Russia
12. Hong Kong	69. Ghana	168. Iran
14. Germany	75. Brazil	158. Cambodia
17. Japan	79. China	162. Venezuela
19. United States	84. India	180. Somalia

Figure 1. Corruption Perception Index, Transparency International, 2009. Ranking of selected countries.

In some countries, for instance in Sweden, civil servants are as clean as the voices of their most celebrated opera singers like that of Anne Sofie von Otter. On average, observers tend to perceive low corruption in high-income countries, medium corruption in middle income countries, and high corruption in low-income countries. By our calculation, the simple correlation between a country's ranking on the corruption perception index and its ranking on income per capita in 2009 is 0.75.[5] This correlation is imperfect, with some wealthy countries like Italy being perceived as more corrupt than some poor countries like Namibia. Also, in states where perceived corruption is high overall, important sectors are uncorrupted. Thus observers agree that Indian elections are as clean as in Western countries; the Indian Supreme Court (APEX) enjoys a reputation for honest judges; and India's space agency (OSRA) launches rockets and satellites that require honest administration. However, experts estimate that up to two thirds of the Indian government's expenditure on cheap food for the poor gets diverted through corruption.[6]

What is the relationship between *perceived* and *actual* corruption? We have little meaningful international data on actual corruption. Rose-Ackerman estimated that approximately three percent of global GDP, or roughly one trillion dollars, goes to pay bribes every year[7].

Optimal crime and corruption

Now we turn to some causes that partly explain international differences in crime and corruption. Increasing the probability and severity of the punishment deters crime because a rational person will not commit a criminal act and offer or accept a bribe when the gain is less than the expected punishment. However, more deterrence requires more money for police, judges, prisons, reform commissions, etc. A good policy towards corruption takes these costs into account. The sum of the cost of the harm from corruption and the cost of deterring it provides a simple and useful measure of corruption's cost to society:

(social cost of crime) = (cost of harm) + (cost of deterrence).

Deterrence that costs less than the harm it prevents reduces the social cost of crime and corruption. Conversely, deterrence that costs more than the harm it prevents increases the social cost. Adjusting deterrence expenditures accordingly

5 Spearman ranks correlation, 175 countries, 2 tailed critical value, 1 per cent: 0.81.

6 E. Luce, 2006. *In Spite of the Gods, The Strange Rise of Modern India*, Abacus p. 87.

7 Cited in J. Svensson, 2005. Eight Questions about Corruption. *Journal of Economic Perspectives* 19(3):19–42.

will minimize the social cost of crime and corruption. At the minimum, economists say that crime and corruption is "optimal." This odd-sounding phrase underlines the inescapable fact that deterrence is costly.

The *optimality hypothesis* asserts that actual deterrence of corruption in most states is roughly optimal if the government follows a rational policy in the public interest. What is the relation between optimal crime and the wealth of a nation, approximated by the GDP? Should, under this hypothesis, poor countries have more or less crime and corruption than rich countries? Countries that optimize deterrence will buy more as they get richer, just as they buy more education and better health. Thus more wealth should cause less crime and corruption. On the other hand in poor countries there is less to steal than in rich countries. Every street robbery in a rich country leads to a higher booty than in a poor country. Therefore, in a rich country each robbery leads to higher costs of crime than in a poor country and the costs of crime are higher in a rich country even when the number of crimes is the same. Moreover, the higher bounty in rich countries can draw people into criminal behavior, such that the number of crimes might be higher in rich countries as compared to poor countries. This effect, however, is again countervailed if, with economic growth, the income of a potential criminal in the legal sector also rises. Wealth distribution also plays a role. If a poor country starts to grow, growth often concentrates in particular regions and sectors. That makes some people very rich very quickly and leaves the incomes of many others unaffected. This concentration of wealth also attracts more crimes. We cannot say which of these positive and negative effects on crime rates and costs of crime prevails. The fact that there is only a weak relation between homicide and GDP is in line with this observation. Under the optimality hypothesis we would predict lower crime rates for those crimes which do not result in an involuntary transfer of wealth or money, such as sex crimes or hate crimes. These crimes should become fewer with more money spent on deterrence as a result of economic growth. For these crimes, however, no reliable statistics exist worldwide. But how, then, can the strong correlation between GDP and perceived corruption and between GDP and perceived organized crime be explained? Probably not with the optimality hypothesis.

There are some observations about corruption and organized crime which differ from those concerning ordinary crime.[8] A robbery, theft or rape is – in economic terms – always a cost for the victim and the society. Corruption is not necessarily a cost. If in a poor country the civil service and the judiciary are corrupt, a bribe might help business people to get things done which otherwise might be impossible. For instance establishing a business in the informal sector and avoiding regulation in exchange for a bribe to law enforcers is widespread but does not necessarily represent a cost to the society. When hiring a worker, buying a machine or bribing an official, businesses expect to get value for money. They would not pay bribes unless their benefit exceeded the cost of the bribe and the anticipated punishment for the crime. Individual firms gain wealth from paying bribes, but what about the nation as a whole?[9] Bribes are sometimes called "speed money" because they enable firms that pay them to grow faster. But do they speed up or slow down the economy?

Whether the services bought with bribes increase or diminish the nation's wealth depends partly on whether the underlying law retards or promotes business. Laws that promote business include property, contracts and business law, as well as laws for building physical infrastructure like railroads and harbors. The state provides many social goods that promote business indirectly, like health, education and security. Conversely, laws that retard business include restrictive

8 For surveys and analytical concepts on corruption see Bardhan, P. 1997. Corruption and development: a review of issues, *Journal of Economic Literature*, vol. 35, pp. 1320–346.

Laffont, J.J. and T.N. Guessan. 1999. Competition and corruption in an agency relationship, *Journal of Development Economics*, vol. 60, pp. 271–95.

Rose-Ackerman, S. 1975. The economics of corruption, *Journal of Public Economics*, vol. 4, pp. 187–203.

Rose-Ackerman, S. 1999. *Corruption and Government, Causes, Consequences and Reform*, Cambridge, UK: Cambridge University Press.

Shleifer, A. and R. W. Vishny. 1992. Pervasive shortages under socialism, *RAND Journal of Economics*, vol. 23 (3), pp. 237–46. Reprinted in Shleifer and Vishny (1998) chapter 6.

Shleifer, A. and R. W. Vishny. 1993. Corruption, *Quarterly Journal of Economics*, vol. 108, pp. 599–618.

9 Osterfeld distinguishes between corruption that increases output and corruption that decreases it. D. Osterfeld. *Prosperity versus Planning: How Government Stiles Economics Growth*, Oxford University Press, 1992. For empirical application of this distinction, see Douglas A. Houston, Can corruption Ever Improve an Economy, 27 *Cato Journal* 325 (2007), and Mushfiq us Swaleheen and Dean Stansel, Economic Freedom, corruption, and Growth, 27 *Cato Journal* 343 (2007).

licenses to suppress competition, non-competitive bidding for state contracts, most cross-subsidies, and confiscatory taxes.

Effective administration of laws that promote business increases the nation's wealth. Bribes make laws less effective by deflecting them from their purpose. To minimize social costs, the state should use its resources to deter the corruption of laws that promote business.[10] Conversely, ineffective administration of laws that retard business increases the nation's wealth. Bribes may do some good by deflecting laws that retard business. To minimize social costs, the state should not focus on deterring corruption of laws with bad consequences such as laws retarding business.

A bribe paid to powerful politicians who protect the briber's property against private or official predators might not cause a cost, because otherwise a business might become unfeasible. The same observation holds for some organized crime activities, like collecting protection money or enforcing contracts with the help of gangs. We will show that the overall effects of corruption and organized crime are clearly negative for society. But there exist some conceptual differences between ordinary crime and corruption as well as organized crime.

Figure 9.4 summarizes this analysis. Optimal deterrence of bribes is high for laws that lubricate beneficial activities, as indicated by the figure's upper left cell. Examples include registering property, enforcing contracts, collecting debts, incorporating businesses, liquidating bankrupt firms, inviting competitive bids on government contracts and supplying passports. Similarly, optimal deterrence is high for laws that retard harmful activities, as indicated by the lower right cell. Examples include protecting property against theft or trespass, withholding an occupancy permit from an unsafe building, prosecuting fraud in contracts and stocks, blocking a merger that creates a monopoly, seizing illegal drugs and weapons and taxing polluters.

Conversely, optimal deterrence of bribes is low for laws that retard beneficial activities. Examples include many process rules that slow down business activity in order to provide more bribes to the officials who administer them. Optimal deterrence of bribes is also low for laws that lubricate harmful activities, according to the lower left cell. Examples include laws that create and sustain cartels.

Ideally, the state should repeal or reform bad laws that retard the economy. After repeal or reform, people no longer need to bribe officials for permits,

10 An economist would be quick to add this phrase to the end of the sentence: "... at the margin."

licenses, exemptions, cross-subsidies, etc. However, entrenched interests often block repeals or reform, in which case the state should *not* focus its scarce resources on deterring corruption of laws that are bad for the economy. Should the state go even further by tolerating corruption of bad laws? Many developing countries tolerate a massive "informal sector" of gray and black market activity, as we will discuss later. Over-regulation feeds profits for illegal activities that bribed officials overlook. Tolerating bribes brings the law into disrepute, and so does enforcing bad regulations. Is the legal system worse if you can pay a bribe to compete with the friend of a politician, or if you cannot compete with the friend of a politician no matter how much you pay? After the best policy of repeal or reform, the second best policy is objectionable, like suppressing a black market for penicillin.

Politicians create many laws to take wealth from the people who make it, and build loyalty by redistributing wealth to their followers. To reward their friends, politicians impose restraints on competition to create monopolies, enact subsidies, restrict supply below demand so that buying is a privilege, create queues to jump, etc.[11] The desire of politicians to reward loyalty is ubiquitous, and so laws that retard growth are pervasive. Bad policy is good politics in most countries.[12] Even so, effective administration of law and policy is better on average than the collapse of administration. If all laws become ineffective, a nation regresses into anarchy, which produces the worst economic conditions in the world, not to mention appalling abuses of human rights. Hence the average effect of corruption on national wealth is negative, as statistical studies confirm.[13]

Corruption in states with strong and weak governments

Having discussed deterrence, next we explain how the structure of political power affects corruption. A modern state consists of politicians at the top (the "govern-

11 V. Tanzi. 1998. Corruption Around the World, Causes, Consequences, Scope and Cures, IMF Staff Papers, Vol. 95/4 pp. 559.

12 This phrase is from Hilton Root, *Capital and Collusion: The Political Logic of Global Economic Development.* 2005. Root argues that redistribution to political allies builds committed loyalists.

13 Jan van Dijk finds a substantial negative effect of corruption on nation wealth. Jan van Dijk (2007) *The World of Crime, Breaking the Silence on Problems of Security, Justice and Development Across the World*, Pine Forge Press, ch. 12.

ment") and administrators below (the "civil service"). In a corrupt state, these two groups compete for bribes. Bribery is centralized when top politicians control it, not the administrators.

The top politicians who control bribes can collect them by two different means. First, politicians can take bribes directly from firms. Direct bribery works best when a few top politicians work with a few large firms. In a centralized industry with a few large firms, top politicians maximize their bribes by preventing administrators from collecting them. Thus a large firm might have to bribe a cabinet minister, who subsequently protects it from extortion by other officials. This is a system of political corruption and honest administration – politicians can take bribes and administrators cannot.

South Korea under Park Chung-hee illustrates a strong authoritarian state with corrupt politicians at the top and a mostly honest administration. The same seems true for the Soviet Union under communism, where corruption was widespread but tightly controlled from above. Other possible Asian cases include the Philippines under Marcos and Indonesia under Suharto, although the top politicians in these countries were not so successful in controlling lower level corruption.

Second, politicians can use administrators as their agents to collect bribes. The top politicians need administrators to collect bribes when small firms produce much of the nation's wealth. In a decentralized industry with many firms, top politicians maximize their bribes by requiring administrators to collect them and then sharing the proceeds, like a large firm that maximizes its sales revenue by paying commissions to its salesmen. Thus a small firm might bribe a low-level administrator who kicks back most of the bribe to the minister. The minister then protects the small firm from further extortion by others. This is a system of delegated corruption – administrators take bribes for politicians. (In game theory, this is a "principal-agent problem." The delegation of bribes may be especially important in a democracy where politicians require extensive support of voters, as opposed to a dictatorship that requires intensive loyalty on the part of the army and police.[14])

14 Root argues that democracy requires more extensive support than dictatorship, so democratic politicians will spread largess broadly to gain a lot of votes, whereas dictators will focus largess more intensively to gain greater loyalty from fewer people. See Hilton Root, *Capital and Collusion: The Political Logic of Global Economic Development.* 2005.

In Afghanistan senior police and anti-narcotics staff at the provincial level are reported to have paid up to 150,000 USD to politicians who post them[15]. In the Philippines the state sets up countrywide developing agencies for public projects, which serve as pork barrel funds for local and national politicians. Contractors pay up to a third of the contract value to the fund. Most of this kickback money is channeled to powerful politicians[16].

We have explained that the top politicians in a centralized state may collect bribes directly and forbid civil servants from doing so, or politicians may use civil servants as their agents for collecting bribes. The direct approach may prevail in one country or industry, especially if the economy is centralized and direct collection is relatively easy. The indirect approach may prevail in another country or industry, especially if the economy is decentralized and direct collection is difficult.

Top politicians who feel secure in their power tend to take a long-run viewpoint towards their wealth. They can collect more bribes in the long run from thriving businesses than from failing ones. For businesses to thrive, the politicians must extort moderate bribes, not confiscatory bribes, just as the state must collect moderate taxes. To keep bribes moderate, the top politicians must discipline civil servants so they do not compete with each other and extort too much. Business investment in a stable state with centralized corruption resembles commerce on the Rhine River in the 19th century after the emergence of nation-states. Ships on the Rhine previously paid to pass each baron's castle, which added up to a lot of money. The nation-states suppressed the barons and then the ships on the Rhine had to pay a small number of state officials, which was cheaper.

Conversely, when a centralized state is unstable and the top politicians feel insecure, they may take a short-run viewpoint and impose confiscatory bribes that bankrupt firms. Unstable politics shrinks the time-horizon for officials and destroys economic growth. Thus Mobutu in the Congo and Mugabe in Zimbabwe used cleptocracy to prolong the power of their failing dictatorships by destroying their national economies.

Having discussed strong, centralized states, we will discuss bribery in weak,

15 Anthony Loyd, Corruption, bribes and trafficking: A cancer that is engulfing Afghanistan, *The Times*, November 24th, 2007.

16 See inquirer.net, http://opinion.inquirer.net/inquireropinion/columns/view/20090522-206417/Pork-barrel-is-root-cause-of-corruption (last visited March 2010).

decentralized states. Weak government provides an opportunity for corruption to proliferate among minor officials. The effect on business is mostly negative, but it can also be positive. The effect is negative when a business needs permission to act from many different officials. The effect of this is comparable to successive monopolies, which lead to a markup higher than in a monopoly. Thus an investor might have to bribe the officials who register companies, license production, collect taxes and tariffs, and impose environmental regulations, as well as the police officer, the electricity company, the water supplier, etc. When a firm needs permission from many different officials, business activity resembles commerce on the Rhine River in medieval times when more than 60 robber barons collected tolls from each ship that passed by. Even highly productive ventures may never launch, like the many ships that never sailed down the Rhine.[17]

In a contemporary example, Silicon Valley attracts engineers from many countries, and they often outsource production to their homeland, especially China and India. An Egyptian engineer we know manages an investment fund for other Egyptians like himself in Silicon Valley. He is unwilling to outsource to Egypt for fear that Egyptian officials would demand confiscatory bribes. When unscrupulous officials have this discretion, every business is at risk. African nations provide more examples of weak states with decentralized corruption. In Kenya businesses were regulated by a multiple licensing system which required each line of business to be approved separately[18]. In India, Shah and Sane found that even after liberalization, licensing requirements which follow no sound policy still exist. The requirements are so difficult to meet that their only rationale seems to be to generate a possibility for bribe extortion by inspectors and the police. To run a small business like a tea stall, to become a street hawker or a cycle-rickshaw puller or to work as a railway porter all require a license. The authors point out that more than 80 percent of the approximately 500,000 cycle-rickshaws in Delhi are illegal.[19] In a study by the team of Hernando de Soto in Lima the researchers resolved to open a garment factory and to do so legally without paying bribes.

---

17 See Michael Heller, *The Gridlock Economy: How Too Much Ownership Wrecks Markets, Stops Innovation, and Costs Lives,* Basic Books, 2008.

18 C. Abuodha, R. Bowles. 2000. Business licence reform in Kenya and its impact on small enterprises, *Small Enterprise Development,* Volume 11, Number 3, September 2000, pp. 16–24.

19 Shah, Parth J. and Renuka Sane. 2008. India: The Elephant in the Age of Liberation, in Benjamin W. Powell, ed., *Making Poor Countries Rich: Entrepreneurship and the Process of Economic Development.* Stanford: Stanford Economics and Finance and The Independent Institute, pp. 309–341, here p. 324.

They found that "a person of modest means must spend 289 days on bureaucratic procedures" to fulfill the requirements.[20]

We explained that decentralized corruption suppresses businesses that need multiple permissions to operate. Conversely, the effect of decentralization is positive when many officials can give permission and no single official can deny it, so officials compete with each other. Thus an investor might have to bribe an official to register his firm, but he can choose the official who demands the lowest bribe. When officials compete, business activity resembles a commercial enterprise in Central Europe that can choose to ship down either the Oder River or the Vistula River. Competition between rivers keeps down the tolls and bribes charged on either one of them. Thus a firm can reduce its burden of bribes in a federal system such as that of India or Brazil by locating in a relatively low-bribe state. If one measures decentralization as the sub-national share of government expenditures, empirical research strongly supports this hypothesis[21].Thus among the rich countries, the USA, Germany and Sweden are decentralized in this sense and have lower corruption than the much more centralized countries such as France, Italy and Spain. Among developing countries the highly decentralized countries (in terms of sub-national government spending) India and Brazil are less corrupt than the more centralized countries Indonesia and Mexico.[22]

An economy that is open and with low customs duties, thereby forcing local suppliers to compete with foreign suppliers, also loosens the grip of corrupt bureaucrats on companies and on customs offices they can control. Cross country analysis shows that the level of corruption decreases significantly with the quota of imported goods as per cent of GNP.[23] This leads to a related insight, that small countries tend to be less corrupt than big countries, because they tend to have a more open economy than large countries. The 13 least corrupt countries in the world are small, like New Zealand, Singapore, Norway or Switzerland, with the one exception, Australia.[24]

---

20 De Soto, Hernando. 1989. *The Other Path*. New York: Basic Books. p. 151.

21 Fizman, R. and R. Gatti. 2002. Decentralization and Corruption: A Cross Country Analysis, *Journal of Public Economics*, Vol 83, pp. 325–345.

22 See op. cit. table A1, p. 340.

23 Ades, A. and R. Di Tella. 1999. Rents, Competition, and Corruption, AER, Vol. 89, No. 4 pp. 982–993.

24 Transparency International Data for 2008.

Figure 3 summarizes the three preceding arguments. First, permission to act is *unique* when only one official can give it. Centralized power tends to produce a system of unique permissions and suppress competition for bribes. The one official who holds unique power is a monopolist in the extortion of bribes, so the cost of bribes is high. However, in a stable state with a secure monopolist, bribes remain at a level where business can thrive. Second, permission to act is *conjunctive* when any one of many officials can deny it. In the conjunctive case, permission to act must come from officials A and B and C and D, etc. In this constellation each official has a veto position, which can easily lead to closed markets. To get a license to enter the market requires multiple bribes. But for an incumbent to prevent somebody from entering the market, he has to bribe only one official with a veto position, which is relatively cheap.

As each official looks to himself, the total cost of bribes is very high, which causes many businesses to fail. This is a state in which officials dominate firms. Third, permission to act is *disjunctive* when any one of many officials can give it. In the disjunctive case, permission to act may come from A or B or C or D or... Competition among officials drives the cost of bribes to a low level. This is a state in which firms dominate officials by making them compete with each other.

Power Structure	Permission to Act	Cost of Bribes
centralized	unique	high
decentralized with officials dominating firms	conjunctive	very high
decentralized with firms dominating officials	disjunctive	low

Figure 3. Power structure and bribes.

Combining the two previous figures suggests the best structure of power with corruption. To encourage beneficial acts creates competition among officials to permit them (disjunctive permission), as with the chartering of corporations by states in the USA and the EU[25] or the creation of trusts in

25 A firm can incorporate in any state in the United States, regardless of the location of its headquarters or business activity. This fact created a chartering competition mostly won by Delaware. Many scholars believe the competition was benign on the whole. See Roberto Romano, 1993, *The Genius of American Corporate Law*, American Enterprise Institute.

London.[26] For the same reason Bulgaria has introduced competition between offices for hygiene control and those for veterinary-medical control[27].

To discourage harmful acts creates competition among officials to forbid them (conjunctive permission), as with police protection against crime. Thus Italian firms prefer to locate in the north where they face less extortion from the mafia than in the south. Unfortunately, however, most activities that fall under state authority are not always beneficial and can instead be directly harmful. To illustrate, issuing a passport is beneficial when the traveler is a legitimate businessman and harmful when the traveler is an arms dealer. Approving a new medicine is beneficial if it is properly tested and harmful if not. When an activity can be beneficial or harmful, it is unclear whether decentralized competition to permit the activity is better or worse than centralized power. Adequate exploration of this problem requires a more detailed theory of centralization and decentralization than we can develop here.[28]

Building distrust

Now we explain policies to suppress bribery that any state can use with the will to do so.[29] Most contracts involve exchange that is consecutive, not simultaneous. Perhaps the buyer pays now for the seller's promise of future performance, or perhaps the seller performs now for the buyer's promise of future payment. With consecutive exchange, the parties need to trust each other. A contract enables them to make legal commitments to do what they say, which provides a basis for

---

26 The trust exists in common law, but not in civil law. With the creation of the European Union, many Europeans in civil law countries have gone to London to create trusts, and this in turn has put pressure on bankers in Frankfurt and Paris to develop instruments under civil law that substitute for the trust. See Hansmann and Mattei.

27 National Center for Agrarian Sciences (Sofia 2008) http://agris.fao.org/agris-search/search/display.do

28 For a more complete sketch of the theory of centralization and decentralization of the state, see Robert Cooter, Part III: The Optimal Number of Governments, *The Strategic Constitution,* Princeton University Press, 2000, and Robert Inman and Daniel L. Rubinfeld, Rethinking Federalism, *J. Economic Perspectives* 11 (1997): 43–64.

29 For an overview, see Johann Graf Lambsdorff, *The Institutional Economics of Corruption and Reform: Theory, Evidence, and Policy,* Cambridge University Press, 2007.

trust. Like contracts, many bribes are consecutive and not simultaneous. Perhaps a builder pays now for the promise of a future permit, or perhaps an official delivers a permit now on the promise of future payment. Bribes, however, are illegal, so the state will not enforce the promises that the parties make. Furthermore, bribes provide opportunities for the parties to abuse each other – perhaps the official partially performs and then extorts another bribe to complete the job, or perhaps one of the parties extorts the other with the threat of reporting the bribe to the police. Since bribes create an especially difficult problem of distrust, a basic strategy for disrupting them is to aggravate distrust.

Disrupting trust is the subject in point of the "prisoner's dilemma," which is one of the first and most famous applications of game theory. Two people who jointly commit a crime are arrested and interrogated separately. Each one knows that if neither of them confesses, they cannot be convicted. Each one also knows that if only one of them confesses, he will receive a lenient punishment and the other one will receive a severe punishment. Thus the separate interrogation of the prisoners creates a dilemma of trust. If they trust each other sufficiently, neither will confess. If they distrust each other, both will confess.

This logic applies to bribes. The citizen who gives a bribe and the official who receives it both benefit from the bribe, provided that neither of them reports it. Like the prisoners, each one must trust the other not to confess.

To disrupt bribery, the state can reward officials for reporting attempted bribery. To get incentives right, the reward should exceed the official's gain from accepting the bribe. Thus an official might receive a reward of $125 for a report that convicts a citizen for offering to pay the official $100 for an illegal driving license. The state could pay for the reward by collecting a fine of at least $125 from the citizen. Foreseeing such incentives, not many citizens will attempt to bribe officials.

The next logical step in extending this law is to give immunity and a reward to the first party who reports that he gave or received a bribe. Thus a citizen who pays an official $100 for an illegal driving permit should be able to report the crime, hand over the illegal permit and other evidence to convict the official, and receive immunity plus a reward of $125. Similarly, the official who received the bribe should be able to report the crime, hand over the money and other evidence to convict the citizen, and receive immunity plus a reward of $125. The first one to file a successful report would receive immunity and the reward, and the other one would get prosecuted and convicted. If this rule were in place, the citizen giving a bribe and the official receiving it would fear that the other one will sprint to the police with a report as soon as the bribe is paid. Faced with such incentives, even fewer citizens or officials will participate in bribes.

Disgruntled employees provide a lot of information on wrongdoing in firms. To protect them, many countries have "whistle-blower statutes." These statutes provide mechanisms to protect employees who report illegal activities in the organizations where they work, such as guaranteed anonymity, immunity against prosecution, protection against retaliatory firing, and the right to disclose government information to the media.

Besides employees, firms provide information about illegal activities of their competitors. Paying an illegal bribe, a firm often gains a competitive advantage. To blunt this advantage, a firm may report information about its competitors' illegal activities, especially if the reporting firm is honest. Thus competitors will police each other against corruption to some extent, provided that some of them are not in on it.

Kickbacks in public procurement are easier to detect when the state buys standardized goods at market prices, rather than specialized, idiosyncratic, or novel goods without market prices. Without a market for close substitutes, an inflated price is easily hidden. As a result, corrupt officials prefer to buy specialized, idiosyncratic and novel products. For example, bribes can be disguised more easily if an irrigation project involves a gigantic dam rather than many small wells; or a school project involves a new building rather than uniforms for the children; or a military project involves a new rocket instead of more rifles.

Oversight discourages corruption, as demonstrated by a field experiment in Indonesia, whereby increased government audits of village road projects significantly reduced missing expenditures.[30] Traditional top-down monitoring can play an important role in reducing corruption.

We have been discussing ways that publicity sows distrust in bribery. Perhaps the most important watchdog against corrupt politicians, managers and civil servants is a free press.[31] A free press can publicize corrupt practices, and it can protect its sources by not divulging them. The corruption perception index

---

30 Olken, Benjamin A. 2007. Monitoring Corruption: Evidence from a Field Experiment in Indonesia, 115 *Journal of Political Economy*, pp. 200–249.

31 Brunetti, A. and B. Weder. A free press is bad for corruption, *Journal of Public Economics*, Volume 87, Issues 7–8, August 2003, pp. 1801–1824.

(Transparency International) for countries has a strong negative correlation with the freedom of the press rating. As usual there are outliers, such as Singapore, that have no perceived corruption and limited freedom of press.

Distrust in organizations

Ineffective contract law channels transactions into repeat dealing among people with enduring relationships. Similarly, the illegality of bribes channels them into relational transactions. Within small groups, people feel loyalty and social sanctions enforce it so they can establish the trust necessary to give and receive bribes. Thus corruption especially involves kinship, affection, caste, ethnicity and communities where officials and businesses have enduring ties.[32]

Just as bribery depends on promises that contract law will not enforce, so organized crime depends on governance that corporate law will not enforce. If the law of contracts, corporations, labor and crimes can incentivize employees to be loyal to the firm, reversing the incentives provided by these laws can undermine loyalty in a criminal organization.[33]

Long-run relationships, repeat transactions and reciprocity build loyalty in any organization. When does a favor become a bribe? Suppose that a policeman stops a speeding car. When the policeman asks for the driver's license, a $20 bill "accidentally" sticks to it. This is a bribe. But suppose the driver knows the policeman and offers to donate $20 to his church? Or the driver remarks that he also works for the city government, or that they are active in the same political party, or that he gave the policeman's cousin a building permit last month? Donations,

---

32 Christopher Kingston. 2007. Parochial corruption, *Journal of Economic Behavior & Organization*, Volume 63, Issue 1, pp. 73–87.

33 See especially Fiorentini, G. and S. Peltzman. 1995. *The Economics of Organized Crime*, Cambridge University Press, Cambridge, and CEPR, 1–30; Aubert, C., W. Kovacic and P. Rey. 2006. The Impact of Leniency and Whistleblowing Programs on Cartels, *International Journal of Industrial Organization*, 24: 1241–1266; Spagnolo, G. 2003. *Optimal Deterrence Mechanisms against Cartels and Organized Crime*, mimeo, Mannheim. We cannot discuss other reasons for organized crimes. For example, a criminal organization can reduce aggregate punishments by assigning crimes to the member of the gang who can be expected to receive the most lenient treatment. Besides reducing aggregate punishment, criminal organizations can spread it among the members, rather like insurance spreads the collective costs of accidents.

gifts, intimidation, reciprocity and loyalty all serve to dull the sharp edge of a bribe. People can agree about the hard-edged bribes, which they hide from view, whereas dull-edged bribes shade into personal favors. When Japanese businessmen exchange gifts, Japanese see the cementing of relationships, whereas Americans see bribery.

Disrupting trust in relationships is the key to destroying criminal organizations. The police can reward gangsters who report on their organizations by giving them immunity or reduced punishment, as well as by helping them to relocate and change their identity. Thus an accomplice-witness program helped to reduce the number of Mafia killings in Italy from about 700 in 1991 when it was introduced to about 200 in 2007. It has also increased the number of prosecutions.[34]

Organized crime is a business that cannot succeed unless it is profitable. Besides disrupting trust, another successful strategy is to reduce the profitability of organized crime by seizing the assets of mobsters. Assets can be seized for tax evasion or money laundering, which is often easier to prove than the underlying crimes.[35]

As with bribes, organized crime's overall effect on the economy is negative, but it can also have some positive effects. Whenever the state does not protect property or enforce contracts, organized crime profits by doing so. For example, the Sicilian mafias originated partly to protect small farmers from crime;[36] drug cartels in Columbia protect small farmers who grow coca; and the Taliban protects poppy farmers in Afghanistan. Criminal gangs are heavily involved in debt col-

34 Antonio Acconciay, Giovanni Immordinoz, Salvatore Piccolo, Patrick Rey. 2009. Accomplice-Witnesses and Organized Crime: Theory and Evidence from Italy, Discussion Paper.

35 A jurimetric study of 107 countries shows the effectiveness of assets forfeiture programs for combating organized crime. Buscaglia, Edgardo (2008) The Paradox of Expected Punishment: Legal and Economic Factors Determining Success and Failure in the Fight against Organized Crime, *Review of Law & Economics:* Vol. 4 : Iss. 1, Article 14. DOI: 10.2202/1555-5879.1206 Available at: http://www.bepress.com/rle/vol4/iss1/art14.

36 Bandiera has shown this for the rise of the Sicilian mafia. During Nalopeonic times the kingdom of Naples abolished the feudal system and distributed land to small famers. Stealing and robbery during harvest times became a much bigger problem than before, as the large farm holdings required less policing. As the police force was not increased with the land reform, the small farmers took refuge with the evolving mafia, which protected their property against protection money. See O. Bandiera (2003), Land reform, the Market of Protection and the Origins of the Sicilian Mafia, *Journal of Law, Economics and Organization* 19(1), pp. 218–44.

lection in many countries, including Russia,[37] Indonesia[38] and Ghana.[39] Similarly, Japanese bankruptcy law prescribes sufficiently unworkable procedures that illegal firms play a pervasive role in the resolution of financial distress.[40] While organized crime substitutes for weak state protection of property and contracts, it is a crude substitute.[41]

Black and gray markets

Earlier we explained that some organizations exist in fact, and the law may recognize or not recognize them. In every country of the world, the law does not recognize some organizations that significantly affect the economy. Some of these organizations are criminal, such as gangs that market drugs, and they operate in black markets. Other organizations systematically violate state regulations, such as unlicensed street vendors. They operate in gray markets. These firms seldom

---

37 J.O. Finckenauer and Y.A.Voronin. 2001. US Department of Justice. 2001. The Threat of Russian Organized Crime, National Institute of Justice, http://www.ojp.usdoj.gov/nij.

38 S. Christiansen. 2003. Violent Youth Groups in Indonesia: The Cases of Yogyakarta and Nusa Tenggara Barat, *Journal of Social Issues in Southeast Asia,* Vol. 18.

39 M. Fafchamps. 1996. The Enforcement of Commercial Contract in Ghana, *World Development,* Vol. 34, No. 3. pp. 427–448.

40 The Japanese Bar Association estimated that more than a thousand illegal "fixers" provided their services in bankruptcy procedures in 1995. "Fixers" *(Seiriya)* can paralyse or speed up foreclosure, intimidate debtor or debt collectors, or evict tenants whom the law tries to protect. See C.J. Milhaupt and M.D. West. 2000. The Dark Side of Private Ordering: An Institutional and Empirical Analysis of Organized Crime, *University of Chicago Law Review,* Vol. 67, p. 41, 2000.

41 See Geneva Declaration, The Global Burden of Armed Violence, Geneva, Sept. 2008. The underlying theoretical problem concerns natural monopoly and public goods. Effective protection of property and enforcement of contracts requires an organization with more power than any competing organization. Thus a gang cannot protect property effectively unless it is more powerful than any rival within its territory. Instead of diminishing returns, there are increasing returns to power in protecting property and enforcing contracts. Besides the characteristics of a natural monopoly, these enforcement activities also have the characteristics of a public good. To illustrate, the police who make a street safe protect everyone on it, regardless of whether or not they have paid their taxes. Since people benefit without paying, protection activities are difficult to finance voluntarily. The state finances protection activities through taxes, whereas the mafia finances protection activities by extortion. Extortion and gang warfare are much cruder than courts and taxes as ways to capture economies of scale and solve the public goods problem of protecting property and enforcing contracts.

pay taxes and frequently break regulations. Labor law, health and safety regulations, corporate law and banking law are ineffective in gray markets. Because these firms have no legal existence, they belong to the "informal sector".

This freedom comes at a terrible price: firms in the informal sector hesitate to draw the state's attention to themselves by seeking its protection. They must use their own private means to protect their property and enforce their contracts.

Weak legal systems preclude enforcing many laws on most small firms, who belong consequently to the informal sector. In poor countries, the informal sector (gray plus black) occupies a larger fraction of the economy than in rich countries.[42] According to one estimate, the informal sector produces less than 17% of GDP in the richest countries, and the informal sector produces between 25% and 40% in poorer countries. The gray market's share of total employment is even higher than its share of GNP. The informal sector apparently employs three-quarters of the non-agricultural labor force in Sub-Saharan Africa, and two-thirds in a selection of important Asian countries.[43]

As a firm gets larger, however, hiding it from the law gets harder. Most large firms, consequently, belong to the formal sector, which is expensive. They must pay taxes and conform to regulations such as licensing laws and labor laws. Thus corporations must exist in law in order to exist in fact. They mostly operate in white markets, which constitute the "formal sector." In return, firms in the formal sector enjoy more advantages of law such as protection of property, enforcement of contracts and banking services.

The following figure summarizes the characteristics of the formal and informal sectors.

---

42 See Delhi Group on Informal Sector Statistics, Geneva, 28–30 August 2000, The Contribution of Informal Sector to GDP in Developing Countries, Assessment, Estimates, Methods, Orientations for the Future. Also see Edgar L. Feige, Defining and estimating underground and informal economies: The new institutional economics approach, *World Development,* Volume 18, Issue 7, July 1990, pp. 989–1002.

43 William E. Cole and Bichaka Fayissa, The urban subsistence labor force: Toward a policy-oriented and empirically accessible taxonomy, *World Development,* Volume 19, Issue 7, July 1991, pp. 779–78.

	Formal sector	Informal sector
Firm size	Large	Small
Legal status	Registered	Unregistered
Ownership	Corporate	Family, partnership
Government role	Promote, protect	Unprotected

Figure 4. Characteristics of formal and informal firms.

Productivity in the informal sector would increase sharply if the state recognized the firms in it, protected their property and enforced their contracts. However, luring firms out of the gray market and into the white market requires reducing the advantage of informality. The advantage of information would fall from repeal of burdensome regulations and taxes.

The division between small firms in the informal sector, and large firms in the formal sector, changes the pattern in growth in poor countries as compared to rich countries. In Western countries a firm often starts as a small business and fails within a few years, but a few grow to be very large firms. In developing countries, however, small firms have difficulty crossing from the informal to the formal sector. Small companies have almost no access to formal credit. Informality deprives them of finance and limits their growth. Instead of starting as small firms in the informal sector, most large firms in poor countries start as relatively large firms in the formal sector,[44] especially in Sub-Saharan Africa.[45]

---

44 See J. van Biesebroeck. 2005. Firm Size Matters, op. cit. p. 546 and G. Ranis. 1988. Analytics of Development: Dualism, in *Handbook of Development Economics*, vol. 1, H. Chenery and T. Srinivasan, eds. New York: North-Holland. Also note that large companies seldom go public. The number of stock listed companies in Africa (except South Africa) is extremely low compared to other regions in the world.

45 Growth and Productivity Growth, in African Manufacturing, Economic Development and Cultural Change, *Economic Development and Cultural Change*, volume 53, pp. 545–583. Remarkable counterexamples do exist for some family enterprises. Thus the Ndegwa Group in Kenya and the Mukwano Group in Uganda developed out of tiny enterprises. Also, the number of stock listed companies in Africa (except South Africa) is extremely low compared to other regions in the world. In 2004 the number of listed firms per million of population was 1.2 in Ghana, 1.8 in Kenya, 1.5 in Nigeria 0.1 in Uganda and 12.0 in South Africa. The world average was 27.7. See S. Djankow. 2005. The Law and Economics of Self Dealing, World Bank Research Papers 1–80.

Trust in civil service

To protect officials against improper influence, modern countries have developed the civil service system. The civil service guards the state administration from improper influence within (cronyism), above (political interference) or outside (firms and citizens). To avoid improper influence, the civil service reduces personal influence. In hiring and promotions, the civil service relies maximally on exams, seniority and performance ratings. Abstract rules make detecting improper influence easier for outside observers. Thus outsiders can easily observe a violation of the seniority principle if a political crony gets promoted. In general, civil servants are difficult to fire, and judges are almost impossible to fire – except for corruption.

Besides abstract rule, the civil service has other methods by which to reduce corruption. We already explained that bribes require trust that often develops through enduring relationships. Another method to undermine trust is to rotate civil servants in and out of positions that are particularly vulnerable to corruption. Or civil servants can act in teams, which take decisions together. Bribing a team involves trusting too many people.

High salaries for civil servants are also a mechanism to stop bribery. Some states like Singapore have wiped out bribes almost completely among judges by paying them princely wages.[46] How did high pay eliminate judicial corruption in Singapore? Not because rich people are less corrupt than poor people. Rather, high pay makes an official hesitate to take a bribe that might cause him to lose his job. High pay reduces corruption when taking a bribe carries with it the risk of getting fired. If a civil servant's wage substantially exceeds the income he could earn outside the civil service, he fears being dismissed. Dismissing a civil servant

46 The Judges Remuneration Act of 1994 fixed the yearly salary of a Judge of Appeal at 253,000 Singapore Dollars, which was then 166,000 US Dollars. In 1997 "High court judges (received) A$835,020, besides other perks and privileges, like a motor car, a government bungalow at economic rent. The chief justice received A$1,260,000 (equivalent to 700,000 US dollars) per annum, besides an official residence (or an housing allowance in lieu thereof), a chauffeur-driven car, among other handsome perks and privileges of office. Indeed, he received more than the combined stipends of the Lord Chancellor of England, the Chief Justices of the United States, Canada and Australia", F.T. Seow, former solicitor general of Singapore. The politics of judicial institutions in Singapore, lecture given in Sydney, Australia in early 1997. While judges do not take bribes, they allegedly take instruction from politicians in some cases.

for suspicion of accepting a bribe is much easier than convicting him of the crime of accepting a bribe. Thus a high relative wage inside the civil service provides a powerful deterrent against accepting bribes when combined with a policy of dismissing employees for small improprieties associated with bribes. However, increasing the wages of judges does not reduce bribery when they have no fear of being fired, as experience in Indonesia suggests.[47]

Rich countries are often lenient with corruption if it targets a poor country. They criticize corruption in poor countries from a high moral ground but sometimes even lend their hand to it. Firms in rich countries with little corruption often pay bribes in poor countries with much corruption.[48] In Germany bribes were tax deductible until this practice was abolished after protests from developing countries like India[49]. The OECD has issued a code of conduct, but it has no teeth.[50] Real progress is the UNCAC (United Nations Convention against Corruption) of 2005, which obliges all signatory states to punish bribery of "foreign public officials" as a criminal offense. In 2009 about 135 states had ratified this convention.[51]

Conclusion

Corruption, metaphorically speaking, is tantamount to the termites in the foundation of economic growth formed by property, contracts and business law. The optimal policy towards corruption minimizes the sum of the cost of the harm it causes and the cost of deterring it. The optimality hypothesis predicts that coun-

---

47 Thus Indonesia reformed bankruptcy law and introduced special commercial courts in 1998. The newly appointed judges received special training and improved pay, but accusations of incompetency and corruption persist. R. Tomasic, 2001, Some Challenges of Indonesian Bankruptcy Reform (Bali), 19.

48 Transparency International also publishes a "bribe payers index," which ranks the world's wealthiest and economically dominant countries by the likelihood of their firms to bribe abroad. It is based on the informed observations of several thousand senior business executives in developing and developed countries.

49 V. von Nell. 2006. Korruption- individuelles Handeln im Zeichen der Globalisierung, p. 17, in: Von Nell, Schwitzgebel, Vollet, Deutscher Universitätsverlag.

50 K. Gordon. 2001. The OECD Guidelines and other Corporate Responsibility Instruments: A Comparison, OECD Working Papers on International Investment, Number 2001/5.

51 United Nations Convention against Corruption, www.unodc.org/pdf/crime/convention_corruption/signing/Convention-e.pdf

tries will allocate their resources for deterrence where they reduce the most harm. Some anecdotes support this hypothesis, but support even more the conclusion that efforts to stop corruption are more political than optimal. In centralized states with a strong but corrupt central government, the politicians on top discipline the corruption of civil servants lower down in the administrative hierarchy. In contrast, the civil servants in weak states with corrupt governments and offices compete for a bribe, which in turn raises the cost of bribes for an activity that many officials can block and lowers the cost of bribes for an activity that any one of several officials can permit.

Large differences in the wealthy nations often have large causes, such as large differences in the productivity of labor. In the case of difference in corruption across nations, some observers think it is caused by large differences in culture. Thus diplomatic immunity protected United Nations officials from enforced parking regulations in New York City prior to 2002. Although every diplomat enjoyed equal immunity from parking tickets, a survey found that diplomats from high-corruption countries accumulated significantly more unpaid parking violations than those from low-corruption countries.[52]

However, some differences in outcomes have small causes which tip a balance, like the last person who jumps on an overloaded boat and causes it to sink. Perhaps large differences in national corruption have small causes. To see why, assume that most civil servants expect each other to be honest. Because they seek the approval of their peers, they will shame and ostracize those who accept bribes. Fearing shame and ostracism, those who may be tempted to accept bribes will refrain from doing so. Thus bribes will then tend to disappear because it does not pay to accept them. Conversely, assume that most civil servants expect others to be dishonest. Because they seek the approval of their peers, they will *not* shame or ostracize those who accept bribes. Without fear of shame or ostracism, bribes will proliferate because it pays to accept them.

In the preceding example, a country ends up with a corrupt civil service if officials expect others to take bribes, and a country ends up with an honest civil service if officials expect others to refuse bribes. The expectation fulfills itself. Small accidents in history that change expectations about corruption can have

52 Raymond Fisman and Edward Miguel. 2007. Corruption, Norms, and legal Enforcement: Evidence from Diplomatic Parking Tickets, *Journal of Political Economy* 115: 1020.

large effects on it. (This is a model of multiple equilibria characteristic of social norms.[53])

Is corruption a deep problem of culture or an accident of history? No one can answer this question decisively based on existing data. There is, however, a remarkably jagged distribution of corruption across countries and sectors that suggests an important role for history. Thus Jordan, unlike other Arab countries, has a corruption rate similar to that of France. The same applies to Botswana, where corruption is dramatically lower than in the rest of Africa, and to Chile where it is dramatically lower than in the rest of the Latin America. And Lithuania, a protestant country, has corruption similar to Catholic Poland or Moslem Turkey. Only recently has Singapore become one of the "cleanest" states in the world, comparable to the Scandinavian countries.[54]

These facts inspire a hopeful thought. Bribery relies on trust between the citizen who gives the bribe and the official who receives it. Public policy can often block corruption by eroding trust between the giver and taker of bribes. Perhaps relatively modest expenditures on deterring bribes can cause large reductions in the harms resulting from corruption.

---

53 On multiple equilibria in the emergence of corruption see Andvig, J.C. and K.O. Moene. 1990. How corruption may corrupt, *Journal of Economic Behavior and Organization* 13, pp. 63–76.

54 See Transparency International, Corruption Perception Index 2008.

Reputation and Character

Jon Elster

I. Introduction

According to OED (Oxford English Dictionary), a main meaning of "reputation" is "The common or general estimate of a person with respect to character or other qualities; the relative estimation or esteem in which a person or thing is held." I shall retain one implication of this definition, while discarding another. The one I shall discard is that the reputation of a person is something that necessarily exists in the opinion of others than the person herself. Discarding this idea allows us to explore the idea of self-reputation or, if you prefer, self-image. The one I shall retain is that reputation attaches to character rather than, say, to actions. Actions flow from character. At the same time, character is revealed by action.

My main concern in this paper is with the ways in which the desire for a good reputation may inspire action. This desire may rest either on instrumental or on intrinsic grounds. In Section II I explore this distinction as it applies to the relatively straightforward case of other-related reputation, and in Section III I repeat the exercise with regard to the trickier issue of self-reputation. In Section IV I offer an analysis that to some extent subverts the two preceding sections, by arguing that the "character" to which reputation attaches is more fragmented, and reputation-building, for that reason, more complicated than is usually assumed. I conclude in Section V by considering three ways in which the concept of character may, at least partly, be rehabilitated.

A central question in the paper is whether reputation-building requires some form of deception. In other-related reputation-building, it seems that the agent has to deceive others, by pretending that the actions were undertaken for other ends than acquiring the reputation. In self-reputation building, it seems that he has to deceive himself as to the true nature of his motivation. These claims seem to be a matter of logic, not of psychology. How, indeed, can you impress others by good actions if they know they were taken only to impress them? How can you get a "warm glow" from helping others if you know that the only motive for helping them was to acquire the warm glow? Roughly speaking, you can't, but we shall see (in Section III) that matters are a bit more complicated.

Although I shall use examples from various domains, I shall be particularly concerned with the reputation for being farsighted, that is, for having a low rate of time discounting. As this reputation is often useful, we might ask how an agent might take steps to acquire it. This is in fact the central issue of a thought-provoking book by Eric Posner, *Law and Social Norms*.[1] Another recurring issue is the reputation for being altruistic.

II. Other-related reputation

To be thought badly of by others, to be the object of their contempt, is among the most aversive experiences one can have. To be thought well of by others, to enjoy a good reputation, is intrinsically satisfying. A. O. Lovejoy (1961) coined a word, "approbativeness", for the desire to be well thought of by others, and noted acutely that others may not approve of this desire. The same idea was stated by La Bruyère: "Men are very vain, and of all things hate to be thought so" (*Characters* XI.65). As the negative reaction of others to the desire for approval causes "a vast deal of insincerity", Lovejoy argued that "disapproval of approbativeness [...] ought [...] to be disapproved". I have suggested (Elster 1999, p. 90 n.90) that in some societies, for example in ancient Greece, there was no opprobrium attached to approbativeness.

From a moral point of view, showing your approbativeness is indeed harmless. Acting on the desire is, however, morally questionable and, if the motive is understood by others, self-defeating. To perform a good action merely to look good in the eyes of others cancels the goodness. As Montaigne (1991, p. 1158) noted, "The more glittering the deed the more I subtract from its moral worth, because of the suspicion aroused in me that it was exposed more for glitter than for good-

1 In a perceptive review of the book, McAdams (2001, p. 630) asks: "How does one convince others than one has a low discount rate? That is the story of the book."

ness; goods displayed are already halfway to being sold".[2] Similarly, when Nazi collaborators in German-occupied countries engaged in last-minute acts of resistance to restore their bad reputation, their visible opportunism tended (with some exceptions) to defeat the intention (Elster 2006).

The last example is ambiguous, in that the "résistants de septembre" may also have had instrumental reasons for restoring their reputation, viz. the desire to avoid prosecution after the war. We observe a more clear-cut case of reputation as intrinsically good in the behavior of individuals who had merely been passive during the occupation, and now wanted to build a reputation as "good French" or "good Norwegians". Not infrequently, these would be among the most active in shaming collaborators or shearing the hair of women who had been intimate with Germans, and the most vindictive in trials of collaborators.[3] In many cases, their effort at reputation-building was too transparently only that, to succeed. Whereas deliberate efforts to build a reputation for *competence* need not be self-defeating when the motivation is known, efforts to build a reputation for *integrity* cannot tolerate daylight.

The instrumental usefulness of a good reputation is obvious. If you have a reputation for being able to defer gratification, for instance, others will be more inclined to trust you to stick to the cooperative strategy in an iterated Prisoner's Dilemma and hence more willing to engage in mutually beneficial long-term cooperation. A reputation for altruism will bring the same benefits. Conversely, a reputation for being vindictive and willing to punish others even at no benefit and some cost to oneself may cause others to believe threats that otherwise would not be credible.[4]

As Descartes noted, these benefits create an incentive to build a reputation for having (in his example) an altruistic character:

> The reason that makes me believe that those who do nothing save for their own utility – and who ought also, **if they wish to be prudent, work, as do others, for the good of others** and try to please everyone as much as they can – is that one ordina-

---

2 For the opposite view, see Hume (1995, pp.157–8): "To love the glory of virtuous deeds is a sure proof of the love of virtue".

3 A French defense lawyer explained the severity of the first sentences after the Liberation by "the fact that many jurors were latecomers to the resistance and were eager to demonstrate a zealousness which they had not shown earlier. Later, when the deported came back from Germany, one had much more thoughtful jurors who [...] did not feel the need to prove themselves" (Lottman 1986, p. 272).

4 This effect may be cancelled, however, by the fact that other people may actively avoid bullying or vindictive types. Even if the bully gets her way in every encounter, she has fewer of them.

> rily sees it occur that those who are deemed obliging and prompt to please also receive a quantity of good deeds from others, even from people who have never been obliged to them; and these things they would not receive did people believe them of another humor (To Elisabeth, January 1648).

Following the seminal work by Kreps and Wilson (1982) and by Kreps et al. (1982), one now has a fairly good understanding of the mechanics of reputation-building in finitely iterated games. In an iterated Prisoner's Dilemma, "both players may believe that there is a small chance that their opponent may be altruistic. For instance, the opponent may get extra pleasure from mutual cooperation [preferring CC to DC] or may even adopt a tit-for-tat strategy. Then it could be in each player's best interest to **pretend, at least for some time, to be an altruistic** player in order to build a reputation for cooperation" (Andreoni and Miller 1993, p. 570). Similarly, in the Chain Store Paradox the monopolist chain store may seek to develop a reputation for being irrationally rapacious or vindictive in order to deter potential rivals from entering the market. In both cases, we obtain the surprising result that even a very small subjective probability that the other player is, respectively, altruistic or vindictive is sufficient to induce, respectively, cooperation and non-entry.

We need to distinguish here between reputation-building and signaling. When you engage in reputation-building, other people may be uncertain whether your actions flow from your character or whether they are merely chosen to induce the belief that they do so. To resolve the uncertainty, they observe your behavior over time, using Bayesian theory to update their beliefs. In signaling, one tries to overcome this problem by choosing an action that only someone with the relevant character trait could afford. A poor man might dress up like a Wall Street banker to appear trustworthy to the taxi driver whom he intends to rob, but is unlikely to do so since the costs would be greater than what he could expect to get from the robbery. By contrast, waving the *Wall Street Journal* in order to hail a taxi is something anyone can afford and hence does not discriminate between the trustworthy and untrustworthy (Gambetta and Hamill 2005). Or suppose there is an opportunity to gain 10 the following year by investing 8 today. A person with a one-year time discounting rate of 10 % would be willing to make the investment, whereas another with a discounting rate of 30 % would not (Posner 2000, p. 19). The willingness to make the investment reveals the ability to defer gratification.[5]

5 Later, the existence of this alleged ability will be put into question.

III. Self-reputation

We care deeply about what others think about us, but even more about our own self-image. In a variation of the phrase I cited earlier, "Men are very vain, and of all things hate to think they are". For "vain", we may also substitute "envious" or "self-interested". In fact, I believe an argument can be made for the proposition that the two things that matter most to many of us are our self-interest and our self-image as not being moved only by self-interest (Elster 2009).

The desire for a good self-image often operates though the mechanisms of self-deception and wishful thinking. As is well known, in any given domain or activity most people think they are above the median (most of them might of course be above the average). Also, in their evaluation of the relative importance of different activities most assign higher scores to the things they do well. Self-serving beliefs of this kind are extremely common. Whether they are genuine beliefs, in the sense that people use them as a premise for action, or merely "quasi-beliefs" that are entertained for their consumption or consolation value, can be hard to tell.

In some cases, at least, it seems clear that self-serving beliefs about one's character do serve as a premise for action. Alcibiades may offer an example. "He had everything going for him. He had too much. How could he not think that his person came before everything else. [...] Beautiful, noble and rich, he ceased to take any account of others and thought that, in practice, everything was his due" (Romilly 1996, pp. 32, 37). In the following, however, I want to explore the converse possibility: that the aim of action may be to strengthen self-serving beliefs about one's character, not by causally affecting the character but by making certain beliefs about it more credible.

As with other-related reputation, self-reputation may be sought either for its intrinsic or for its instrumental value. The desire to see oneself as not merely self-interested is an intrinsic motivation. The desire to see oneself as having strong will power may be either an intrinsic or an instrumental one. The desire, finally, to believe that one is in good health is a purely instrumental one. To realize any one of these desires, an individual may take action to make the target beliefs more credible. In the three cases I just mentioned, this might take the form of donating money, abstaining from an opportunistic sexual encounter, or working hard on some test that is supposed to be diagnostic of good health.

Let me begin with the last case, which is illustrated in a classic experiment by Quattrone and Tversky (1984). The subjects were first asked to hold their hands in cold water until they could no longer tolerate the pain. Next, they were induced to believe that the length of time they could keep their hand in the water was a good predictor (for subjects in one condition) of a long life-expectancy or (for subjects in a different condition) of a short life-expectancy. Finally, they were asked to do the cold-water test again. Subjects who had been told that tolerance to cold water predicted a long (short) life kept their hands in the water for a longer (shorter) period than in the first test. Although the output utility of the action was negative (for subjects in the first condition the pain was almost intolerable), this effect was more than offset by its positive diagnostic utility, that is, by the utility the subjects derived from their belief in a long life expectancy.

As interpreted by Quattrone and Tversky, these findings imply that the subjects were deceiving themselves. This is not the garden variety of self-deception I referred to earlier, where people simply adopt the belief they would like to be true, but a two-step operation in which they act to produce confirming evidence for the belief. It would seem that the same mechanism operates in the person who donates to charity in order to prove to himself that he has an altruistic character, or the person who abstains from taking a drink before noon to prove to himself that he does not have an alcoholic disposition. Since the acts in question were undertaken only for their diagnostic value, they do not have any intrinsic value.

Drazen Prelec and Ronit Bodner have challenged this conclusion in recent articles (Prelec and Bodner 2003, Bodner and Prelec 2003). Their argument can perhaps be summarized by saying that when taking actions for their diagnostic value, people are engaged in motivated self-discovery. Hence they argue that actions taken to bolster self-reputation may be perfectly rational (and provide genuine information), rather than self-deceptive. Bootstrapping can work.

For an example, suppose I would like to believe myself to be altruistic rather than selfish. Although I do not know exactly where I am located on the altruism scale, I have a subjective probability distribution over the positions on the scale. My initial endowment of self-esteem equals the expectation of this distribution. I then take an action (e.g. donating to charity) that generates both outcome utility and diagnostic utility. The latter is the difference between the expectation of self-esteem based on the new distribution that is conditional on having taken that action, and the expectation that corresponds to the initial endowment.

> Where does this [new] distribution come from? The simplest assumption, though perhaps not the most accurate one psychologically, is that inferences are true, which

> means that the revised distribution [...] is consistent with maximization of both components of total utility. What does this mean psychologically? It means that the decision maker is fully aware that he or she is partly motivated by the desire to get good news. (Prelec and Bodner 2003, p. 283)

The central claim is that such rational self-signaling can induce a new distribution that makes the person better off overall. Even if the outcome-utility component of the reward should fall, diagnostic utility may increase to offset it. Moreover, even though "the diagnostic value of an action is properly discounted for the presence of diagnostic motivation" (ibid.), the discounting does not drive the value all the way to zero. Given an underlying character trait of altruism, an action chosen for the purpose of revealing its strength will reflect not only my desire to see myself as altruistic but also the strength of the trait. A very selfish person would not be willing to invest a lot in building a self-reputation as an altruist. Knowing this fact, a rational agent will see a generous contribution as an indicator of an altruistic character.

At the same time, he will know that his contribution is deceptively high, in the following sense. Let us distinguish between a concern for disinterestedness (desire for self-reputation) and a disinterested concern for other people's welfare (altruism). Harry has both concerns, but Jane has only the latter. The strength of their altruism is the same. Although Harry will donate more than Jane, he cannot rationally infer that his altruism is stronger than hers, since he knows that part of his contribution is due to his desire to strengthen his self-reputation.

By contrast, in self-deceptive self-signaling "You generously give yourself *full* credit for doing the good thing, even when *part* of the motive was precisely to get the credit" (Prelec and Bodner 2003, p. 294; my italics). In other words, a self-deceptive Harry would conclude that he was more altruistic than Jane. Bodner and Prelec (2003, p. 109) refer to this inference as a "face-value interpretation" of the behavior. As they write, "A person [such as Jane in my example] whose actions were made innocent of their diagnostic implications would be justified in maintaining face-value inferences. Diagnostic utility would be experienced as an unintentional byproduct of choice, not something that can consciously affect choice" (ibid.). For someone like Harry to maintain that inference would, however, be self-deceptive.

In many publications since 1975, George Ainslie has developed a related but somewhat different line of argumentation for self-reputation effects. He agrees with Prelec and Bodner (or rather they agree with him) that "Doing good for its diagnostic value may not invalidate that diagnostic value" (Ainslie 1992, p. 203). The context of this statement is his theory of hyperbolic discounting: its bad consequences, the remedies for those bad consequences, and the bad consequences of the remedies. I shall address the last aspect in Section V.

Very roughly speaking, hyperbolic discounting is the tendency to weigh utility today compared to utility tomorrow more heavily than utility tomorrow compared to utility the day after tomorrow. Since tomorrow will ultimately become today, this tendency makes it difficult for us to stick to plans that require us to sacrifice a small early reward for the sake of a larger delayed reward. Each morning a student may form the intention of going to bed early so that he can study efficiently the next day, but each evening he succumbs to the temptation of watching a late night movie. The trick – the remedy – is to reframe the situation so that each choice is seen as showing a deep-seated disposition ("action reveals character") and hence as a predictor of future choices ("action flows from character"). By raising the stakes in this way, the student can enable himself to defer gratification.

Yet the self-fulfilling nature of the diagnosis does not make it rational. Rather, in my opinion, it involves a form of magical thinking. The procrastinator may ask himself, "If not now, when?", the implicit answer to this rhetorical question being "Never". Similarly, a person who is asked to make a donation to charity may ask himself, "If not me, who?", the implicit answer to the question being "No one". These answers have immense persuasive force and are no doubt conducive to an immense amount of socially desirable behavior, but they are false. In this case, I believe that the building of self-reputation does involve self-deception. The difference between Ainslie and Prelec-Bodner is that uncertainty and self-discovery have no role in his argument.

IV. Dismantling "character"

Folk psychology, as represented by proverbs, affirms the unity of character. "Who tells one lie will tell a hundred." "Who lies also steals." "Who steals an egg will steal an ox." "Who keeps faith in small matters, does so in large ones." "Who is caught red-handed once will always be distrusted."

People often make strong inferences from the private conduct of others to their reliability in other domains. A member of the French Academy reportedly voted for de Gaulle because of the dignity of his private life, the tacit premise being that someone who would betray his wife is also liable to betray his country (Veyne 1998). In Vietnam, Communist leaders were able to win "the minds and the hearts of the population" because of their incorruptible personal style, in stark contrast to the less self-denying organizers from other political groups (Popkin 1979). Among Mafiosi, having affairs is thought to be a sign of a disorderly and weak character (Gambetta 2006). We tend to impute medical competence to doctors with good beside manners.

According to Posner (2000, p. 21), "good types [with low discounting of the future] signal by being business-like, in contrast to bad types, who fail to plan, are poorly organized, are chronically late, and are likely to be obese or to be addicted to alcohol and drugs". One is either myopic across the board, in all situations, or farsighted across the board. According to Bodner and Prelec (2003, p. 111), "the diagnostic value of an action may be all out of proportion to its scale – a small gesture can reveal character quite effectively (e.g. stealing 25 cents still counts as theft)". Similarly, the "altruistic personality", the "authoritarian personality" and the "narcissistic personality" are supposed to exhibit these character traits with cross-situational consistency.

If this view were correct, building (and losing) reputations would be disconcertingly easy. Consider again Posner's *Law and Social Norms*. In his review of this book, McAdams (2001, p. 630 ff.) shows how according to Posner, each of the following might be used to signal a low discounting rate: engagement rings, deferred sex and unprotected sex, obedience to law, voting, patriotic displays, self-censorship, race discrimination, nationalism, education, conspicuous consumption (but not saving!) and philanthropy.

The "characterological theory" is, however, now generally recognized by psychologists as being false (see notably Mischel 1968). The "power of the situation" (Ross and Nisbett 1991) often has as much explanatory power as the dispositions of the agent. To cite only the most dramatic evidence, in the laboratory experiments by Stanley Milgram (1983), two thirds of the subjects were induced to behave heartlessly, to the point of imposing (what they believed to be) severe electrical shocks (about 450 V) on a confederate of the experimenter. Yet there is no reason to believe that their behavior was due to an underlying trait of sadism, cruelty or indifference to the suffering of others.

This discovery is actually a rediscovery of old insights. In his essay "On the

Inconstancy of Our Actions", Montaigne contrasts the behavior of the younger Cato with that of ordinary humans such as himself:

> [S]trike one of [Cato's] keys and you have struck them all; there is in him a harmony of sounds in perfect concord such as no one can deny. In our cases on the contrary everyone of our actions requires to be judged on its own: the surest way in my opinion would be to **refer each of them to the immediate circumstances**, without looking farther and without drawing any firm inference from it. [...] If [a man] cannot bear slander but is resolute in poverty; if he cannot bear a barber-surgeon's lancet but is unyielding against the swords of his adversaries, then **it is not the man who deserves praise but the deed.**

Commenting on the apparent contradiction between Swann's "exquisite dissimulation of an invitation to Buckingham Palace" and his boast that the wife of a lower functionary had visited Mme Swann, Proust (2003, p. 6) wrote that

> The main reason was (and this is one that holds for all of humanity) that even our virtues are not extraneous, free-floating things which are always at our disposal; in fact they come to be so **closely linked in our minds with the occasions for acting** on which we feel they should be deployed that, if we are required to engage in some different activity, it can take us by surprise, so that we never even think that it too might entail the use of those very virtues.

Accordingly, Swann would have very different reputations among those who knew him only from his life before Odette and among those who met him through her. Being victims of folk psychology, those in each category would think that his behavior reflected his "character" rather than specific "occasions for acting".

Adopting this perspective, I shall discuss the alleged character traits of altruism and low rates of time discounting.[6] Consider first the fact that some Germans acted to rescue Jews from the Nazi regime. On a "characterological" theory, one

6 Dishonesty, too, may be studied in this perspective. In a letter to the ethicist Randy Cohen (*New York Times Magazine,* January 15, 2006) an academic asked whether the fact that an untenured colleague claimed discounts at the Faculty Club to which he was not entitled warranted a vote against him for tenure "because of his dishonesty and its potential extension to his research". Cohen said no, on the grounds that "People who behave badly in some situations often behave well in others".

would assume that the rescuers had an altruistic character that non-rescuers lacked (Monroe, Barton and Klingemann 1990). It turns out, however, that the factor with the strongest explanatory power was the "situational" fact of being asked to rescue someone (Varese and Yaish 2000). Similarly, "Fund raisers know that to get money donated, you have to ask for it" (Andreoni 2006, p. 1225). Although in both cases it has been argued that being asked is important by virtue of providing information about potential targets of altruism, I believe that the shame of saying "No" in a face-to-face encounter is equally crucial.

Or consider the apparent paradox that some voters seem to be both selfish and altruistic. They are selfish or "egotropic" rather than "sociotropic" because they vote as a function of their personal economic interest. Not all vote on that basis, but some certainly do. At the same time, any voter must be altruistic (or motivated by duty) as shown by the very fact of bothering to vote at all (Blais 2000). This duality in behavior ceases to be a puzzle if we recognize that altruism may be just as context-specific as courage (Montaigne) or discretion (Proust).

From altruism, I now turn to the ability to defer gratification. It is clearly implicit (although never stated) in Posner's analysis that people have the same rate of time discounting across the board. The "good types" are invariably able to defer gratification, the "bad types" never do so. That is indeed why good types may signal their character by any kind of costly behavior that a bad type would be unable to afford.

There is, however, plenty of anecdotal and experimental evidence against this view. Louis XVIII was legendary not only for his obesity (a sign of high discounting rate) but also for his perseverance in adversity (a sign of low discounting). The jazz musician Charlie Parker was characterized by a doctor who knew him as "A man living from moment to moment. A man living for the pleasure principle, music, food, sex, drugs, kicks, his personality [sic] arrested at an infantile level" (Russell 1973). Another great jazz musician, Django Reinhardt, had an even more extreme present-oriented attitude in his daily life, never saving any of his substantial earnings, but spending them on whims or on expensive cars, which he quickly proceeded to crash. In many ways he was the incarnation of the stereotype of "the Gypsy". Yet you do not become a musician of the caliber of Parker and Reinhardt if you live in the moment in all respects. It takes years of utter dedication and concentration. If these two musicians had been myopic, impulsive and carefree across the board – if their "personality" had been consistently "infantile" – they could never have become such consummate artists.

Experimental studies have focused on comparing rates of time discounting with regard to money, health and drugs. Two studies (Madden, Bickel and Jacobs 1999, Giordano et al. 2002) found that drug addicts discounted delayed hypothetical drug rewards much more than they discounted delayed hypothetical monetary rewards. The latter study found, more specifically, that both drug-deprived and drug-satiated addicts displayed this difference.

In a series of articles, Gretchen Chapman and her co-authors have explored "domain independence" of rates of time discounting with regard to health and money. An early study (Chapman 1996) found that although the average rates of time discounting in subjects in these two areas were roughly the same, there was little correlation at the level of the individual. This finding is inconsistent with normative utility theory, as well as with explanatory theories based on "types". According to a more recent study, some findings "might indicate that time preferences are even more domain specific than previously thought, such as the discount rate applied to getting a flu shot is not the same as the discount rate applied to a scenario about getting the flu. That is, *decision makers do not possess a single discount rate that is broadly applied*" (Chapman et al. 2001, p. 248; my italics).[7] To my knowledge, no similar empirical studies exist of the possible "domain independence" of altruistic dispositions.

V. Restoring "character"

The findings I have described undermine what one might call "crude essentialism" in the study of character. It is simply not true that people are aggressive, altruistic, impatient, extrovert or talkative across the board. At the same time, the findings do not imply that the situation is all-powerful in explaining behavior. Rather, we have to decompose "the" character into a set of contingent response tendencies (Mischel 2004). Instead of characterizing a person as altruistic, we might describe him or her by the phrase "helps when asked, but does not volunteer to help", or by the phrase "helps when unstressed, but is neglectful when stressed". Each of these phrases might characterize one aspect of a person, and thus underwrite a more subtle form of essentialism. A person might scold a

7 This study also found a disturbingly low correlation between time preferences as measured by responses to hypothetical questions and actual behaviors exemplifying inter-temporal tradeoffs.

spouse for never cleaning up around the house ("you're lazy") or for never cleaning up unless asked to ("you're thoughtless"). In the latter case, the spouse might be proactive rather than reactive in other matters, such as monitoring the health of the children in the family. There would be no across-the-board trait of reactiveness.

In this perspective, explanation of behavior rests on the particular situation plus the person-specific relation between situations and behavioral propensity. One person might be highly aggressive with individuals over whom he has power, but exceptionally friendly with those who have power over him, whereas another person might show the opposite pattern. If we observe both of them behaving in a friendly manner, we might be tempted to conclude that they both are of a friendly disposition. As should be clear by now, however, the similarity of behavior might be due to differences in situation and in response contingencies that exactly cancel each other.

The conclusion, then, seems to be: don't look for inter-situational consistency in behavior, only for intra-situational, inter-temporal consistency. Let me discuss, however, three mechanisms that might contribute to greater cross-situational consistency in behavior than the findings enumerated in Section IV might suggest.

First, folk psychology, although mainly wrong, may to some extent be self-fulfilling. While the first four proverbs are false, the fifth ("Who is caught red-handed once will always be distrusted") is actually somewhat true because people believe what the other proverbs (falsely) assert. If a person believes that others will predict her behavior in a situation of type A on the basis of her behavior in a situation of type B, she will act in situation B with situation A in mind. If the belief in a link between private and public morality is widespread (and known to be so), it creates an incentive for politicians to behave honestly in private life, assuming that any misbehavior would be made known to the electorate. Or suppose that it is widely believed (and known to be believed) that people have the same rate of time discounting in all situations. If they care too little about their future to take care of their bodies, they are also (according to folk psychology) likely to break a promise to realize a large short-term gain. Hence to be able to make credible promises about mutually profitable long-term cooperation, one should also cultivate a slim and healthy appearance.

Second, recent work by Chapman (2002) suggests that we may observe greater consistency of rates of time discounting when health and money are tradable. The issue had already been raised by Giordano et al. (1997, p.180), who entertained the idea that "subjects might have calculated the quantity of heroin they could purchase while completing the discounting ask for money", but rejected it on the grounds that "degree of discounting should be equal if subjects used money as a proxy for heroin; however, heroin was discounted two or three times more rapidly than money". Chapman (2002, p. 415) found, however, that "agreement between health and money discount rates was greater when the 2 domains were presented as tradable than not tradable. The agreement seen in the tradable condition was also noticeably higher than that seen in previous studies that examined domain independence".[8] Hence consistent time preferences are in some sense forced upon the individual by the fungibility of the goods rather than constituting a preexisting character trait. Since the study by Giordano et al. (1997) did not include tradability as a variable, we cannot tell whether the difference between the discounting rates for drugs and money would have been even greater in a non-tradable situation.

Finally, Ainslie's work on personal rules suggests a third way in which character may be built from the bottom up. These rules are intended to protect the agent from procrastination, impatience, backsliding, yielding to temptation and other consequences of hyperbolic discounting. They do so by setting up strict injunctions: "Never do it", or "Always do it". The stratagem of laying down in advance what will count as a legitimate occasion is easily eroded. When people resolve not to drink alcohol before dinner, they may find themselves scheduling dinner earlier. The rule of drinking wine only at restaurants, never at home, may cause one to dine out more frequently. Kant's rule of smoking only one pipe after breakfast was not unambiguous enough to give him full protection, since as time passed he bought himself bigger and bigger pipes (Kuehn 2001, p. 222). Mark Twain tells the same story about the increasing size of his cigars (Ainslie 1992, p. 163). When feasible, the rules "Never do it" and "Do it every day" may be the only ones that can be stably upheld.[9]

A personal rule relies on a "private side bet", which "forms when an individual perceives a series of similar choices as each predicting the direction of the choices

---

8 By contrast (and against the author's prediction), when subjects were asked to imagine themselves in the role of policy makers, for whom there is always a tradeoff between health and money, domain independence was unaffected.

9 Since this policy is not feasible with regard to eating, obesity may be more recalcitrant than are addictions to private rules.

to come, that is, as precedents" (Ainslie 1992, p. 373). The rule can easily turn into a compulsion, however:

> A person with little skill at formulating rules or with unusually strong impulses is apt to compensate for these effects by increasing the number of behaviors that he classifies as covered by each private side bet, or by connecting each bet with some or all of his other bets.[10] Either way of making his choices more interdependent will increase the differential reward for turning down each temptation, but at the expense of making his behavior more rigid: Increasing his tendency to classify his behaviors as impulsive or not will give his experience a dry, rational, lawyerlike quality, because he will choose his actions less and less for their intrinsic value, and more according to whether or not they meet the terms of a bet. (Ainslie 1992, p. 206)

In this way, a person may indeed develop consistent across-the-board attitudes, as a by-product of the fear of losing control. This is reputation-building with a vengeance. In Max Weber's phrase, the "character" has become "an iron cage".

References

Ainslie, G. 1992. *Picoconomics.* Cambridge University Press.

Andreoni, J. 2006. Philanthropy, in S.-C.Kolm and J.-M. Ythier (eds.), *Handbook of the Economics of Giving, Altruism and Reciprocity*, vol. II, Elsevier, pp. 1201–69.

Andreoni, J. and J. Miller. 1993. Rational cooperation in the finitely iterated Prisoner's Dilemma: Experimental evidence. *Economic Journal* 103, 570–85.

Blais, A. 2000. *To Vote or not to Vote: The Merits and Limits of Rational Choice Theory.* University of Pittsburgh Press.

Bodner, R. and D. Prelec. 2003. Self-signaling and diagnostic utility in everyday decision making, in I. Brocas and J. Carillo (eds.), *The Psychology of Economic Decisions*, vol. I, Oxford University Press, pp. 105–23.

Chapman, G. 1996. Temporal discounting and utility for health and money. *Journal of Experimental Psychology: Learning, Memory, and Cognition* 22, 771–91.

10 E.g., "If I stay up late at night, I shall skip my exercises tomorrow" and "If I skip my exercises, I shall not be able to resist having dessert", etc.

Chapman, G. 2002. Your money or your health: Time preferences and trading money for health. *Medical Decision Making* 22, 410–16.

Chapman, G. et al. 2001. Value for the future and preventive health behavior. *Journal of Experimental Psychology: Applied* 7, 235–50.

Elster, J. 1999. *Alchemies of the Mind.* Cambridge University Press.

Elster, J. 2006. Redemption for wrongdoing: The fate of collaborators after 1945. *Journal of Conflict Resolution*, 324–338.

Elster, J. 2009. *Le désintéressement.* Paris: Seuil.

Gambetta, D. 2006. Trust's odd ways, in J. Elster et al. (eds.), *Understanding Choice, Explaining Behavior: Essays in Honour of Ole-Jørgen Skog.* Oslo Academic Press, pp. 81–100.

Gambetta, D. and H. Hamill. 2005. *Streetwise.* New York: Russell Sage.

Giordano, L. et al. 2002. Mild opioid deprivation increases the degree that opioid-dependent outpatients discount delayed heroin and money. *Psychopharmacology* 6, 174–182.

Hume, D. 1995. *Essays.* The Liberty Press.

Kreps, D. et al. 1982. Rational Cooperation in the Finitely Repeated Prisoners' Dilemma. *Journal of Economic Theory* 27, 245–252.

Kreps, D. and R. Wilson. 1982. Reputation and Imperfect Information. *Journal of Economic Theory* 27, 253–79.

Kuehn, M. 2001. *Kant: A Biography.* Cambridge University Press.

Lottman, H. 1982. *L'épuration.* Fayard.

Lovejoy, A.O. 1961. *Reflections on Human Nature.* Baltimore PA: Johns Hopkins Press.

Madden, G., W. Bickel and E. Jacobs. 1999. Discounting of delayed rewards in opioid-dependent outpatients: Exponential or hyperbolic discount functions? *Experimental and Clinical Psychopharmacology* 7, 284–93.

McAdams, R. 2001. Review of Posner (2000). *Yale Law Journal* 110, 625–90.

Milgram, S. 1983. *Obedience to Authority.* Harper.

Mischel, W. 1968. *Personality and Assessment.* Wiley 1968.

Mischel, W. 2004. Towards an integrative science of the person. *Annual Review of Psychology* 55, 1–22.

Monroe, K., M.C. Barton and U. Klingemann. 1990. Altruism and the theory of rational action: Rescuers of Jews in Nazi Europe. *Ethics* 101, 103–22.

Montaigne, M. de. 1991. *Essays.* Penguin Books.

Popkin, S. 1979. *The Rational Peasant.* University of California Press.

Posner, E. 2000. *Law and Social Norms.* Harvard University Press.

Prelec, D. and R. Bodner. 2003. Self-signaling and self-control, in G. Loewenstein, D. Read and R. Baumeister (eds.), *Time and Decision.* Russell Sage, pp. 277–98.

Proust, M. 2003. *In the Shadow of Young Girls in Flower.* Penguin Books.

Quattrone, G. and A. Tversky. 1984. Causal versus diagnostic contingencies: On self-deception and on the voter's illusion. *Journal of Personality and Social Psychology* 46, 237–248.

Romilly, J. de. 1996. *Alcibiade,* Editions de Fallois.

Ross, L. and R. Nisbett. 1991. *The Person and the Situation.* Temple University Press.

Russell, R. 1973. *Bird Lives: The High Life and Hard Times of Charlie (Yardbird) Parker.* Charterhouse.

Varese, F. and M. Yaish. 2000. The importance of being asked: The rescue of Jews in Nazi Europe. *Rationality and Society* 12, 307–24.

Veyne, P. 1998. Pourquoi veut-on qu'un prince ait des vertus privées? *Social Science Information* 37, 407–15.

On the Pareto-optimality of Contract Rules

Henrik Lando

Introduction

A central insight of law and economics applied to contract law stipulates that when parties are well-informed and act rationally when negotiating their contract, only one contract rule is Pareto-optimal[1]. In essence, the rule that leads the contracting parties to adopt value-maximizing actions (when acting rationally under that rule) should be preferred by both parties, since they can distribute this maximum value between themselves in setting the price of the contract. But does this insight rely on the parties actively negotiating the contract? For example, what happens when the price does not emerge through negotiation but is set by one of the parties as is the case when the seller is a monopolist who can unilaterally set a (high) price? Or what happens if the price is set by anonymous market forces: is it still the case that the two parties should be in agreement about which rule should govern their contract?

These questions were recently analyzed by Professor Erling Eide in the context of consumer sales law (Eide 2009). Eide demonstrated that the insight holds, irrespective of how the price is set in the market, i.e. independent of the market structure. This result is both surprising (an economist colleague recently refused to believe it), and rich in its consequences, and it seems worth elaborating on Eide's analysis. While Eide showed the result graphically, I discuss the intuition, and prove it mathematically. I discuss also the underlying assumptions concerning the parties' knowledge of the rule and of its effect and take up a related point,

1 A rule is Pareto-optimal when there does not exist a rule that makes one person better off without making some other person worse off.

also discussed by Eide, about whether the whole cost of a Pareto-suboptimal rule is borne by the consumer, or whether the inefficiency is shared between seller and consumer. In a recent consumer law case[2], Norwegian Supreme Court Judge Flock stated that the consumer would bear the whole cost, but Eide disagreed, showing in his graphical analysis that the cost is generally shared between the parties. I would argue that Judge Flock is correct in the long run, and that Eide's view pertains to the short run. Thus, not only will the consumer be disadvantaged by a Kaldor-Hicks inefficient rule that seems to benefit her, she will carry the whole of the cost of the inoptimality in the long run under perfect competition (free entry).

On the efficiency of repair versus replacement under monopoly

While the results are general, and pertain to any contract rule and to any set of sellers and buyers, we can analyze the rule taken up by Eide, namely whether it should be consumer or seller that is allowed to choose between repair and replacement of a non-performing good. While replacement is generally preferred by consumers, and repair is generally (for goods of sufficient value to warrant repair) preferred by sellers, the idea behind the Coase theorem is that if the difference in the cost to the seller, which we will term c (following Eide's notation) is greater than the advantage to the buyer (measured in money, i.e. in terms of willingness to pay), denoted by v, then repair should be preferred by both parties, since the seller could bribe the buyer to accept repair, through a lower price. What Eide shows is that this holds true, regardless of market structure, e.g. even when the seller is a profit maximizing monopolist. Let us consider first how this could hold true under monopoly, which will make it immediately clear why it also holds under perfect competition.

2 The case is referred to in the Norwegian notation as HR-2006-00299-A-Rt-2006-179.

The intuition about why Eide's result holds under monopoly

To understand why Eide's result holds, we could first consider the reasons why one might doubt it, and then refute this counterargument. My aforementioned colleague offered the following reasons for not believing Eide's result: if replacement is the legal rule, the (variable) cost to the seller will be higher under this remedy, and therefore he will charge a higher price. But, as monopoly pricing theory shows, the price will generally not increase as much as the cost, since the monopolist will be forced to accept a part of the loss as a consequence of his/her own cost increase. Hence, when the monopolist takes on part of the adjustment, the consumer should be expected to be better off if the consumer's advantage from the repair remedy is greater than that part of the seller's cost increase, which the buyer has to bear. My colleague argued that whether the consumer is better or worse off must depend on the incidence, i.e. on the extent to which the monopolist can make the buyer bear the cost increase through a higher price.

To understand what is wrong with this argument, consider the demand curve in the given market, representing the consumers' willingness to pay for the product.

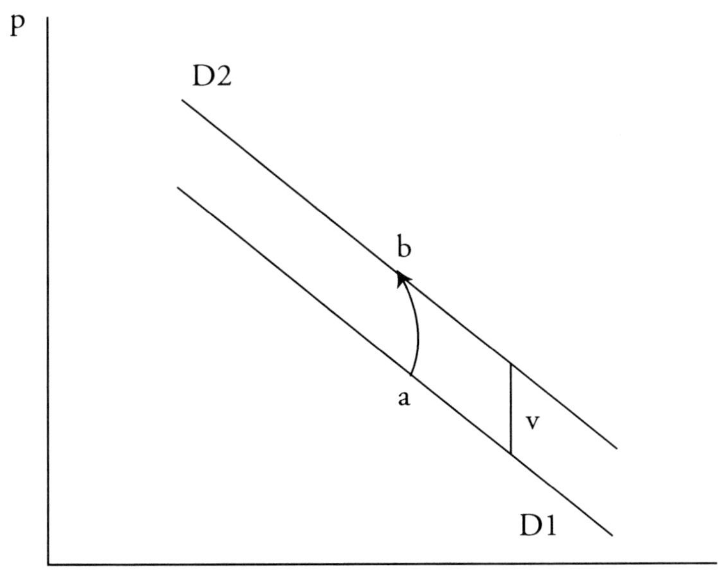

Diagram 1

When the remedy is repair the demand curve is D1 and when the remedy is replacement, the demand curve is D2. The difference is the benefit to the consumer of replacement over repair, *v*, reflecting the cost of returning to the store to fetch the repaired product, the possibility of an insufficient repair, etc.

The important point here is the simple fact that the price will end up on the demand curve, moving from some point *a* to some point *b* as indicated, and that the demand curve shifts upwards by the benefit to the consumers of choosing the rule that they prefer (all other things being equal). That the price will end up on the demand curve must be true when the parties are fully informed: the monopolist, of course, has no reason not to obtain the highest possible price, given the quantity sold. From this simple fact, consider the consumer's surplus, depicted in diagram 2 as the area under the graph lines.

Whether repair or replacement is advantageous for the group of consumers as a whole is determined by the size of the area. Note, that, if the price increases

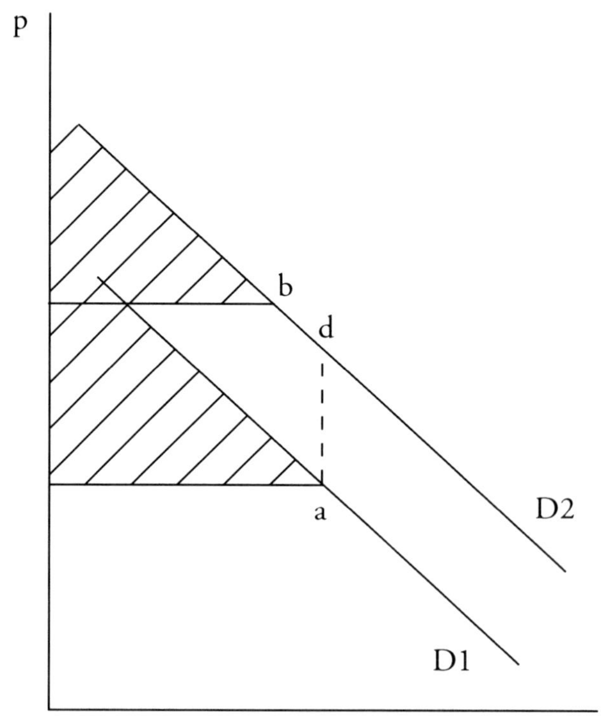

Diagram 2

from a to d, the surplus will remain constant. Clearly, then, if the total quantity sold falls under replacement, total consumer surplus also falls, but if the total quantity sold goes up, so does consumer surplus. So this is the refutation of the refutation: the traditional analysis of the incidence of a cost increase on the price assumes a constant demand curve, but the demand curve rises by an amount that equals the benefit to the consumer, which thus provides the monopolist with an opportunity to raise the price. When the consumer prefers replacement over repair, but the monopolist prefers repair over replacement, the price will be higher under replacement for two reasons: the marginal cost of producing and selling an extra good will be higher for the monopolist (by c), which will tend to lower output and increase price. And the demand curve goes up (by v), reflecting consumer's higher utility from the good, which also increases the price. In fact, the logic which stipulates that the consumer cannot negotiate with a monopolist seller and therefore cannot gain from accepting repair (if repair is the overall efficient rule, i.e. if $c > v$) is the opposite of the truth: under the assumption that the monopolist realizes what is the value of the good to the consumer, accepting repair as a remedy means the consumer will automatically gain a price decrease by virtue of the fact that her value of the good will decrease. Or, put differently, if the rule is replacement, the monopolist can utilize his/her bargaining power and extract the consumer's gain through a price increase.

Following this logic, we need now to demonstrate that the quantity sold must go down when $c > v$, since this implies that consumer surplus also must decrease.

That the quantity sold and hence the consumer surplus will go down when the increase in the marginal cost to the monopolist is higher than the increase in the consumer's marginal willingness to pay, can be understood by noting that if the quantity sold stays constant, the marginal cost to the monopolist will have become higher than the marginal revenue. The marginal revenue increase is simply the extra marginal revenue gained by selling one more unit, and this equals the consumer's extra willingness to pay, v,[3] while the marginal cost increase is c. If $c > v$, the marginal cost will be higher than the marginal revenue, at the given level of output, and it will be profitable for the monopolist to reduce the quantity.

If this is not sufficient to convince, a mathematical proof, showing that the quantity will decrease when $c > v$, is provided in the appendix.

3 This is demonstrated as part of the general proof in the mathematical appendix.

Some implicit assumptions behind the result

The traditional demand and supply analysis is so second nature to all economists that it may not always be detected that it actually relies on a set of assumptions which may not be fulfilled. I would mention the following:

a) Consumers perceive the change in the law and increase their demand for the good;
b) Given a) the monopolist is aware of the shift in the demand curve and raises the price to take advantage of the higher demand;
c) The monopolist realizes that his marginal costs have gone up, and reacts by lowering the quantity produced.

In a sense, when either of these assumptions is not fulfilled, one might say that the market is not in equilibrium in the sense that there are unexplored opportunities for gain for either of the parties. Let us briefly consider the consequences if one of these assumptions does not hold.

Ad a) If consumers do not perceive the change (but only recognize it when the rule takes effect for them individually), the demand curve will remain constant. Consumers may e.g. not realize that they have been given a right to replacement. If the monopolist is aware of this and of his/her cost increase, i.e. if c) still holds, the price will go up but not as much as the benefit v. In this case, the Kaldor-Hicks optimal rule will still be repair when $c > v$, but both rules will be Pareto-optimal when the price increase that is due to the cost increase is not larger than the advantage v. What then becomes important is hence the incidence, which depends on the slope of the supply and the demand curves. It may still be to the advantage of the consumers to accept repair, when $c > v$, but it is not certain to be so.

This case where the demand curve is unaffected may prevail in the short run, but it seems realistic to assume that consumers will become aware of their right to a replacement, at least if replacement is considerably better than repair. Moreover, if the difference between the two remedies is so small as to remain unnoticed by consumers, then arguably, there may also be little reason to implement replacement for the sake of the consumers. So it is doubtful that much should be made of the fact that assumption a) may not hold.

Ad b). If there is a shift in the demand curve that the monopolist does not notice, but he or she does notice her/his own costs increasing, the price will be set according to the old demand curve (on the assumption that this is known by the monopolist). Thus, the price will be increased in accordance with incidence theory, which holds the demand curve constant, and the increase will hence be strictly lower than when the monopolist realizes the demand shift. Consumers may then be better off under the rule of replacement. However, this case may seem somewhat unrealistic.

Ad c). If the monopolist does not realize that his costs have gone up, the outcome depends on whether there is a demand shift and whether the monopolist notices this shift. I mention this possibility but do not pursue it further, as it seems to be the least realistic assumption.

Admittedly, the above is far from a full analysis of the case of market disequilibrium. A fuller analysis would involve a full description of what the seller and the buyer know and what mainly the seller assumes about the buyer's knowledge and foresight. Such an analysis, however, is beyond the scope of the present article.

Why Eide's result extends to other market structures

It is evident that the reasoning set out above extends to other market structures. Thus, regardless of the market structure, in equilibrium price and quantity will be a pair that lies on the demand curve which will shift upwards by v when consumers obtain their preferred remedy (replacement). So, regardless of market structure, the essential question becomes whether the quantity sold increases or decreases. Let us consider perfect competition. Under perfect competition, the supply curve is essentially equal to the sum of the MC curves (their increasing parts), so shifts upwards by c. while the demand curve shifts upwards by v. Naturally, if $c > v$, the quantity sold will decline (by the same marginality reason as under monopoly). Hence, under perfect competition, the result holds true that consumer surplus will increase, if $c > v$, while it will decrease if $c > v$. Again, sellers and buyers should agree on the remedy. Since monopolistic competition falls between monopoly and perfect competition, it seems clear, and is shown graphically by Eide, that the result also holds true here. Mathematical proofs are not be provided here, but it is evident that they would follow the same logic as the proof for the case of monopoly.

Finally, one caveat should be mentioned: Eide's result hinges on the absence of a price fixing agreement between sellers. If they have implicitly or explicitly agreed on a price, and this price is unaffected by the legal rule, obviously both rules may be Pareto-optimal.

Who bears the cost of inefficiency in the long run

In the case mentioned in the Introduction that was decided in the Norwegian Supreme Court (HR-2006-00299-A-Rt-2006-179), Judge Flock remarked:

> I add that I can hardly see any element of consumer protection worth mentioning in a rule that should give a right to replacement in a case like this. In my opinion, repair will constitute a sufficient protection of the interest of the consumers. Moreover, in the end it will be the consumers that have to cover the additional costs.

However, this is criticized by Eide (2009), mainly in section 4.1., who writes that the buyer will only bear part of the cost increase: essentially, Eide argues that the price will not increase by $v + c$ but by less than this. The reason by now is familiar: as the quantity sold will be smaller, the marginal cost will be lower (assuming increasing marginal costs of production!), and this will attenuate the effect on price. Hence, consumers will not bear the full cost increase; part of it will be borne by the suppliers whose surplus will go down.

This analysis, however, considers only the short run. If we consider a long run equilibrium before and after the increase in cost and the increase in the willingness to pay, and if we assume free entry and competitive equilibrium, we immediately obtain the result that consumers must bear the whole cost increase. According to conventional price theory, in the long run price equals marginal cost equals average total cost (ATC) for each seller (producer) in the market, where the condition that price equals ATC is the zero profit condition (if profits were positive, entry would continue until profits were zero). Given that both the MC and the ATC curves shift upwards by c, for each seller who remains in the market, the quantity must remain the same as before (since the two curves intersect only at that quantity), and so the price must go up by the cost increase. The number of firms adjusts. Put differently, if profits are zero before and after the change in the legal rule, the difference in the total surplus must be borne by the consumers.

Conclusion

This note elaborates on Eide's result that contract law is uniquely determined by the criterion of Pareto-optimality, regardless of market structure. With only a slight simplification, the main conclusion is that this (remarkable) result holds for the simple reason that market equilibrium must be a point on the demand curve, which shifts upwards with the benefit to the buyer of a buyer-friendly rule.

I have argued further that this result hinges on informational assumptions, mainly that buyers are aware of the consequences of the legal rule, and that the sellers are aware of the shift in the demand curve. If these assumptions are relaxed, there will still be a unique Kaldor-Hicks optimal rule, but not necessarily a unique Pareto-optimal rule. Finally, I showed that buyers pay for the whole extra cost of an inoptimal rule in the long run when the market structure is perfect competition.

Appendix:

This appendix formulates Eide's result and proves it mathematically for the case of monopoly.

Proposition: When each consumer's marginal willingness to pay goes up by v and the monopolist's marginal cost goes up by c as a consequence of a change in the legal rule, both consumers' total surplus and monopolist's profits will decrease when $c > v$ and increase when $v > c$, assuming that the monopolist knows the demand curve.

Proof: In equilibrium, marginal cost equals marginal revenue. Marginal revenue is derived from the demand curve. Let the former demand curve be given by the equation: $p = f(\mathrm{q})$, and the new demand curve be given by the equation $p = f(\mathrm{q}) + v$. Then, total revenue is given by $f(\mathrm{q})\mathrm{q}$ before, and by $(f(\mathrm{q}) + v)\mathrm{q}$ after. Marginal revenue becomes $f'(q)q + f(q)$ before, and $f'(q)q + f(q) + v$, after. Thus, the MR curve shifts upwards by v. The monopolist's MC-curve also shifts upwards, but by c. If we denote the former MR curve by MR_1 and the new MR curve by MR_2, and denote the MC curves similarly, we can state the former equilibrium condition (determining the equilibrium quantity q_1^*), as $MC_1(q_1^*)$ = $MR_1(q_1^*)MC_1(q_1^*) = MR_1(q_1^*)$, and the new as $MC_1(q_2^*) + c = MR_1(q_2^*) + v$. Note that $MR_1(q) - MC_1(q)$ is decreasing in q, since $MR_1(q)$ is decreasing in q and$MC_1(q)$ is increasing in q. Given this, the $MR_1(q) - MC_1(q)$ equals $v - c$ at a higher q when $v - c$ is positive (than when it is zero), and at a lower q, when $v - c$ is negative. Thus, $q_1^* < q_2^*$, when $v > c$ and vice versa.

To see that consumer surplus is greater when $q_1^* < q_2^*$ (and smaller when $q_1^* >$ q_2^*, note that consumer surplus increases as quantity increases, down a given demand curve, and that consumer surplus at the former demand curve equals consumer surplus at the point of the second demand curve where $q = q_1^*$, as the price will be v higher at this point, eliminating the higher surplus due to v. However, when $v > c$, the point realized on the new demand curve will lie further down the demand curve (and this will mean a higher surplus), whereas a lower surplus will by the same reasoning be realized when $v > c$.

References

Eide, Erling. 2009. Is the consumer directive advantageous for the consumers? *European Journal of Law and Economics* **28** (3)

Law and Economics from Lawyers' Point of View

Kalle Määttä

Very many textbooks as well as articles in law and economics have been written as if economists analyse the issue. On the contrary, this paper approaches law and economics in the way in which lawyers may think about the topic. On the other hand, it may be said that lawyers are interested in legal interpretation but law and economics often provides a toolbox to the economic analysis of norm formulation, not so often to the legal interpretation, at least in civil law countries.

Studies of law and economics deal so largely with common law that it may be said that they have dealt with questions of common law and economics. However, this paper claims that an economic analysis of law is a suitable approach in civil law countries, too. Much depends, of course, on the approach adopted. For instance, economic analyses of norm formulation as well as econometric analyses of law are important and appropriate on both sides of the Atlantic Ocean. On the other hand, the most problematic approach in this respect is legal dogmatics, i.e. the interpretation of law in civil law countries.

1. In which ways have the functions of law and economics been characterized?

The functions of law and economics have been analysed in different ways by different authors. For instance, Cento Veljanovski (2006) has characterized law and economics at a general level as follows: "The economics of law can be defined rather crudely as the application of economic theory, mostly, price theory, and statistical methods to examine the formation, structure, processes and impact of the law and legal institutions."

Moreover, it has been referred quite often that economic analysis of law seeks to answer two basic questions about legal and non-legal norms.[1] First: What are the effects of these norms on the behaviour of relevant actors? Second: Are these effects of norms socially desirable?

The distinction between approaches in law and economics that follows is a familiar one, and one step further from the above-mentioned classification.[2] The positive approach is concerned with the predictions. What will the effects of the law be? That is, positive economics is the empirical branch of economics. The prescriptive approach is concerned with showing how society might actually reach one shared goal. The normative approach is concerned with what the legal system should do.

A somewhat different approach has been adopted by A. Klevorick (1975) according to whom economists may have three approaches to law and economics. First, the economist can accept the legal problem as formulated by lawyers and seek to solve it by applying economics. Here the economists are assisting lawyers in applying the law without challenging their authority. Second, economists can treat an area of law, such as tort law or criminal law, as if its objective were to improve the allocation of resources in the economy. The third role is to employ economic concepts and terms to provide new vocabulary for lawyers.

The tasks of law and economics have also been outlined as follows. On the one hand, law and economics studies whether law promotes economically efficient outcomes, and, on the other hand, if they do not, suggests how they can be changed in order to do so, always provided the cost of the change falls short of benefits.[3] In more legal terms, in the former case law and economics is directed towards *de lege lata* studies, while in the latter law and economics is directed towards *de lege ferenda* studies.

Some of the functions of law and economics mentioned are such that they are unfamiliar for lawyers, and especially lawyers' way of thinking about legal studies. Against this background, it is understandable that legal scholars have not been very interested in economic analysis of law, and they have left it to the economists. What is of great importance, too, is that there seems to be no close connection between economic analysis of law and legal interpretation. However, in order to awaken the

1 See also Eide and Stavang (2008).

2 See e.g. Sunstein (2000).

3 Veljanovski (2006). Foreword written by Professor Geoffrey E. Wood.

interest of lawyers in law and economics, this connection should be closely knit and the questions of interest should be presented in another manner. Moreover, it is not only legal interpretation that legal studies are interested in, but rather a broader range of topics, i.e. informational needs.[4] They have been referred to in law and economics literature quite often, however without being systematized at all.

2. A brief overview of the functions of law and economics as seen through lawyers' eyes

It is well known that *legal dogmatics* refers to the interpretation and systematization of law. What is not so well known, and what has created controversies among legal scholars and legal economists, is the position of efficiency considerations when the legal provision is interpreted. Because this issue is analysed later in this paper, we will jump to the next function of law and economics.[5]

Economic analysis of norm formulation can be characterized by the following statement: "To regulate or not to regulate, and if to regulate, how? These are the questions."[6] Regarding the economic analysis of norm formulation, *Coase theorem* is one benchmark, since it helps to analyse under which circumstances law is needed, or when an agreement between parties may be sufficient. On the other hand, transaction costs may be in a critical position in estimating the opportunities for self- or co-regulation.[7] If transaction costs are very high, the opportunities for enterprises to agree about self-regulation and its design are very limited. On the other hand, there are quite many mechanisms by which to minimize transaction costs in this respect, too.[8]

Economic analysis of norm formulation covers plenty of regulatory problems. One such issue is the debate over *rules* and *standards*.[9] Rules are those legal commands which differentiate legal from illegal behaviour in a simple and clear way, i.e. they are bright-line in nature, which helps the work of the adjudicators.

4 See closer Määttä (2006).

5 The aim is not at being exhaustive in the presentation. Therefore, e.g. comparative law and economics has been omitted from the paper. See closer about it, in particular, Mattei (1997).

6 Määttä (1997).

7 See e.g. Ogus (1995) about self-regulation.

8 See e.g. Milgrom and Roberts (1992).

9 See e.g. Kaplow (2000).

Standards, instead, are general legal criteria which are unclear and fuzzy and require complicated judiciary decision-making.[10] Moreover, economic analysis of regulatory options may be directed e.g. at *ex ante* and *ex post* instruments as well as direct regulation and economic instruments.

One approach may be labelled *law and econometrics* (or legal econometrics). Criminal law has been the target of a broad range of econometric studies, for instance, partly thanks to Professor Erling Eide.[11] Most empirical testing of the relationship between crime and deterrence variables has analysed data on recorded crimes using standard statistical procedures, normally multiple regression analysis. Three basic types of studies which can be distinguished are cross-sectional comparisons of areas at a point of time, such as countries in a particular year; analyses of a particular area (region, country) over a period of time; and longitudinal studies of individuals, usually related to prisoners.[12]

Nevertheless, lack of empirical research is a characteristic of many separate fields and topics in law and economics.[13] This is not only a problem as such, but it has other additional implications as well. For instance, follow-up on the impacts of legislation is all-important in order to study whether the legislation enacted has reached its goals. Otherwise the legislator's work is tantamount to shooting in the dark. Moreover, from a comparative point of view, it is not only merely interesting to study the impacts of legislation abroad, but it may help government when it plans to introduce a similar kind of legislation domestically. In addition, lack of empirical research may also have impact with respect to the usefulness of the economic analysis in legal interpretation. For instance, the law and economics literature may present competing recommendations, and the problem is, of course, how to select the "right" recommendation.

Economic analysis in legal history has not been a systematic approach in law and economics, but textbooks and articles sometimes mention anecdotes about the usefulness of economic analysis in this respect, too. Criminal law provides an example of economic analysis explaining the development of law. According to Gary S. Becker (1968), there was tendency during the 18th and 19th centuries

10 Of course, the distinction between different legal norms is not so clear-cut in practice, since many norms can be located somewhere between pure rules and pure standards.

11 See especially Eide et al. (1994). See also Eide (2000).

12 Pyle (2000).

13 See e.g. Faure (2008) regarding tort law and economics.

in Anglo-Saxon countries to punish those convicted of criminal offences severely, at the same time that the probability of capture and conviction was set at rather low values. A promising explanation of this tendency may have been, according to Becker, that an increased probability of conviction obviously absorbs public and private resources in the form of more policemen, judges and so forth. Consequently, a "compensated" reduction in this probability obviously reduces expenditures on combating crime, and, since the expected punishment is unchanged, there is no "obvious" offsetting increase in either the amount of damages or the cost of punishment.[14]

Finally, *legal planning* concentrates on finding the best possible legal solution for the enterprise among all possible legal solutions. The approach is familiar in tax law, so-called tax planning, but it can be extended to cover every field of legislation. Tort law, for instance, may provide an example in this respect. The fact that injurers may be able to avoid liability costs by being found judgment-proof creates an incentive for firms to act strategically by, for example, divesting themselves of risky activities and locating them in small subsidiary firms, given the limited liability of assets within a corporation.[15] This may be privately profitable for the firm, even though it distorts incentives for precautions.

3. Interpretation of law

3.1 Economists versus lawyers

Economists tend to criticize lawyers' focus on the details of the legal system and thereby the tendency to overlook the purpose of legal institutions. Moreover, the attitude of lawyers has been regarded as inward looking and conservative.[16] To some extent this point of view is right, but only to some extent. We should recognize that lawyers concentrate on the interpretation of the law in their daily work, and in that respect it is a question of legal details. Moreover, the approach

14 See also Dnes (1996) and Friedman (2000).

15 See closer Ringleb and Wiggins (1990) and Brooks (2002). See also Miceli (2004) from which the example has been taken.

16 See e.g. Guellec and van Pottelsberghe (2007) concerning, however, only patent system. In any case, this kind of point of view may be extended to cover all fields of legislation.

of legal dogmatics is different when compared with the economics approach. Traditionally, lawyers have behaved like judges making decisions, as if they were located inside the legal system. However, the legal economist's point of view is at the same time an insider's as well as an outsider's approach, even though they concentrate only on the legal interpretation. Simply put, this is due to the emphasis on substantive arguments in legal reasoning.[17]

It has also been a matter of concern that the legal approach addresses issues of fairness and balance of rights, of internal consistency of the legal system, and of consistency of a certain law with other bodies of law.[18] Even though these issues sound unfamiliar to economics, they are necessarily germane. For instance, the relationship between fairness and efficiency has been an eternal issue in law and economics. And many authors claim that the difference is not drastic, if there is a difference at all.[19] Furthermore, internal consistency of the legal system is important also from an economic point of view. This may be justified, for example, by the minimization of administrative costs and improvement of the predictability of legal treatment. Moreover, from an economic point of view it is good if the different parts of the legislation serving similar goals fit together. In this way, for instance, the risk of over-regulation may be minimized.

The difference between lawyers' and economists' way of thinking can also be exemplified by the distinction between deduction and induction.[20] Deduction implies that the focus is from the theory to reality, starting with assumptions, deriving hypotheses from them, and testing them by empirical observations, e.g. the rational choice approach by Gary S. Becker (1968). On the other hand, an inductive approach is oriented from reality to theory starting with empirical observations, and thereafter making generalizations in order to develop a theory. What is of great importance here is that the legal studies concentrating on the interpretation of law are often characterized by the inductive approach: there are plenty of court decisions and the purpose of the legal study is to make generalizations about this material.

According to Robert Cooter and Thomas Ulen (2008), lawyers focus on individual cases, whereas economists focus upon statistics. This point of view is easy

17 This issue is explained later in a more detailed fashion.

18 Guellec and van Pottelsberghe (2007).

19 See e.g. Posner (2003).

20 See also Kerkmeester (2000).

to share, that is, that economists concentrate on *aggregates*, e.g. the position of poorest households if the unconscionability doctrine is applied broadly. Lawyers emphasize too much that the decision by the court concerns only the individual case at hand. To a certain extent this is paradoxical since the decisions of supreme courts are used as precedents.

A static or historical point of view is a characteristic of conventional legal interpretation, whereas a *dynamic point of view* and the future impacts are crucial positions in economically-oriented legal interpretation. For instance, Richard A. Posner (2003) has emphasized that sunk costs are sunk and therefore the crime committed, for example, is not critical in interpreting criminal law, but rather how the interpretation affects committing crimes in the future so that the crime rate would be at the optimal level. As a general point of view, it may even be claimed that judicial decision-making will be driven to crisis, if dynamic argumentation is omitted. This is simply because of the rapidly changing world around us in which the legislator is always late, to lesser or greater extent. An item of great importance, too, is that the concept of efficiency assumes that all that matters is the consequence, not non-consequential criteria, such as justice.[21] On the other hand, these consequences are often theoretical (or hypothetical) in nature, not based on empirical evidence. In any case, empirical research may help us move in the latter direction, and to increase the weight of economic principles.

Moreover, are economists able to make an essential contribution to ensuring that the necessary legal principles are adapted to economic and social realities? One significant problem here is that judges are "essential facilities" who finally decide whether economic reasoning may be taken into account. This claim is supported to some extent by the fact that authorities where economists are working make decisions which are compatible with economics. For instance, US antitrust agencies hired and integrated economists already in the 1960s, with the result that the approach of agencies became more economic and less legalistic.[22]

On the other hand, studies in law and economics have often been written in such a fashion that "outsiders" may think that lawyers are only party addressed. However, several examples show that lawyers, law or legal studies have been the initiators. The Coase Theorem was based on court decisions. The Learned Hand

---

21 See e.g. Friedman (2000).

22 Eisner (1991). See also Monti (2007), 5.

rule is based on a court decision. The economists of the late nineteenth century saw no need for antitrust legislation. However, the Sherman Act was signed in 1890 in spite of the fact that economists opposed the act.[23] These examples show that lawyers have been in the forefront when remarkable advances have been made in law and economics. Thus, law and economics has been a two-way road, and it should remain two-way in nature in order to stay vital.

Finally, emphasizing economics in legal interpretation may save – to some extent paradoxically – transaction and administrative costs. For instance, many fields of the economy, such as new economy and financial markets, are very dynamic, entailing the emergence of new problems of interpretation all the time. If legal dogmatics is based on historical argumentation, i.e. on government bills and earlier court decisions, courts would be always late. At worst, the Supreme Court could give precedent after the law has already been amended. On the other hand, more flexible legislation and the economic approach in the interpretation of these statutes may help greatly in this respect.

3.2 Economic mission as a mission of legal interpretation

R.H. Bork (1978) has emphasized the need for knowing the goals of antitrust law. This requirement could and should be extended to other fields of law as well. Against this background, we may speak about the economic mission, economic function or economic principles of the law under consideration.

But what is involved in making economic mission the benchmark of the interpretation of law? The Trademark Act may highlight the issue. Primarily, one trademark should not be similar to another because the trademark's function is to minimize search costs. However, what is the situation if an identical trademark is used in a separate market? First, if firms are active in entirely different fields of business, there is no risk of confusion among customers. Moreover, if another firm is not taking advantage of the *goodwill* of the other, there is no reason to change the conclusion mentioned. In addition, a generic term for a product, such as a camera, cannot be registered as a trademark.[24] This is one way to prevent monopolization and to emphasize that the function of the trademark is to promote competition.[25]

23 See e.g. van den Bergh and Camesasca (2001), 355.

24 Landes and Posner (1987).

25 See also Dnes (1996).

One problem here is that individual function may be easily legitimated by economics but it may have no clear-cut grounds in preparatory drafts of legislation. Moreover, the function or mission mentioned in the preparatory drafts of legislation (i.e. explicit goal) may not correspond with the actual goal of the legislation. For instance, tobacco tax may be justified by health policy concerns but the real goal is only a fiscal one, i.e. to collect proceeds for the government. In addition, the goals of the law may be controversial. For instance, even the objectives of the competition law – especially in the European Union – are far from clear-cut: What is the weight of market integration as a goal compared with efficiency considerations? And should other objectives be taken into account, too, such as industrial competitiveness? Giulio Monti (2007) has referred to multiplicity of goals behind the competition legislation, and that the goals of legislation vary over time, which makes it difficult or almost impossible to adopt Bork's approach. Even though Monti's remark concerns only competition law, it can be extended to other fields of legislation, and perhaps with better reason than under competition legislation.

3.3 Sources of law

The basic question here is: What is the weight of economics or efficiency considerations in the interpretation of law, for example in the Nordic tradition?[26] For instance, the culture in the Finnish judicial system and the authorities have been described as fairly formal and focused on the authority of the written law. While the role of the courts in independently developing the law has become more pronounced from the 1980s and onward, the courts have not gained the kind of independent status typical of courts in common law countries. Instead, the role of the courts in Finland is still primarily to apply the legislation or, at most, to supplement it.

Sources of law and their bindingness are in a critical position in the interpretation of laws in Nordic countries. Sources of law have been divided into three groups: strongly-binding, weakly-binding and permissible sources of law. This also shows the priority of these sources.

Strongly-binding sources of law are *law text* and customary law.[27] If the answer

26 See e.g. Timonen (1996).

27 Customary law has been omitted here since it is not at all as important as the law text as a strongly-binding source of law in civil law.

to the interpretative problem can be found from the law text, there is no need to outline other sources of law. An important aspect, however, is that not all concepts are defined at all in law.[28] This feature of course opens for taking advantage of economics in legal interpretation. On the other hand, these kinds of *definitional gaps* do not oblige courts and other judicial bodies to take economics into account in legal interpretation.

Taking the wording of the law as a benchmark may sound much more unambiguous than it is *de facto*. In principle, the problem is whether to prefer the *ordinary meaning* of the legal text or to stress *contextual meaning* in the legal text.[29] In practice, many cases show that *literal interpretation* is far from clear-cut. For example, consumer protection legislation concerns – of course – consumers, but competition legislation does this as well. However, the definition of consumers is completely different in these laws. In a similar fashion, the concept of "undertaking" in competition law is not identical to the question of legal personality for the purposes of company law and fiscal law.[30]

A reference can be made to Finnish business name legislation, too.[31] A case in the Finnish Supreme Court (KKO:1994:110) concerned a situation in which the surname of the sole proprietor changed (which may occur, for example, through divorce or marriage). On the other hand, Finnish legislation requires that this kind of entrepreneur shall use only her own name as a business name. Thus, the legal problem was whether the sole proprietor had the right to use her old surname as a business name. If the law text had been interpreted literally, this possibility would have been rejected. But the Supreme Court used common sense: the woman had the right to maintain the old business name even though her surname had changed.

The decision could be justified by the minimization of administrative and transaction costs. In other words, the sole proprietor did not have to give any notification to the authorities regarding the change of business name and she was under no obligation to pay fees either. Transaction costs were saved, too, since the sole pro-

---

28 See also Veljanovski (2006).

29 See e.g. Sunstein (1995) about these problems.

30 See also Posner (2001).

31 Economic missions of business names are similar as missions of trademarks; reducing the search costs of customers, signaling the quality of services and products traded, and the promotion of competition.

prietor did not have to change the business names on invoices, brochures and other documents of the enterprise. On the other hand, the net impact on search costs among customers is more difficult to estimate. However, because customers of sole proprietors constitute in practice only a limited group of people, they may very well know who the owner of the firm is even though the business name has not changed and although the surname of the owner of the firm has changed. In summary, taking into account the minimization of all the costs related to the change of the surname of sole proprietor, the Supreme Court's decision is well justified.

The analysis of the position of strongly-binding sources of law may be continued by the following arguments. When a literal interpretation is emphasized, there are increasing pressures to amend the statutes, which generate administrative costs as well as uncertainty about the reform of the statute. On the other hand, if the wording of the statute is not appreciated, the predictability of the legal treatment is eroded, and in this way uncertainty among enterprises and consumers is created – uncertainty which hinders the efficient allocation of resources. Consequently, it is not only a question of automatic adoption of the doctrine about the sources of law, but a more analytically critical approach to the doctrine.

What is of great importance here, too, is the distinction between rules and standards. If the legislator uses primarily bright-line rules, courts and other judicial bodies do not have discretionary power or they have it only superficially. Under these circumstances, the use of economic reasoning is not even facilitated broadly at the level of interpreting statutes, and we can bid – almost – farewell to law and economics in this respect. On the other hand, the more standards are applied in the legal system, the broader the discretionary power of courts and adjudicators becomes, and the broader the scope for economic reasoning will be. Nonetheless, even this does not mean that economics is applied; it is only facilitated to be applied.

Because laws are always imperfect, there is a need for outlining *weakly-binding sources of law*, i.e. preparatory drafts of legislation and court decisions. For instance, in Finland nowadays among preparatory drafts of legislation the most important are government proposals; on the other hand, in Sweden also, Committee reports are of great importance. By court decisions, we refer particularly to the decisions of the Supreme Court and Supreme Administrative Court.

It is easy to show that the justifications of law reforms are often based on market failures, even though nothing is explicitly mentioned about externalities, asymmetrical information, public goods, commons or imperfect competition.[32] On the other hand, why are the justifications mentioned in the preparatory drafts not sufficient "guides"? First of all, the absence of justifications is a characteristic of government bills as well as the fact that they are often vague. In other words, preparatory drafts of legislation are always imperfect, too. Moreover, the justifications may be contradictory to each other: what is the justification followed in legal praxis? In addition, explicit justifications of the law do not necessarily correspond with the actual justifications of the law.[33]

One problem in law and economics is to explain why the courts do not use economic reasoning explicitly if they use it in any case.[34] However, in the US the Supreme Court has sometimes quoted the publications of law and economics scholars in support of the decision. Unfortunately, it seems that in some cases the research results have not been the final truths. For instance, mention can be made of Isaac Ehrlich's (1975) study about the deterrence effect of capital punishment, the results of which have been made questionable later. Moreover, representatives of the Chicago School argued that predatory pricing is not a rational pricing strategy for a dominant firm. The Supreme Court also quoted these publications in the *Matsushita* case, even though more recent economic literature has shown that predatory pricing may sometimes be a rational pricing strategy.[35]

These examples show that it is not at all so straightforward to use economic reasoning as justifications in the court decisions. First, there may be multiple contradictory studies already when the decision is made by the court. How to make the choice, then, particularly since judges are not experts in the field of economics? Second, later studies may show that the original studies quoted are misleading. The problem faced by the courts, however, is how the courts can be sure that these later studies are "better" than the original ones. Finally, if research results are appreciated, the legal treatment is not developed by the law but rather by the economic theory and empirical studies regarding it. It is not astonishing that this thought may seem to be very unfamiliar to lawyers.

It is not uncommon that weakly-binding sources of law are mute in the face of the interpretative problem. Under these circumstances, *permissible sources of law*

---

32 Määttä (2009).

33 See closer Määttä (1997).

34 See also Monti (2007).

35 See e.g. van den Bergh and Camesasca (2001) about predatory pricing.

could be used: legal principles, legal literature, moral as well as substantive arguments belong to these sources of law. And what is critical here, is that *economic arguments (or efficiency considerations) usually belong to the substantive arguments.*[36] From this point of view, the position of economics in legal interpretation seems to be weak. First, both strongly-binding and weakly-binding sources of law should in principle be silent in front of the interpretative problem before we could even think of using the economic toolbox. Second, substantive arguments are not alone in the group of permissible sources of law, that is, there is even competition between these sources of law. Third, substantive arguments may be constructed not only on the basis of economics but on other bases, too.[37]

Against this background, one may also ask immediately where there is any point in concentrating on legal dogmatics (in civil law countries) in law and economics, but whether one should instead pay more serious attention to studies which somehow help norm formulation and impact analysis, such as criminometrics.[38] However, the situation is not as hopeless as it seems. First, efficiency considerations are not only part of permissible sources of law; they may have been written into law. Partly, therefore, competition law is some kind of core of law and economics studies.[39] Moreover, and as was mentioned above, preparatory drafts of legislation involve argumentation which quite often refers to efficiency considerations, or which can be translated into economic jargon. In addition, genuine interpretative problems are such that strongly-binding and weakly-binding sources of law do not provide guidance for the decision. From this point of view, economics may be a useful toolbox especially in this respect.

4. Challenges of economics in legal interpretation

Anthony Ogus (2004) has emphasized well the strengths of the economics point of view in legal studies. But this does not tell the whole story; there are also prob-

36 See closer Timonen (1996).

37 See closer Määttä (2006).

38 See closer about criminometrics Eide et al. (1994).

39 However, van den Bergh and Camesasca (2001) have mentioned that the harmony between competition law and economics is not complete.

lems in this respect, particularly regarding the interpretation of law. And it is good to identify these drawbacks, even though they may weaken the status of law and economics among lawyers. On the other hand, no other approach is perfect in this respect. Thus, it is question of competition between imperfect approaches to legal interpretation.

It is easy to refer, for example, to the transaction costs, but *empirical evidence* about the level of transaction costs is scarce. According to Douglas W. Allen (2000), there are only a few studies that have attempted to measure the level of transaction costs. Moreover, Roger van den Bergh and Peter Camesasca (2001) have mentioned with respect to the competition law that economics does not necessarily lead to better legal policy, because it has little empirical content. Even though they refer only to competition law, their argument is not without importance in other fields of law. On the other hand, the argumentation could be reversed. Cento Veljanovski (2006) has argued that economics can be used to develop antitrust doctrine based solely on theoretical concerns that have not been tested by the regulator (or economists) and which at best have questionable empirical relevance.

Moreover, it may be easy to refer to the efficiency, or more specifically to Kaldor-Hicks criterion or Pareto efficiency as benchmarks in law and economics. Sometimes, of course, these efficiency considerations may help a lot, when, for instance, the legality of the resale price maintenance is analysed.[40] On the other hand, problems emerge already here. First, it is not written in stone whether to use the Pareto efficiency or the Kaldor-Hicks criterion; this is a problem since different efficiency criteria may lead to different results. Second, if the latter criterion is used, there may be problems in estimating the benefits and costs in borderline cases. Moreover, problems are not exhausted in the above-mentioned issues, since there are difficulties in determining the dynamic impacts of legal measures (i.e. dynamic efficiency).[41]

In addition, economic theory does not provide the efficient outcome for every possible legal problem. One might mention bilateral accidents and how efficient activity level may be reached. None of the liability rules could yield efficient out-

40 See e.g. Posner (2003).

41 See also Brodley (1987) regarding the efficiency considerations under the competition law. Of course, there are also problems whether to emphasize consumer welfare of total welfare in decision-making (particularly under competition law).

come. Therefore, the best rule depends – in this case – on a comparison of overall accident costs under each of the rules.[42]

One difficulty of economic analysis in legal interpretation is that the "theory is theory but practice is practice". For instance, *perfect expectation damages* create incentives for efficient performance and breach of contracts, that is, damages which restore the promisee to the position that she would have enjoyed if the promise had been kept. However! *Practical difficulties* have resulted in expectation damages actually awarded by courts in the US usually being imperfect, for instance, because foregone profits have been difficult to estimate.[43] One solution to the problem concerned is that the economic analysis of law should be approached at two stages. The first stage consists of the ideal analysis, which pays no heed to the practical difficulties. These rules may be labelled as *theoretical norms*. Another stage takes into account practical considerations. Recommendations made on this basis are called as *practical norms*.

In any case, some problems of interpretation are so sticky that they cannot be solved by economic argumentation even though economic mission is indisputable and clear-cut. For instance, it is self-evident that business names which could be confused with each other should not be accepted, because search costs would increase – not decrease – due to the confusion. Of course, it is very difficult to determine the point at which similar business names can be confused. Moreover, practical problems may concern many stages, not only one. Suppose that your house is infested with termites, and that the case will go to the court. The following kinds of questions must be answered:[44] What are the costs of extermination? If termites are not detected, what is the extent of damage they may cause? What is the fraction of houses with termites? What are the costs to acquire information about the termites? In summary, answering these questions is obviously demanding, perhaps sometimes too demanding to provide clear recommendations to the adjudicator.

Economic analysis of law has *not been completely consistent across different fields of legislation*. A reference can be made to tort and environmental law. Under tort law, the negligence rule is regarded as efficient if courts can determine the due care standard efficiently. Under environmental law, direct regulation has been

---

42 See e.g. Miceli (2004), 67–68.

43 Cooter and Ulen (2008).

44 See closer Miceli (2004).

heavily criticized from a cost-effectiveness point of view, since environmental authorities lack information enabling them to set directives in a cost-effective manner. However, what is worth noting is that the asymmetrical problem is similar in nature both under the negligence rule and under direct regulation.

One problem under law and economics is that the decisions of courts are sometimes compatible with economic reasoning, but only sometimes. The application of the Learned Hand rule may provide an example in this respect. What can we say under these circumstances about the usefulness of economic reasoning? On the other hand, nothing prevents the use of economics regarding sticky interpretation problems by solicitors, for example. Another example is provided through the punitive damages awarded. In economic theory, the so-called punitive multiplier is crucial when the amount of punitive damages is determined. However, A. Mitchell Polinsky and Steven Shavell's (1998) conclusion has been in this respect that courts do not pay systematic attention to the probability of escaping liability, even though it is a crucial factor in economic theory.

A controversy between economic reasoning and legal praxis in many countries is that economists recommend harsher punishments for repeat offenders without taking into account the similarity of crimes, time period between crimes and how many crimes the offender has committed. And these are just the issues which have been crucial in legal praxis. Roughly speaking, harsher punishments for repeat offenders have been the exceptions in legal praxis, whereas in economics only harsher punishments for repeat offenders have been explained. Thus, the problem is *why one should explain something which does not exist in practice*! It is clear-cut that the economic analysis of law has to be linked much more closely and credibly to law; otherwise it may lose its value before it has even warranted losing it.

Multiplicity of different schools in law and economics may cause problems, too. For instance, antitrust law provides a case in point, since a kind of "revolution" occurred after 1970s when the tide turned from Harvard School to the Chicago School's arguments. If law and economics is taken as a whole, there are plenty of schools which may be paid attention to. The problem for lawyers under these circumstances is to select which kinds of arguments are preferable, or remain eclectic.[45] Moreover, the problem is one of anticipating the developments in a

45 See e.g. Kerkmeester (2000). Monti (2007) has paid attention to how divided opinions of economists are (e.g. in analysing markets and in predicting the potential developments in the market).

(dominant) economic theory. Today's truth may be tomorrow's heresy! On the other hand, different schools in law and economics may be regarded as hallmarks of law and economics. It shows that the approach is analytical and that even legal interpretation could be something more than basing the decisions on the authoritative arguments, like the law text, government bills and court cases. It compels the adjudicator to approach the legal problem analytically. A quite new challenge is whether to give priority to the results of mainstream law and economics or behavioural law and economics. Of course, before this can be done, the legal economist has to decide what is meant by mainstream or what kind of behavioural approach should be preferred.

Still another problem is whether to take into account only efficiency considerations or whether *fairness* or *social justice* should also be included in the argumentation. Moreover, during EC competition law deliberations, an intensively discussed problem has been whether the law should serve only efficiency goals or at the same time also integration goals.[46] Conflicting aims characterize legal interpretation in many other respects as well.

5. Concluding remarks

The position of efficiency considerations in front of the problems of interpretation is not at all clear-cut. First, it may be argued that judges unwittingly decide cases in a way that encourages a more efficient allocation of resources. This is a familiar discussion particularly in common law countries, but not in civil law systems. Second, the absence of any reference to economics in decided cases has been enough for many legal scholars to reject outright any economic analysis in legal interpretation.

At any rate, this paper has adopted the approach that economic analysis of law should not be omitted even among lawyers.[47] The critical issue, however, is under which circumstances law and economics is useful, when it is not. First, the economic approach is not only a theoretically fascinating field of study, but it facilitates analysis of sticky interpretation problems better than the conventional point of view. What is worth noting, among other things, is that law and economics

46 See e.g. Motta (2004) and Kirchner (2007).

47 See also Ogus (2004). Cf. Klevorick (1975) about economist's point of view to law and economics.

perhaps does not always provide suitable answers, but does identify more specific questions than are otherwise provided. In particular, competition legislation regarding collusion of undertakings, abuse of dominance and mergers constitute such a field of law. Moreover, civil law systems involve plenty of standards – and also gaps – in the legislation, which facilitate the use of the economic approach in interpretation. In addition, laws are always imperfect, which strengthens the position of economics even more.

Second, law and economics opens our eyes to the fact that legal studies are not only the domain of legal interpretation, but also a fruitful agenda of many other sub-disciplines of legal studies. Some of these sub-disciplines are also important for lawyers, such as economic analysis of norm formulation. This is simply due to the fact that lawyers often prepare new legislation. In addition, legal planning – or business law planning – is worth noting. Lawyers in business life do not merely frequent the courts, but they devise, for example, compliance programmes for customers.

Nevertheless, there are also approaches to legal studies of an economic nature which are not so suitable for lawyers. For instance, impact analyses of new legislation *ex ante* as well as the *ex post* evaluation of existing legislation are such fields in which lawyers are not masters. In any case, even under these circumstances lawyers may have a role to play, but it should be played on a stage shared with economists and statisticians.

References

Allen, Douglas W. 2000. Transaction Costs, in Bouckaert, Boudewijn and Gerrit De Geest (eds.), *Encyclopedia of Law and Economics, Volume I, General Works, History and Methodology.* Cheltenham: Edward Elgar, pp. 893–926.

Becker, Gary S. 1968. Crime and Punishment: An Economic Approach. *Journal of Political Economy*, **76**(2), 169–217.

Bork, R.H. 1978. *The Antitrust Paradox: A Policy at War with Itself.* New York: Basic Books.

Brodley, Joseph F. 1987. The Economic Goals of Antitrust: Efficiency, Consumer Welfare, and Technological Progress. *New York Law Review*, **62**, 1020–1053.

Brooks, Richard. 2002. Liability and Organizational Choice. *Journal of Law and Economics*, **45**, 91–125.

Cooter, Robert and Thomas Ulen. 2008. *Law & Economics*, 5th ed. Boston: Pearson.

Dnes, Antony W. 1996. *The Economics of Law.* Oxford.

Ehrlich, Isaac. 1975. The Deterrent Effect of Capital Punishment. *American Economic Review*, **65**, 397–417.

Eide, Erling. 2000. Economics of Criminal Behavior, in Bouckaert, Boudewijn and Gerrit De Geest (eds.), *Encyclopedia of Law and Economics, Volume V. The Economics of Crime and Litigation.* Cheltenham: Edward Elgar, pp. 345–389.

Eide, Erling, J. Aasness and T. Skjerpen. 1994. *Economics of Crime, Deterrence and the Rational Offender.* North-Holland: Elsevier Science B.V.

Eide, Erling and Endre Stavang. 2008. *Rättsökonomi.* Oslo: Cappelen Akademisk Forlag.

Eisner, M.A. 1991. *Antitrust and the Triumph of Economics.* Chapel Hill: University of North Carolina Press.

Faure, Michael. 2008. Calabresi and Behavioural Tort Law and Economics. *Erasmus Law Review*, **1**(4), 75–102.

Friedman, David. 2000. *Law's Order. An Economic Account.* Princeton University Press.

Guellec D. and B. van Pottelsberghe de la Potterie. 2007. *The Economics of the European Patent System. IP Policy for Innovation and Competition.* Oxford: Oxford University Press.

Harrison, Jeffrey L. 1995. *Law and Economics in a nutshell.* St. Paul, MN: West Publishing Co.

Kaplow, Louis. 2000. General Characteristics of Rules, in Bouckaert, Boudewijn and Gerrit De Geest (eds.), *Encyclopedia of Law and Economics. Volume V. Economics of Crime and Litigation.* Cheltenham: Edward Elgar, pp. 502–528.

Kerkmeester, Heico. 2000. Methodology: General, in Bouckaert, Boudewijn Gerrit De Geest (eds.), *Encyclopedia of Law and Economics. Volume I, General Works,* History and Methodology. Cheltenham: Edward Elgar, pp. 383–401.

Kirchner, Christian. 2007. Goals of Antitrust and Competition Law Revisited, in Schmidtchen, Dieter, Max Albert and Stefan Voigts (eds.), *The More Economic Approach to European Competition Law.* Tuebingen, pp. 7–26.

Klevorick, A. 1975. Law and Economic Theory: An Economist's Perspective. *American Economic Review*, **65**(2), 237–243.

Landes, William M. and Richard A. Posner. 1987. Trademark Law: An Economic Perspective. *Journal of Law and Economics*, **30**(2), 265–309.

Määttä, Kalle. 1997. *Environmental Taxes, From an Economic Idea to a Legal Institution.* Jyväskylä: Kauppakaari Oy, Finnish Lawyers' Publishing.

Määttä, Kalle. 2006. *Oikeustaloustieteen perusteet* (*Introduction to Law and Economics*). Helsinki: Edita.

Määttä, Kalle. 2009. *Oikeustaloustieteellinen näkökulma kotimaiseen lainvalmisteluun* (*Law and Economics Point of View for Finnish Law-Making*). Oikeuspoliittisen tutkimuslaitoksen julkaisuja 242, Helsinki.

Mattei, Ugo. 1997. *Comparative Law and Economics.* Ann Arbor: The University of Michigan Press.

Miceli, Thomas J. 2004. *The Economic Approach to Law.* Stanford Economics and Finance, Stanford, California.

Milgrom, Paul and John Roberts. 1992. *Economics, Organization & Management.* New Jersey.

Monti, Giorgio. 2007. *EC Competition Law.* New York: Cambridge University Press.

Motta, Massimo. 2004. *Competition Policy: Theory & Practice.* Cambridge: Cambridge University Press.

Ogus, Anthony. 1995. Rethinking Self-regulation. *Oxford Journal of Legal Studies*, **15**(1), 97–108.

Ogus, Anthony. 2004. What Legal Scholars Can Learn from Law and Economics. *Chicago-Kent Law Review*, **79**(2), 383–401.

Polinsky, A. Mitchell and Steven Shavell. 1998. Punitive Damages: An Economic Analysis. *Harvard Law Review*, **111**, 869–862.

Posner, Richard. 2001. *Antitrust Law.* Second edition, Chicago and London: The University of Chicago Press.

Posner, Richard A. 2003. *Economic Analysis of Law.* Sixth Edition, Aspen Law & Business.

Ringleb, Al and Steven Wiggins. 1990. Liability and Large-Scale, Long-Term Hazards. *Journal of Political Economy*, **98**, 574–595.

Sunstein, Cass R. 1995. Problems with Rules. *California Law Review*, **83**(4), 953–1023.

Sunstein, Cass R. 2000. Introduction, in Sunstein, Cass R. (ed.) 2000. *Behavioural Law and Economics.* Cambridge: Cambridge University Press, pp. 1–10.

Timonen, Pekka. 1996. Taloustieteen ja sen tulosten käyttö oikeustutkimuksessa, in Kanniainen, Vesa and Kalle Määttä (eds.), *Näkökulmia oikeustaloustieteeseen (Viewpoints to law and economics),* Tampere, pp. 129–159.

van den Bergh, Roger J. and Peter D. Camesasca. 2001. *European Competition Law and Economics, A Comparative Perspective.* Intersentia, Anwerpen – Groningen – Oxford – New York.

Veljanovski, Cento. 2006. *The Economics of Law.* Second edition, The Institute of Economic Affairs, London.

Legal Uncertainty and Collective Decision Mechanisms: An Analysis of the Norwegian Supreme Court

Gunnar Nordén

> [D]espite the complex and implicit nature of adjudication, its institutional structure determines the path of legal development…
>
> L. A. Kornhauser

1. Introduction

Legal systems contain complex decision mechanisms. At higher levels of the adjudicative system, decisions are typically made by panels of judges. A panel's competence characteristically depends on intricate "law" and "fact" distinctions. Furthermore, legal and factual questions are typically determined under different voting rules and with different "standards of proof" applying to the individual finders of law or facts.

The role of collective entities in determining factual questions has been thoroughly studied. Core results are variants of the Condorcet Jury Theorem (CJT), showing how decision quality varies with group size and individual capabilities.

CJT-style arguments are not directly transferable to legal decision-making. If available legal resources determine outcomes uniquely under all admissible complexes of conditioning facts, panel composition and voting rules would be irrelevant: all collectives would necessarily reach the same conclusion. In such a world, it would make little sense to commit resources to panels and legitimate decisions by panel size. Only a limited hierarchical structure would be needed to check for compliance.

Yet, even when questions of law and fact are unambiguously separated by mechanisms intrinsic to the legal system, on appeal legal questions are decided by panels in the context of an elaborate hierarchical system. I contend that this institutional attribute reflects a structural feature of substantive legal norms: for relevant conditioning complexes of facts, applicable norms do not uniquely determine legal consequences. In this environment, the structure of the adjudicational mechanisms have systematic effects on legal outcomes.[1]

In this paper, I model *norm based legal uncertainty* in a simple manner and study norm and court structure *confluence*. The substantial norms and the adjudicational mechanisms constitute separate sources of legal uncertainty. I use the actual divisions of the Norwegian Supreme Court for illustration. The analysis, of interest in its own right, is but one application of a general framework.

I use the norm-based conception of legal uncertainty to suggest a (stipulative) definition of valid law or law in force, which incorporates basic aspects of the collective legal decision mechanism.

In this development, I abstract from factual uncertainty and take a "local" approach to the legal norm concept. I assume that judges vote over outcomes, not issues or reasons. I will only hint at possible generalizations, but mention that my framework may represent two levels of norm-based legal uncertainty: on the level of doctrine and on the level of sources and interpretation of law.

An alternative approach to legal uncertainty is to assume that substantive norms determine outcomes uniquely, but that judges are imperfectly informed or make errors. Drawing on a well-established literature, I offer some alternative interpretations of the analytical results. Observations concerning court structure design – in particular hierarchical aspects – are prudent to make in the Norwegian context.

The paper is organized as follows. In Section 2 I sketch the norm concept and explain the "local" approach. Section 3 presents the Supreme Court structure and explains how differently sized panels may return different verdicts when judges are randomly assigned to cases. This represents a norm-free or *ex post* perspective. Section 4 integrates legal norms and the adjudication mechanisms and

1 The quote is from Kornhauser (1992a) p. 170, one of the first rigorous studies of adjudication.

suggests definitions of valid law from an *ex ante* perspective. Sections 5 and 6 interpret the analytical results from norm-based and error-based perspectives, respectively. Section 7 concludes. In the Appedix I derive some basic results.

2. Norm-based legal uncertainty

I understand the concept *legal norm* as a *relation* between a set of conditioning ("operative") legal facts LF and a set of legal consequences LC.[2] I assume that the set of consequences has two elements $LC = \{lc_r, lc_w\}$, with lc_r and lc_w denoting a "red" and a "white" outcome, respectively. Each element may be an arbitrarily complex description of properties (a long list).

If to a given complex of conditioning facts $lf^0 \in LF$ there corresponds a unique complex of consequences $lc^0 \in LC$, the legal norm will be said to (locally) have *rule character* or to (locally) be *determinate.* If the norm does not determine a unique complex, it is said to (locally) have *standard character* or be (locally) *indeterminate.* In this case the norm will be represented by a non-degenerate probability distribution $(p, 1 - p)$, see Figure 1.[3] The parameter p represents norm-based *legal uncertainty.*

Factual uncertainty concerns identification of operative facts. I abstract from this question and assume that all judges in the relevant panel identify the same conditioning complex $lf^0 \in LF$. This allows for a simple local approach.

In applied contexts, due to the system-based character of legal norms, it may be hard to distinguish between factual and legal uncertainty: output from one set of norms (reflecting a confluence of legal and factual elements) is input to the next. A prime example is rules of evidence, which filter data and define standards of proof.[4]

---

2 On relations generally, see Suppes (1957) ch. 10.

3 I do not give precise global definitions of the concepts. Furthermore, I do not discuss norms of competence (which require a more elaborate definition). Degenerate probability distributions correspond to functional relations in the ordinary sense (Suppes 1957, ch. 11).

4 The doctrines of *res judicata,* collateral estoppel and the possibility of splitting proceedings and adjudication (e.g. ruling on the scope of a claim may be postponed until a ruling has been made regarding existence) are examples of mechanisms by which the law partitions the world into "givens" and "variables."

Questions regarding which legal norms apply (or how norms are to be interpreted) are in many legal systems answered under a "preponderance of evidence"-standard and under majority voting rules. This may apply even in criminal cases. (I provide a dramatic example in Section 3 below.)

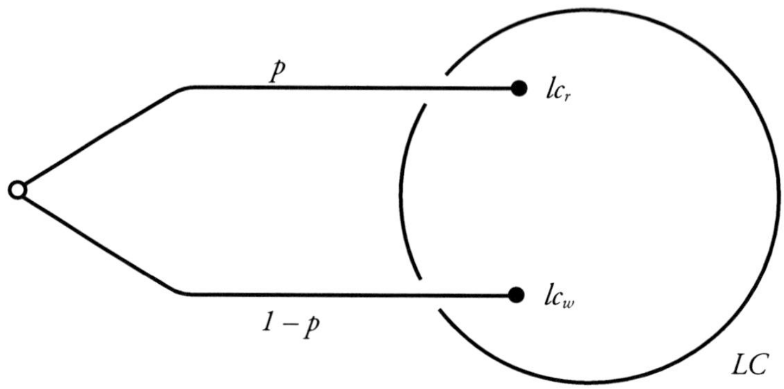

Figure 1 A legal standard locally represented as a probability distribution (chance node) over the set of legal consequences, *LC*.

The general negligence norm in tort law is a paradigmatic example of a legal standard. To illustrate, let the legal fact $lf = x$ correspond to an index of care by a (potential) tortfeasor. The possible legal consequences under the norm are no liability $lc_r = 0$ or liability $lc_w = L$, where L is the loss when risk is materialized according to some underlying accident technology. If F_C is a cumulative probability distribution representing a vague (stochastic) standard of care C, given the level of care $lf^0 = x^0$ the negligence norm locally, that is at $lf^0 = x^0 \in LF$, induces a simple probability distribution over $LC = \{0, L\}$. The distribution is $(F_C(x^0), 1 - F_C(x^0))$.[5]

Different norms are (locally) represented by different probability distributions. A compact notation for a distribution $(p, 1 - p)$ is $p \in \mathbf{P}_{LC}$, where $\mathbf{P}_{LC}$ is the set of probability distributions over LC.

5 The tortfeasor is liable for losses L if and only if the chosen standard of care x^0 is smaller than the required (stochastic) standard of care in the negligence norm, $C > x^0$. The probability of this event is $1 - F_C(x^0)$, where $F_C(x^0) = \int_0^{x^0} f_c(\tau)d\tau$ (f_c is a density function representing the standard of care), see Calfee and Craswell (1984).

Shavell (1987) extends the model. (Note that Section 4A.3.1 may be interpreted as an analysis of (single) judge competence as described in Section 6 below).

Norms operate on two levels in legal argumentation: they constitute the doctrine of sources and interpretation of law ("meta-norms") as well as ordinary norms ("doctrine"). The meta-norms are relations between a set of legal sources and a set of ordinary legal norms (a function space).

Given (local) standard structure of meta-norms, legal uncertainty may derive from *both* levels of argumentation. This corresponds to questions of i) which (ordinary) norm is in fact applicable and ii) under an applicable norm and a constellation of (ordinary) legal facts, what are the legal consequences?

I do not formulate the two-level aspects of legal argumentation explicitly. For a given complex of legal sources and a given complex of legal facts, uncertainty will be reducible to a probability distribution over the set of (ordinary) legal consequences.[6]

3. Supreme Court mechanisms

The Norwegian Supreme Court (SC) has $N = 19$ judges, who sit in plenary session (PL) with $n^{PL} = 19$ members; in Extended Division (ED) with $n^{ED} = 11$ members; in Division (D) with $n^{D} = 5$ members; and as an Appeals Committee (AC) with $n^{AC} = 3$ members. To a first approximation, judges are selected randomly to serve in individual cases. The cases are decided under a majority voting rule requiring $v^j = (n^j + 1)/2$ votes, $j = PL,ED,D,AC$.[7]

---

6 In my framework, uncertainty about which complex of legal *sources* of law in fact prevails is factual. Uncertainty as to the "interpretation" or implications of a complex is part the norm structure.

7 The Constitution requires the SC to have at least five members. Surprisingly, N is not fixed in formal law. Division sizes are defined in the Courts of Justice Act. In absence of specific legislation, all SC decisions are made under a majority voting rule. General voting rules (and to a limited extent the voting protocol) are legislated in applicable sections of the Dispute Act and the Civil Criminal Procedural Act. All legal questions (and factual questions admissible to the SC; it has authority to assess evidence, but particular limits apply in criminal cases) are resolved under a "preponderance of evidence" standard (not formally legislated).

Smaller sized collectives have the authority to make judgments in particular circumstances described in the Courts of Justice Act. I do not discuss these issues here.

Procedural rules regarding allocation of judges have been established by the SC in accordance with the Courts of Justice Act. They define selection to the ED as a formal lottery between N-1 judges (the Chief Justice leads all ED proceedings). The regulation is more lax with respect to the AC. As far as I know, no formal regulation is in place with respect to D. In the analysis below, I assume that the selection to any panel is a random sample.

I start the SC analysis in a mechanical way, abstracting from applicable substantive legal norms. (An alternative interpretation is to imagine that the norm based uncertainty has been resolved.) I label judges that cast votes for lc_r "red", and judges that vote lc_w "white". Reflecting the possible distributions of votes, there might be $N + 1 = 20$ different constellations of the SC. In Figure 2, C_i denotes a court with i red judges and $N - i$ white judges, $i = 0,1,2,...,N$.

The court constellations $C_{10},C_{11},...,C_{19}$ decide lc_r with certainty under the majority rule v^{PL} and are called "red". Likewise, the constellations $C_0,C_1,...,C_9$ decide lc_w and are called "white". The red and white courts are represented by filled and open circles respectively in Figure 2.

Conditionally, it seems reasonable to say that if one of the red SC constellations obtains, lc_r is the correct legal outcome. Similarly, if one of the white SC constellations obtains, lc_w is correct. To the same effect, I note that the Draft Committee for the Norwegian Dispute Act suggests that "the more judges participate in each ruling, the more effective such ruling will be as binding precedent."[8]

However, a possible effect of selecting smaller panels from the SC is that PL-outcomes may not be reproduced: What are the effects of having smaller panels of size n^j drawn randomly from SC-constellation C_i and deciding under voting rule v^j, $j = ED,D,AC$? The answer is easily obtained under random allocation of judges to panels.

For each SC constellation C_i, I calculate the conditional probability $p^j|C_i$ of outcome lc_r when a random sample of n^j judges are drawn and vote under majority rule v^j, $j = ED,D,AC$, $i = 0,1,...,N$.[9]

For many (i, j)-combinations (row i, column j, see Figure 2), $p^j|C_i$ differs from 0 and 1, corresponding to the certain outcomes lc_w and lc_r under v^{PL} given SC constellation $C_0,C_1,...,C_9$ and $C_{10},C_{11},...,C_{19}$, respectively. It reflects the isolated effect of smaller panels.

For example, when nine judges are red ($C = C_9$), the outcome is lc_w for certain under v^{PL}. However, there is more than a 39 percent chance that the ED

8 Report of the Draft Committee for the Norwegian Dispute Act NOU 2001: 32 Vol. B p. 1107.

9 The probabilities are calculated using basic combinatorial principles (counting of certain sets), see the Appendix.

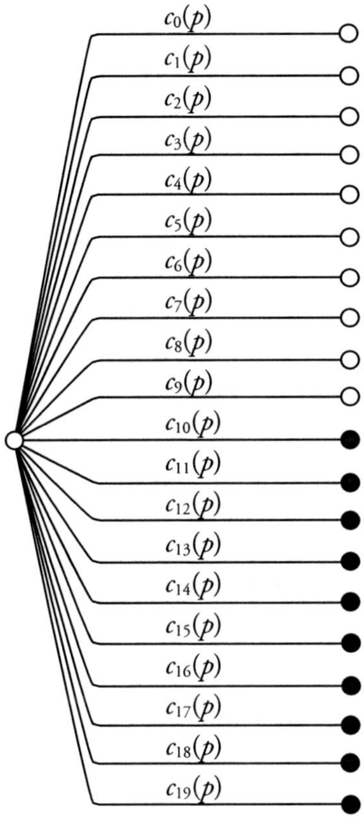

	$p^{ED}\|C_i$	$p^{D}\|C_i$	$p^{AC}\|C_i$
C_0	0	0	0
C_1	0	0	0
C_2	0	0	.0175
C_3	0	.0103	.0506
C_4	0	.0374	.0970
C_5	0	.0844	.1548
C_6	.0170	.1514	.2219
C_7	.0799	.2366	.2962
C_8	.2083	.3359	.3756
C_9	.3950	.4443	.4582
C_{10}	.6500	.5557	.5418
C_{11}	.7917	.6641	.6244
C_{12}	.9201	.7634	.7038
C_{13}	.9830	.8486	.7781
C_{14}	1	.9156	.8452
C_{15}	1	.9626	.9030
C_{16}	1	.9897	.9494
C_{17}	1	1	.9825
C_{18}	1	1	1
C_{19}	1	1	1

Figure 2 The left part is a (probability-) tree representing the possible SC-configurations. The filled and non-filled circles represent red and white outcomes in PL. In the right part matrix cell (i,j) gives the probability $p^j|C_i$ of a red outcome given SC-composition C_i (row) in panel j (column).

decides lc_r. Similarly, there is more than a 44 to 45 percent chance that the D and the AC reach lc_r.

From Figure 2 we may conclude that there are significant differences between the panels for many constellations of the SC. The courts C_0 and C_1 cannot be sources of red panels and C_{18} and C_{19} cannot generate white panels. But given the white courts C_3 to C_9, the AC will make red choices with positive probability monotonically increasing to above .45. Given the red courts C_{10} to C_{17}, the AC will make *white* decisions with a positive, monotonically falling probability $1-p^{AC}|C_i$

from above .45 (symmetry). Similar "deviation probabilities" apply to the ED and D panels.

Notice that given any C_i, deviation probabilities are (weakly) larger the smaller the panel (cf. the Draft Committee remarks on precedent weight above).

The importance of the decision mechanism may be illustrated by the trial of Kriminalassistent Karl-Hans Herman Klinge in post-war Norway.[10] Klinge had been sentenced to death by Eidsivating Lagmannsrett (Oslo) for having ill-treated and tortured Norwegian citizens during interrogations at the Gestapo H. Q. in Oslo from November 1944 to April 1945. The basis for the death sentence was a Provisional Decree of May 1945 amending the Civil Criminal Code. The facts of the case were not disputed. The judgment was appealed to the SC due to questions regarding sources of law and retroactivity.

The case was decided in PL by the SC which then had $N = 13$ members. Nine judges voted to uphold the judgment, four dissented. Under the majority rule, Klinge was executed. If precisely the same questions had been answered by a criminal jury and the "jury" had been drawn randomly from the SC-panel, the probability of Klinge not being executed would have been .294.[11]

4. Definitions of valid law

Judges are not red and white balls. In the absence of factual uncertainty, they vote over tuples (lf^0, lc), $lc \in LC$, under the applicable legal norms.

I assume that each SC judge has complete information and has "internalized" the applicable substantial norms, represented as elements $p \in |\mathbf{P}_{LC}$. Due to the identification of norms and judges, I assume that legal uncertainty is resolved as judges cast votes *independently* of each other (that is, stochastic independence given the constellation of legal facts and legal sources).

10 See *Law-Reports of Trials of War Criminals*, The United Nations War Crimes Commission, Vol. III, London, HMSO, 1948 and Rt. 1947/148 (the judgment in Norwegian).

11 The Norwegian Criminal Jury has ten members and a supermajority of seven or more votes is required for conviction under a specific provision of the Civil Criminal Code. See the Appendix regarding the calculation.

Rt. 1947/148 shows that two of the dissenting judges contemplated alternative arguments for the death penalty, so my thought experiment depends on a specific framing of questions to the "jury".

By abstracting from factual uncertainty, I assume that all judges observe the same constellation of legal sources and the same constellation of legal facts (the same "case"). Both applicable meta-norms and ordinary norms are assumed internalized. The modelling approach to legal norms may in part be motivated by Ross (1959, 1968) ch. 1–4 and 4 respectively.

The applicable substantial legal norms might be determinative or non-determinative (Section 2 above). If all norms (locally) are rules, all judges vote (lf^0, lc_r) or (lf^0, lc_w); C_{19} and C_0 are the only possible SC constellations. It follows that the smaller panels must reach the same result; under determinacy, panel size and voting rules are irrelevant. However, under norm based uncertainty, the structure of the adjudication mechanism matters.

I suggest defining *valid law* as a confluence between the relevant substantive norms represented by the probability distribution $p \in \mathbf{P}_{LC}$ and the procedural rules which define the SC-mechanism.[12] The concept is local and defines a resulting norm (probability distribution) in a two-stage procedure. First, legal sources and legal facts determine the (local) substantial "input norm" $p \in \mathbf{P}_{LC}$. Second, this norm is applied by the relevant SC-panel, producing an "output" norm $p^j(p) \in \mathbf{P}_{LC}$, j = PL, ED, D, AC, in general different from the "input" norm.

The stochastic variable C represents the possible constellations of the SC. Let $c_i(p)$ denote the probability of obtaining exactly i red SC-judges when each judge is identified with the input norm $p \in \mathbf{P}_{LC}$, $i = 0,1,2,\ldots,N$.[13]

Given voting rule $v^{PL} = (N+1)/2$, *valid law conditional on PL* is:

$$p^{PL}(p) = \sum_{i=v^{PL}}^{N} c_i(p). \tag{1}$$

Valid law conditional on panel j *under* $v^j = (n^j + 1)/2$ is:

$$p^{ED}(p) = \sum_{i=0}^{N} c_i(p) p^{ED} | C_i, \tag{2}$$

---

12 I do not discuss the norms that determine which SC-panel is to be used (they are implicitly understood to be rules).

13 $c_i(p) = P(C = C_i | p)$. Under the stated assumptions C is binomially distributed. The norm is simply a "success parameter" in N independent trials. C ~ BIN(N,p) implies $c_i(p) = C(N,i)p^i(1-p)^{N-i}$. ($C(N,i)$ is a binomial coefficient, see Equation (A1) in the Appendix.)

$$p^{D}(p) = \sum_{i=0}^{N} c_i(p) p^{D} | C_i \tag{3}$$

$$p^{AC}(p) = \sum_{i=0}^{N} c_i(p) p^{AC} | C_i \tag{4}$$

To facilitate interpretation of the definitions, I have endowed the branches of the tree in Figure 2 with probabilities. For instance, the branch leading to C_{10} is equipped with the probability $c_{10}(p)$ of having exactly 10 judges voting lc_r given the legal norm p.

The definition of valid law in Equation (1) is the probability that the plenary session PL decides outcome lc_r: $p^{PL}(p)$ is the sum of the branch probabilities of the red court constellations $C_{10}, C_{11}, \ldots, C_{19}$.

The definition of valid law in the smaller sized panels in Equations (2)–(4) corresponds to the following operation in Figure 2: the probability of lc_r in panel

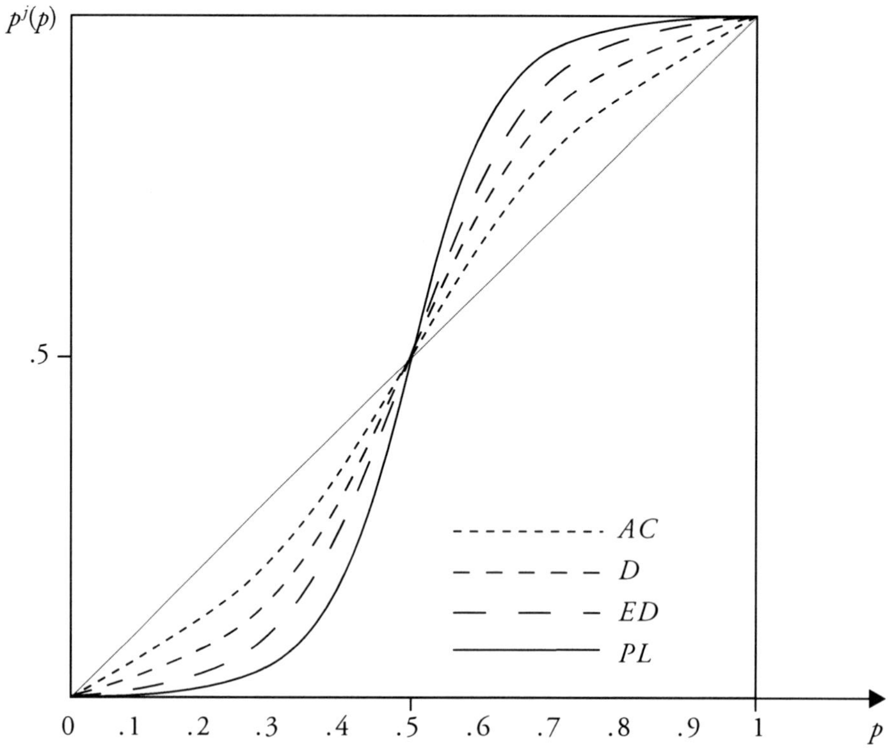

Figure 3 Valid law (transformations).

j, $p^j(p)$, $j = ED,D,AC$, is the weighted sum of conditional probabilities $p^j|C_i$ (line i and column j) over all lines (all elements in column j). The weights are given by the tree-branch probabilities $c_i(p)$.

The resulting valid law functions $p^j(\cdot)$ are illustrated in Figure 3, and values corresponding to nine input-norms are given in Table 1.[14] The functions are strictly increasing, strictly convex on $(0, \frac{1}{2})$ and strictly concave on $(\frac{1}{2}, 1)$, with $p^j(p) = p$ if and only if , $p = 0$, $p = \frac{1}{2}$ or $p = 1$, $j = PL,ED,D,AC$ (see the Appendix).

	.1	.2	.3	.4	.5	.6	.7	.8	.9
$p^{PL}(p)$	.0000	.0016	.0326	.1861	.5	.8139	.9674	.9984	1.000
$p^{ED}(p)$	.0003	.0117	.0782	.2465	.5	.7535	.9218	.9883	.9997
$p^{D}(p)$	.0086	.0579	.1631	.3174	.5	.6826	.8369	.9421	.9914
$p^{AC}(p)$	.0280	.1040	.2160	.3520	.5	.6480	.7840	.8960	.9720

Table 1. Valid law for a subset of input-values.

5. Discussion

Generally, a suggested candidate for valid law, say the substantial legal norm $p^0 \in \mathbf{P}_{LC}$, by the confluence of norm-based uncertainty and adjudicative mechanism structure is transformed to $p^j(p^0) \in \mathbf{P}_{LC}$, with (in general) $p^j(p^0) \neq p^0$, $j = PL,ED,D,AC$. The transformations are illustrated in Figure 3.

The norm $p = \frac{1}{2}$ may be interpreted as maximal legal uncertainty. Abstracted from the fixed points $p = 0$ and $p = 1$ (degenerate probability distributions, the norms are local rules), $p = \frac{1}{2}$ is the only situation in which the panels' output norm is the same as the input norm. For many input norms, the panels produce significantly different norms from the input norm and there are significant inter-panel differences.

---

14 Computationally, under the independence and random selection assumptions the probabilities $p^j(p)$ in Table 1 and Figure 3 are directly obtainable from BIN(n^j,p) by summing from $v^j = (n^j + 1)/2$ to n^j (a cumulative binomial distribution). However, to the extent that underlying assumptions are varied, it is necessary to use the conceptual definitions (1)–(4) also for computations.

It is interesting to note that for all other legal norms than the fixed points, all panels will reduce legal uncertainty compared to the degree of indeterminacy in the substantial input norm itself. From Figure 3 it is clear that the reduction in uncertainty is increasing in panel size. It happens in a symmetric way around $p = \frac{1}{2}$.

The functional differences between the panels motivate the inclusion of procedural-institutional aspects in definitions of valid law. Consideration of "rule of law" or "legal unity" principles suggests that legal norms should determine as clearly as possible which panel decides a case.

These functional aspects are also important for analyses of law that study agent behaviour under norms. Well-informed agents arguably should be modelled basing their decisions not on p but on transformed notions as suggested above.[15]

6. Judgment error interpretation

The analytical results may be given a different interpretation. For simplicity, assume that all norms (locally) are rules, so that given applicable legal sources and legal facts, there is in principle a determinate answer to the legal questions. However, assume that an individual judge might get the answer wrong.

Under these assumptions, it may be assumed that p represents the probability that an individual judge gets the answer right: in the terminology of the theory, p is a measure of judge or voter *competence* (ability). The function $p^j(p)$ may be interpreted as the probability that collective mechanism j returns a correct verdict as a function of the input competence p, $j = PL, ED, D, AC$.

If all judges are fully knowledgeable ($p = 1$), the choice of collective mechanism is again irrelevant; all panels necessarily make the same (correct) decision. However, when judges make errors, but $p > \frac{1}{2}$, larger panels have a higher probability of making the right decision than smaller panels, see Figure 3.

The interpretation corresponds to the non-asymptotic part of the famous Condorcet Jury Theorem (CJT), which has important applications in decision theory and reliability theory (see generally Boland 1989).[16] Most applications to law deal with questions regarding factual uncertainty (the most prominent analyses pertain

15 Uncertainty over mechanisms may be handled along the lines developed above.

16 The asymptotic version: for *any* $p > \frac{1}{2}$, by making a panel sufficiently large, it reaches the correct result with a probability arbitrarily close to 1.

to the criminal jury). The first application to legal theory is probably Kornhauser and Sager (1986), whose discussion of "accuracy" in adjudication corresponds closely to the error interpretation of legal uncertainty (see in particular p. 97–100). However, this type of application is potentially controversial due to the assumption of an underlying "right" answer. Arguably, proper application of the CJT requires one of the outcomes to be unambiguously better for all decision makers (voters).[17]

Under the judgement-error interpretation of legal uncertainty, it is interesting to relax the independence assumption naturally assumed in Section 4 above. For instance, Boland (1989) introduces notions of dependence among units in a majority system, which may be taken to represent the deliberational aspect of the procedural mechanism. Under various notions of stochastic dependence, the curves in Figure 3 "flatten out" and shift down for any $p > \frac{1}{2}$, but retain the qualitative rankings.[18]

Under the judgement-error interpretation, it is also interesting to note that CJT style arguments may be generalized to heterogeneous judges as long as the average judge's competence is sufficiently large. On such result is that

$$\text{if } \bar{p}^j = \frac{\sum_{l=1}^{n^j} p_l}{n^j} > \frac{1}{2} + \frac{1}{2n^j}, \text{ then } p^j\,(p_1,p_2,\ldots,p_{n^j}) > \bar{p}^j,\ j = PL,ED,D,AC,$$

see Boland (1989), Theorem 3. Berend and Sapir (2005) show that if *any* division $\tilde{D}$ is drawn from a larger SC with $n^D \geq 3$ and $p_i > \frac{1}{2}$ for $i = 1,2,\ldots,N$, under majority voting, the probability of deciding correctly increases in division size, $n^{\tilde{D}}$. These results give additional substance to the view that larger panels return better decisions than smaller panels and hence should be used for important decisions.

17 However, I believe that the error correction perspective may be combined with norm-based legal uncertainty (where the "right" answer is a probabilistic one).

In some of the CJT applications in Posner and Sunstein (2006), the problem seems to be to determine which outcome is best, not to identify the (unknown) better alternative.

18 This is an interesting explication of the value of "independent" judges.

Notions of dependence are complicated, since in principle information about an n^j-dimensional distribution is required. The "following the leader" notion discussed in Boland, with one decision maker stochastically influencing all others, might be used to question the Chief Justice's role in the ED (see Boland 1989, Theorem 5a and Section 3 above).

7. Conclusions

Legal norms are central study objects for legal theory. To the extent that the norms do not uniquely determine outcomes, existence of multi-judge decision mechanisms has non-trivial consequences: different collectives systematically return different verdicts.

The confluence of norm-based uncertainty and adjudication mechanisms are illustrated using the structures of the Norwegian Supreme Court. It naturally leads to definitions of valid law which incorporate procedural-institutional details.

Regarding the specific structures of the Norwegian SC, to the extent that its main role is "to contribute to the clarification, unity and development of law", the number of divisions seems high.[19] Considering issues regarding legal reasoning in a collective, a similar remark seems relevant regarding the number judges *N*.[20]

The identification of judges and norms brings the latter to the center stage of the analysis of the collective mechanism. As such, the approach is an alternative to what may be called "preference based" approaches.

By abstracting from uncertainty with respect to legal sources and legal facts, it is sufficient to formulate local versions of legal norms. However, interesting recent work on collective aspects of judicial decisions takes a more global approach. Through the specification of a so-called "case-space" (corresponds to my set of legal facts *LF*), arguments are developed under norms which are determinative (rules): every element in *LF* is mapped into a degenerate probability distribution over *LC*.

Two approaches may be distinguished. In the first, judges are allowed to make different factual assessments (identify different elements in *LF*) but all hold the same view of legal doctrine (rules). In this setting, which may be interpreted as factual uncertainty, Kornhauser and Sager have developed the "doctrinal paradox".[21] The second approach allows different judges to apply different *rules* over the case space. In this setting, which may be interpreted as representing uncertainty with respect to

19 Quote from: Report of the Draft Committee for the Norwegian Dispute Act (NOU 2001: 32 Vol. B p. 1106). I also mention the seemingly somewhat incomplete and partially internal regulation of the SC (Section 2 above).

20 The latter aspect requires considerations that go beyond the scope of this paper, but see the papers by Kornhauser and Sager, and Landa and Lax referred to below.

21 Kornhauser and Sager (1986, 1993, 2004). The case-space approach is introduced in Kornhauser (1992a, 1992b).

legal sources and/or norm based uncertainty on the level of meta-norms, Landa and Lax have developed a "generalized doctrinal paradox".[22]

I believe norm-based legal uncertainty may be expanded to merge with this kind of global analysis. Explicit consideration of the two levels legal argumentation may yield important insights.

Judgement-error interpretation of legal uncertainty may contribute to the design of legal decision mechanisms. For instance, the analyses challenge a widespread belief in the legal profession in substantial hierarchical structures. I make two points:

First, analyses point toward concentrating resources in larger panels rather than spreading them on several levels.[23] In contrast, Norway has a *de facto* five-level hierarchy for decisions regarding law.[24]

Second, the cost of the panels is a fraction of the costs involved in litigation. To the extent that mechanisms for "[d]ispute resolution serves a social function, by ensuring that substantive law takes precedence, that it is respected and that it influences behaviour," functional analysis of the said systems seems necessary.[25] For instance, I contend that risk-averse litigants facing (approximately) risk neutral entities are involved in a game where the mere *existence* of a multi-level court system (compounded by rules allocating litigation costs) places them at a substantial strategic disadvantage.[26]

---

22 Landa and Lax (2008, 2009).

23 In the context of error correction, Shavell (1995) points out that there would be no need to legitimate the decisions (inter alia with large panels) unless things could go wrong (p. 426).

24 In addition to a three-level regular court system, mediation before a conciliation board is a mandatory requirement for bringing legal action before the courts. Conciliation boards have some authority to pass judgements. Regarding the fifth level, I use the term *de facto* to avoid discussing intricate relations between domestic courts and judicial bodies under the Agreement on the European Economic Area, the Convention for the Protection of Human Rights and Fundamental Freedoms and the International Covenant on Civil and Political Rights.

25 Quote from the Draft Committee for the Norwegian Dispute Act, NOU 2001: 32 Vol. B. p. 1099.

26 I know of no systematic analyses of these questions in a Norwegian context.

The Draft Committee for the Norwegian Dispute Act (NOU 2001: 32) stresses the need to restrict the scope for appeals considering proportionality and procedural inequality between parties, and to concentrate resources in an accessible and efficient first-line mechanism. It is regrettable that the suggestions regarding the mandatory role of conciliation boards have not been implemented.

Both from a normative and positive point of view, there are many interesting connections between the structure of legal norms, knowledge of norms and the institutional structures of adjudication. These are important challenges for legal theory.[27]

Acknowledgements

I would like to thank Richard R.W. Brooks and Espen R. Moen for valuable discussions.

References

Bartoszynski, R. and M. Niewiadomska-Bugaj. 1996. *Probability and Statistical Inference.* New York, NY: Wiley.

Berend, D. and L. Sapir. 2005. Monotonicity in Condorcet Jury Theorem. *Social Choice and Welfare* 24(1), 83—92.

Boland, P.J. 1989. Majority Systems and the Condorcet Jury Theorem. *The Statistician* 38(3), 181—189.

Calfee, J. E. and R. Craswell. 1984. Some Effects of Uncertainty on Compliance with Legal Standards. *Virginia Law Review* 70(5), 965—1003.

Cameron, C. M. and L. A. Kornhauser. 2005. Decision Rules in a Judicial Hierarchy. *Journal of Institutional and Theoretical Economics* 2005(?), 264—292.

Kornhauser, L. A. 1992a. Modeling Collegial Courts I: Path-Dependence. *International Review of Law and Economics* 12(2), 169-185.

———. 1992b. Modeling Collegial Courts II. Legal Doctrine. *Journal of Law, Economics, & Organization* 8(2), 441—470.

Kornhauser, L. A. and Sager, L. G. 1986. Unpacking the Court. *Yale Law Journal* 96(1), 82—117.

———. The One and the Many: Adjudication in Collegial Courts. *California Law Review* 81(1), 1—59.

———. 2004. The Many as One: Integrity and Group Choice in Paradoxical Cases. *Philosophy & Public Affairs* 32(3), 249—276.

27 The interesting analyses in Shavell (1995) and Cameron and Kornhauser (2005) attest to this.

Landa, D. and J. R. Lax. 2008. Disagreements on Collegial Courts: A Case-Space Approach. *Journal of Constitutional Law* 10(2), 305—329.
———. 2009. Legal Doctrine on Collegial Courts. *The Journal of Politics* 71(3), 946—963
Posner, E. A. and C. R. Sunstein. 2006. The Law of Other States. *Stanford Law Review* 59(1), 131—179.
Ross, A. 1959. *On Law and Justice.* Berkeley, CA: University of California Press.
———. 1968. *Directives and Norms.* New York, NY: Humanities Press.
Shavell, S. 1987. *Economic Analysis of Accident Law.* Cambridge, MA: Harvard University Press.
———. 1995. The Appeals Process as a Means of Error Correction. *Journal of Legal Studies* 24(2), 379—426.
Suppes, P. 1957. *Introduction to Logic.* Princeton, NJ: Van Nostrand.

Appendix

From a set of N members, the number of distinct *combinations* (sets of size n^j) that can be formed is given by the binomial coefficient[28]

$$C(N,n^j) = \frac{N!}{n^j\,!(N - n^j)!}\,. \tag{A1}$$

Given that court C_i obtains (a court with i red judges and $N - i$ white judges, $i = 0,1,2,\ldots,N$) what is the probability of a red outcome in institution j, $p^j|C_i$ ($j = ED,D,AC$)? Let the stochastic variable X_{n^j} measure the number of red judges in a random sample of n^j judges from C_i. Under the majority voting rule $v^j = (n^j + 1)/2$

$$p^j|C_i = P(X_{n^j} \geq v^j|C_i) = \sum_{k=v^j}^{n^j} P(X_{n^j} = k|C_i), \tag{A2}$$

28 In equation (A1), the symbol ! means that given a non-negative integer k, $k!$ is formed as $k! = 1 \cdot 2 \cdot \ldots \cdot (k-1) \cdot k$ (read "k factorial"; $0! = 1$). The formula implies the possible formation of 75582 different ED-panels, 11628 D-panels and 969 AC-panels.

with point probabilities

$$P(X_{n^j} = k | C_i) = \frac{C(i,k)C(N-i,n^j-k)}{C(N,n^j)}, \tag{A3}$$

$0 \leq k \leq \min(n^j,i)$. (If $i < n^j$ and $k > i$, $P \equiv 0$.) $p^j | C_i$ is a *cumulative hypergeometric distribution.*[29]

Under independence and random selection of SC judges to the panels, the $p^j(\cdot)$ functions in Equation (1)–(4) reduce to simple cumulative binomials. Letting $m = 1,2,5,9$ correspond to $j = AC,D,ED,PL$ respectively, they may be written (Boland 1989)

$$p^m(p) = (2m+1)C(2m,m)\int_0^p \tau^m(1-\tau)^m d\tau. \tag{A4}$$

From (A4) with $k \equiv (2m+1)C(2m,m) > 0$

$$\frac{\partial p^m(p)}{\partial p} = kp^m(1-p)^m > 0, \tag{A5}$$

$$\frac{\partial p^m(p)}{\partial p^2} = k\{mp^{m-1}(1-p)^m - mp^m(1-p)^{m-1}\} = kmp^{m-1}(1-p)^{m-1}\{1-2p\}. \tag{A6}$$

It follows that $p^j(\cdot)$ is strictly increasing, strictly convex on $(0,\frac{1}{2})$ and strictly concave on $(\frac{1}{2},1)$.

---

29 For details see Bartoszynski and Niewiadomska-Bugaj (1996) Sec.9.6.

To illustrate, consider the computation of $p^{AC} | C_{10}$. There are $C(19,3) = 969$ possible ACs with $v^{AC} = (n^{AC}+1)/2$. Hence, $p^{AC} | C_{10} = P(X_{n^{AC}} = 2 | C_{10}) + P(X_{n^{AC}} = 3 | C_{10}) = C(10,2)C(9,1)/969 + C(10,3)C(9,0)/969 = (45 \times 9 + 120 \times 1)/969 = .542$.

Regarding the Klinge case, there are $C(13,10) = 286$ possible jury constellations. $C(4,4)C(9,6) = 84$ do not convict. Hence, under random drawing of the "jury" from the 13 SC judges, it does not convict with the probability $C(4,4)C(9,6)/C(13,10) = .294$.

Regulatory Sanctions: Wheel-clamping and Hassle

Anthony Ogus

It has been my pleasure to have known Erling Eide for many years. Throughout, he has impressed me not only with his scientific rigour but also with his wisdom and insights on the impact of economic reasoning. Within law and economics, his specialism has been, of course, crime and law enforcement (Eide et al. 1994, Eide 2000) and, as a tribute to his powerful work in these areas, I have selected as a topic a form of sanction for regulatory infringements which has not been explored in the literature.

1. Introduction

Wheel-clamping has been used for over two decades in the UK to combat illegal parking (Smith 1992). Along with the removal and crushing of vehicles, it has also been used, if more recently, as a sanction for the non-payment of vehicle excise duty (Comptroller and Auditor General 2003). Two striking features of this penalty are that it is non-financial and that it directly affects the use and utility which the offender derives from an object which was instrumental in committing the offence.

These sanctions are different from the large majority of penalties used for the enforcement of regulation and mainstream crime. Financial penalties, normally fines, predominate for regulatory contraventions as well as minor and middle-scale crimes. Apart from imprisonment, which is widely used for major crimes and for cases where fines prove to be inadequate deterrents, non-financial penalties, such as probation and community service, are in general intended to meet rehabilitative or retributive goals.

In recent years there has been considerable discussion of appropriate strategies for regulatory enforcement but there seems to have been little attention to the phenomenon of wheel-clamping. In this paper I trace the evolution of its use in relation to illegal parking and the evasion of excise duty, and I seek to evaluate its deterrence function.

For my analytical framework, I rely primarily on the economic theory of deterrence. This theory is derived from the simple proposition that individuals will, in general, obey the law, if the costs which they will incur on breaking the law exceed the benefits that will accrue to them from the illegal act (Becker 1968). Although this has given rise to a vast literature (for an overview, see Eide 2000), analysis has focused largely on financial consequences and has under-estimated the importance to many individuals of avoiding hassle and inconvenience, consequences often arising from wheel-clamping.

2. Wheel-clamping in England and Wales

The power to tow away vehicles illegally parked has existed for some time, but it is, of course, a costly enforcement device. Following its apparently successful use in the USA, wheel-clamping was introduced in the UK in 1983 as a means of combating the growing problem of illegal parking in London. Extensive publicity was given to the scheme, and studies undertaken in its early years suggest that it was very successful in reducing the duration of illegal parking on double yellow lines, from 150,000 vehicle hours per day in 1982 to 70,000 hours in 1989 (May and Turvey 1984, Smith 1992).

Although wheel-clamping became subsequently available as an enforcement device for illegal parking in other British urban areas, its use has varied considerably and has been somewhat controversial. There has been some criticism of the practice on the ground that, though effective, it is "unfair" to offenders. This was particularly the case after the Road Traffic of 1991 allowed the decriminalization of illegal parking, removing the matter from the police to local authorities, and leading to exclusive reliance on non-penal sanctions, notably fixed penalty notices. Indeed a circular issued by the Department for Transport to local authorities in 1995 acknowledged that it was necessary for the scheme to have public support and to this end, the guidelines issued suggested that it should primarily be used in relation to persistent offenders (Department of Transport 1995).

A study undertaken by the Camden Culture and Environment Directorate (2006) casts doubt on the effectiveness of wheel-clamping in reducing non-compliant parking. Reviewing a survey of public opinion, the same study revealed that a significant majority of groups and individuals considered that there was excessive use of the device. These findings anticipated a review undertaken by the Government in 2007. A Consultation Paper (Department of Transport 2007) indicated that "very few authorities now use clamping" and that the "Secretary of State is of the view that clamping should only be used in limited circumstances such as where the same contravening vehicle repeatedly breaks parking regulations and it has not been possible to collect payments for penalties" (para. 152). It should only take place where it has "clear traffic management benefits". Local authorities are required to publish guidelines on the appropriate use of clamping and, interestingly, these "should have regard to the costs and benefits of the activities, especially the inconvenience caused to motorists whose vehicles are clamped or removed" (para. 154).

Following the review, the law and practice may be summarized as follows. The normal sanction for illegal parking is a penalty charge notice (PCN) fixed to the windscreen of the offending vehicle or sent to the registered owner's place of residence. The prescribed amount must be paid within 28 days, but payment within 14 days entitles the offender to a 50% reduction. Subject to appeal procedures, a failure to pay the charge results in it being registered as a civil debt and, as such, is subject to the recovery processes undertaken by court enforcement officers.

Although there are powers to clamp a vehicle if it is still illegally parked after 30 minutes following the issuing of a PCN, in practice local authorities use this recourse (if at all) only for persistent evaders, individuals who, as revealed by databases kept by the authorities, have committed three or more recorded contraventions and have not paid the relevant PCNs. The vehicles of such offenders can, indeed, be clamped after a period of 15 minutes from the issuing of the (latest) PCN. To have the vehicle released, the owner (or other user) has then to pay a release fee. The authorities also have analogous powers to remove the vehicle to a pound, with similar consequences.

Wheel-clamping as a sanction for evading the payment of vehicle excise duty (VED) has had a very different history and has led to a very different policy. It began only in August 1997, as a response to increasing concern about the non-payment of duty. Over the decade in which it has been used, the law and practice seem to have changed little. In general, any vehicle parked on a public road and appearing on the list of the Drivers and Vehicle Licensing Agency (DVLA) as untaxed can be clamped. For the vehicle to be released, a prescribed fee must be paid. If, at the same time, a valid tax disc for the vehicle cannot be produced, a surety payment has to be made, and this will be reimbursed on production of the tax disc. There are equivalent powers to remove unlicensed (and abandoned) vehicles and, on failure to produce a valid tax disc within a prescribed period, to dispose of the vehicle by selling it or disposing of it as scrap.

The fact that enforcement of the payment of vehicle excise duty is the responsibility of a single national institution, the DVLA, meant that there was greater consistency in its application than became the case with illegal parking, when the latter became the responsibility of local authorities. Indeed, as a method of dealing with defaulters, the system has been increasingly favoured by the DVLA. Although the agency targets wheel-clamping on what it regards as intentional and persistent evaders, the number of vehicles clamped has risen from about 25,000 in 2001–02 (Comptroller and Auditor General 2003), to nearly 100,000 in 2008–09 (DVLA 2009).

The DVLA has engaged in its own evaluation of the effectiveness of wheel-clamping and has concluded that, though the costs of the process exceed the revenue from release fees, storage charges, surety payments and proceeds from auctions and scrapped vehicles, the scheme nevertheless provides good value since it is assumed to have a significant deterrent effect on duty evasion (ibid. 26). And this view has been endorsed both by the Comptroller and Auditor General (2003) and by an independent appraisal commissioned by the Department for Transport (Brown et al. 2008).

The contrasting experience of wheel-clamping as a sanction for illegal parking and VED evasion is striking. To attempt to explain it we need to begin by exploring the problem of deterring regulatory contraventions relying solely on financial penalties.

3. Deterrence Theory and the Problem of Inadequate Financial Penalties

The simplest version of the economic theory of deterrence predicts that individuals will comply with the law if the benefit they acquire from breaking the law (*U*) is exceeded by the costs arising from the penalty which is imposed by the law (*S*), discounted by the probability of being caught and convicted (p). The condition of compliance is thus $U < pS$. Given that different options for p and S generate different levels of administrative and other cost, from an economic perspective the goal is to select an optimal combination of p and S, that is one which imposes the least costs on society (Polinsky and Shavell 1979).

Economists understandably tend to favour financial over non-financial penalties primarily because the former are cheaper to administer. Nevertheless there are reasons why financial penalties might be inappropriate. First, the amount of the penalty deemed necessary to satisfy the condition $U < pS$, might exceed the defendant's available wealth, and the incentive to comply with the law will be undermined. Then, take a case where reliable estimates of U for a given individual cannot be made *ex ante*, perhaps because the utility which that person derives from committing the offence is idiosyncratically high relative to that of the typical or average offender. The sentencing authority may not be permitted to select an appropriately high value for S, because to do so would exceed the maximum prescribed by legislation or would otherwise infringe the general principles of sentencing law. We should notice, too, that above a certain level of severity administrative financial penalties may fall foul of European human rights law if appropriate procedures, notably a public hearing, are not involved (Guinchard 2005).

If financial penalties, in circumstances such as those considered here, are not adequate for deterrence purposes and traditional non-financial penalties such as probation, community service and imprisonment are inappropriate and/or too costly to administer, how can the problem be solved? If the obstacle is the limited wealth of the offender, then one possibility is to impose liability for the offence on a third party, for example an employer, who is able to exert influence over the decision-making of the perpetrator. Another possibility is to adopt sanctions or procedures which indirectly increase the offender's costs, such as lowering the offender's market reputation by, for example, "naming and shaming". Although there would appear to be a strong case for this strategy in relation to administrative proceedings, care must be taken because such proceedings do not have the procedural safeguards of the criminal law, and harmfully misconceived publicity can give rise to high error costs (Galbiati and Garoupa 2007).

A third possibility is to cause disutility to the offender through personal inconvenience and "hassle". This can take a variety of forms. The procedures associated with investigation and prosecution inevitably generate some such costs. The police, or other enforcement agency, can engage with the offender in protracted interviews and other forms of interaction, involving the discomfiture of psychological pressure and embarrassment, as well as the loss of time; and the costs may multiply if the processes take place in public (Cramton 1964, pp. 432 and 443). Other sanctions may impede the use and enjoyment of the offender's own property or lawful pursuits. Violent football supporters may be barred from attending matches; knives or other dangerous items may be confiscated; car drivers may have their vehicles immobilized or impounded. The fact that it is ordinary and lawful use and enjoyment which is obstructed aggravates the grievance and increases psychic costs.

Of course it is impossible to quantify these inconvenience and hassle costs in any meaningful way, but that does not necessarily imply that they should be treated as trivial. To investigate the matter further, we need to see how economists have analysed the phenomenon.

4. The Economics of Inconvenience and Hassle

Although there is not a large economic literature on inconvenience and hassle costs, it has been recognized that they play a significant role, particularly at the margin, in decision-making in some contexts. Take, for example, the question whether price-matching guarantees offered to consumers by traders facilitate collusion and thereby restrict competition. If firms were automatically to match prices, the prediction can be sustained, but it has been shown that the hassle costs to consumers in enforcing the guarantees will, if they are sufficiently large, inhibit collusion (Dugar and Sorensen 2006).

Traders can also use hassle to deter the unlawful use of their products or services. The economically appropriate strategy here is to adopt measures which maximize inconvenience for unlawful users, while minimizing inconvenience for lawful users. The design and printing of valuable documents can, for example, be devised in such a way as make their counterfeiting particularly difficult and onerous (Herley et al. 2004).

Why might hassle costs constitute an effective deterrent? Adopting a neo-classical view of utility maximization, we might be tempted to treat these costs as relatively insignificant, particularly when the disutility is ephemeral. The individual is assumed rationally to weigh up the costs and benefits, both long term and short term, of contravening, or complying, with the law. The (generally short-term) hassle costs will, on this basis, often be exceeded by the benefits, both short-term and long-term, arising from the unlawful behaviour. But this can be challenged by reference to behavioural law and economics. Drawing on empirical studies by social psychologists, this approach, rather than repudiating rationality, recognizes that it operates within certain parameters (hence "bounded rationality"), and shows how decision-making is typically biased. From these studies, we can identify two behavioural characteristics which help to explain the deterrence power of hassle costs.

The first of these is referred to as "hyperbolic discounting" (Laibson 1997). Individuals generally attribute a much higher value to short-term costs and benefits than is assumed in rational utility-maximising models. One consequence is the deferring of welfare-generating activity when the present costs of immediate action appear to be large relative to future costs (Akerlof 2001). The effect, in a law enforcement context, is to raise the value of *S* where potential offenders know that if they break the law they are likely to be subjected to immediate costs. This leads to a prediction that the earlier the imposition of the sanction, the more effective the deterrent (Utset 2005), and there is empirical evidence to support this (Banks and Vogel-Sprott 1965). Some sanctions, for example the removal or immobilization of a vehicle, are imposed as the immediate consequence of the detection of an offence. Given the existence of hyperbolic discounting, we can now see why the inconvenience and hassle costs to which such sanctions give rise are perceived by offenders to be relatively onerous and why, in terms of the economic theory of deterrence, that should make the sanctions particularly effective.

Additional deterrence may nevertheless result from the second relevant behavioural characteristic. This relates to the salience of phenomena which influence decision-making and is referred to in the social psychology literature as the "availability heuristic" (Kuran and Sunstein 1999). The easier the phenomena are brought to mind, the greater the influence they will have on the formulation of preferences. So, if the salient feature appears attractive, the individual is likely to exaggerate its benefits relative to its costs.

Of course, the converse also applies, so that if the feature is unattractive, the subjective perception of costs increases. This may have considerable importance for law enforcement. By way of example, Jolls, Sunstein and Thaler (1998, p. 1538) contrast the likely impact of two different systems of administering illegal parking tickets. The first has an unobtrusive colour and is placed under the windscreen wiper on the kerb side of the street; the second has the inscription "VIOLATION" in large orange letters and is placed on the window on the other side, so that it can be clearly seen by other drivers. The second is likely significantly to increase deterrence at no additional cost.

A clamped vehicle is generally highly visible, hence the salience of this sanction. But phenomena can come easily to mind also for emotional reasons; and the fact that clamping impedes vehicle use and enjoyment is likely also to provoke a strong emotional response, leading to a distortion of rational choice.

5. An Appraisal of Wheel-clamping

As indicated above, there is a perception that wheel-clamping has been an effective sanction in relation to VED evasion but not in relation to illegal parking. I now explore possible reasons for these contrasting views.

We may first attempt to evaluate the use of wheel-clamping in the two contexts by reference to cost-effectiveness. This economic criterion involves the minimization of costs for a given benefit (Ogus 2006, pp. 290–292). If we take the given benefit of regulatory enforcement to be a reasonably high degree of compliance with the law, then it is not immediately obvious why the cost of achieving this by means of wheel-clamping should be lower in relation to VED evasion than in relation to illegal parking. The processes of applying and releasing the clamp are sufficiently similar that any differences in administrative expenditure are likely to reflect institutional arrangements, rather than relate to the substance of the offence.

As regards the deterrent effect, it is reasonable to assume that, in both contexts, the hassle factor involved in getting a vehicle released adds significantly to the costs to the offender of the sanction (S). Also, the visual impact of a clamped wheel may be so salient to those who observe it that, in accordance with the availability heuristic, many individuals in both situations may subjectively attribute a relative high probability to the sanction being imposed (p). In relation to parking, the immediacy of the event may increase the perceived costs still further, but account has to be taken here of the fact that summary administrative penalties inevitably give rise to wrongful or inappropriate impositions and therefore high error costs, because the procedures for verifying guilt are limited (Ogus 2009). It is therefore a question of balancing the welfare gains from increased deterrence against the error and other costs of early impositions.

Subject to this last consideration, the perceived value of *pS* is likely to be sufficiently high to exceed *U*. In a parking case, *U* will largely comprise savings from the non-payment of any parking charge and/or from the time and inconvenience in not having to travel from another place where parking is legal; in the VED case it will primarily be the savings from the non-payment of the tax.

However, while in theory the weight of the sanction might not vary between the two applications, the practice of the enforcement agencies might suggest otherwise. As we have seen, the DVLA has had a strong belief in the deterrence value of wheel-clamping. Indeed it explicitly refers to "inconvenience" (to the vehicle owner) as playing an important role in relation to such deterrence (Comptroller and Auditor General 2003, para. 43). Contrast that with the following statement which appeared in the Department for Transport's guidance (1995, para. 8.17) to local authorities on the enforcement of parking regulations: "it is important that motorists who have paid their declamping charge and associated penalty charge should be able to use their vehicle as soon as reasonably possible. The punishment of wheel-clamping should be the cost of the release fee, not the time and inconvenience in arranging and waiting for the vehicle to be declamped". There is apparently here a concern to minimize the hassle costs experienced by the vehicle owner! Moreover, as it became increasingly apparent during the 1990s that most local authorities were reluctant to use wheel-clamping, so the perceived probability of the sanction being imposed would have been reduced. This might have led to a vicious circle: the lower the offender perceived the probability of the vehicle being clamped, the less effective became the sanction; and as the local authorities perceived clamping to be less effective, the greater the reluctance to use it.

If, notwithstanding the practice described in the last paragraph, it can be shown that in theory wheel-clamping is cost-effective as a deterrent in both the parking and the VED contexts, that does not necessarily mean that the economic case for adopting it is equally strong. Cost-effectiveness analysis provides only a partial input to the normative issue of what enforcement policy is appropriate, because it takes no account of any variations in the benefits to society of deterring different illegal acts by wheel-clamping. From this broader perspective, the policy goal should be that of optimal enforcement of the law, the point where the (marginal) social benefits of reducing illegal behaviour approximate to the (marginal) costs of achieving those benefits.

The question thus arises as to how the social benefits of deterring illegal parking compare with those of deterring VED evasion. As regards the former, the primary benefits would appear to be: an increase in the payment of parking charges; reduced obstruction on the roads, if the illegal parking impedes traffic flow; and, to the extent that vehicle owners decide to use alternative means of transport, some general environmental benefits, including reductions in noise, emissions and congestion (Calthrop et al. 2000). It might also be appropriate to add, perhaps, a reduction in the indignation costs of those (for example, residents) entitled lawfully to park in the place taken by the offending vehicle, and of those incurred by law-abiding vehicle owners. These benefits are difficult to quantify, but are by no means trivial. However, they have to be compared with the costs of wheel-clamping which are perhaps in the region of £200 per vehicle clamped (Comptroller and Auditor General 2003) and on an intuitive evaluation we cannot be confident that the benefits decisively outweigh the costs.

When we turn to VED evasion the picture is clearer, since the benefits of compliance can be assumed to be very much larger. This is not only because the direct consequence of regulatory compliance, the payment of excise duty, involves substantial sums (Brown et al. 2008). It is also because VED enforcement generates major external benefits. In particular, wheel-clamping assists in the identification and prosecution of individuals responsible for other forms of illegality. It has been estimated that for each VED offence detected there is an average of 1.31 other serious motoring offences revealed (Brown et al. 2008, para. 4.1), including for example, the absence of third-party insurance or of a Ministry of Transport certificate. Insofar, then, that wheel-clamping for VED evasion facilitates the deterrence of these other offences, it generates additional benefits in reducing the social costs associated with them. It also helps to alleviate the environmental costs associated with abandoned vehicles, since the clamping and removal of these are included in the same enforcement exercise (Comptroller and Auditor General 2003).

The cost-benefit perspective can make an important contribution to the normative question of when wheel-clamping is an appropriate sanction and, on the basis of the reasoning in the last paragraph, helps to justify its use in relation to VED evasion, but not for illegal parking. It can also provide an explanation for what has happened in England and Wales and described in section 2, the increase in enthusiasm for the former but in disillusionment with the latter.

There is, moreover, another economic theoretical framework which can be invoked to explain that experience: public choice. This approach explores how interest groups stand to benefit from changes to the law and, by means of lobbying and other methods, are able to persuade politicians and bureaucrats to supply them with those benefits. Key determinants of successful lobbying are the degree of homogeneity of interest in relevant groups and their ability to coordinate the pressure they bring to bear at relatively low cost (Olson 1965). Applying this framework to wheel-clamping requires us to ask what interest groups stand to gain and lose from the use of the sanction and what are likely to be the relative lobbying strengths of those groups. Perhaps the most important such group to gain are those private organizations which are engaged, normally under franchise arrangements, to undertake the clamping and declamping of vehicles. Now, although this applies to both parking and VED evasion, in the former context different franchisees are engaged by different local authorities and coordination costs of the firms will not be trivial; in contrast, the DVLA has a franchise contract with a single operator throughout the UK (DVLA 2009), and its lobbying power must be significantly greater.

Identification of the groups which are likely to oppose wheel-clamping provides an even sharper contrast between the two situations. The only private interests motivated to oppose VED wheel-clamping because it imposes significant costs on them are those comprising the VED evaders themselves. These individuals (and firms) are likely to lack the resources for serious opposition and in any event constitute a disparate group, unable to coordinate except at high cost. Contrast this with likely opponents of wheel-clamping for illegal parking. Most obviously the characteristics of offenders are very different, since they include a wide range of otherwise law-abiding citizens. Although the group is very diverse, and therefore lobbying activities are difficult to coordinate, there is the compensating factor that many will be wealthy and some are likely to be themselves politicians. Moreover, opposition might also come from traders in urban areas who benefit from temporary, illegal parking outside their premises.

Acknowledgements

I wish to thank participants for comments received at workshops at the Institute for Law, Economy and Global Governance, University of Manchester, and at the Centre for Socio-Legal Studies, University of Oxford where earlier versions of the paper were presented.

References

Akerlof, G.A. 2001. Procrastination and Obedience. *American Economic Review* (Pap & Proc) 81(2), 1–19.

Banks, R.K. and M.D. Vogel-Sprott. 1965. The effect of delayed punishment on an immediately rewarded response in humans. *Journal of Experimental Psychology* 70, 357–359.

Becker, G.S. 1968. Crime and Punishment: An Economic Approach. *Journal of Political Economy* 76, 169–217.

Brown, M, M. Jeffcott and E. Gilles-Smith. 2008. The Costs and Benefits of DfT's Traffic Enforcement Activities, European Transport Conference Proceedings.

Calthrop, E., S. Proost and K. van Dender. 2000. Parking Policies and Road Pricing. *Urban Studies* 37, 63–76.

Camden Culture and Environment Directorate. 2006. Wheel Clamping – The Effect of Wheel Clamping on Compliance with Parking Regulations On-Street.

Comptroller and Auditor General. 2003. Report on the Driver and Vehicle Licensing Agency Trust Statement 2002–03. National Audit Office, London.

Cramton, R.C. 1964. Driver Behavior and Legal Sanctions. *Michigan Law Review* 67, 421–454.

Department of Transport. 1995. Local Authority Circular 1/95: Guidance on Decriminalised Parking Enforcement Outside London, Dft, London.

Department of Transport. 2007. Better Parking – Keeping Traffic Moving, Operational Guidance Draft Consultation DfT, London.

Dugar, S. and T. Sorensen. 2006. Hassle Costs, Price-Matching Guarantees and Price Competition: An Experiment. *Review of Industrial Organization* 28, 359–378.

DVLA. 2009. Annual Report 2008–09. DVLA, Swansea.

Eide, E. 2000. Economics of Criminal Behavior, in B.Bouckaert and G.De Geest (eds.), *Encyclopedia of Law and Economics.* Cheltenham: Edward Elgar, vol. V, pp. 345–389.

Eide, E. with J. Aasness and T. Skjerpen. 1994. *Economics of Crime: Deterrence and the Rational Offender.* Amsterdam and New York: Elsevier.

Galbiati, R. and N. Garoupa. 2007. Keeping Stigma Out of Administrative Law: An Explanation of Consistent Beliefs. *Supreme Court Economic Review* 15, 273–284.

Guinchard, A. 2005. Fixing the Boundaries of the Concept of Crime: The Challenge for Human Rights. *International and Comparative Law Quarterly* 54, 719–734.

Herley, C., P. Vora and S. Yang. 2004. Detection and Deterrence of Counterfeiting of Valuable Documents. Proceedings of IEEE International Conference on Image Processing 4, 2423–2426.

Jolls, C., C.R. Sunstein and R. Thaler. 1998. A Behavioral Approach to Law and Economics. *Stanford Law Review* 50, 1471–1550.

Kuran, T. and C.R. Sunstein. 1999. Availability Cascades and Risk Regulation. *Stanford Law Review* 51, 683–768.

Laibson, D. 1997. Golden Eggs and Hyperbolic Discounting. *Quarterly Journal of Economics* 112, 443–477.

May, A.D. and I.G. Turvey. 1984. The Effects of Wheel Clamps in Central London: Comparison of Before and After Studies, Institute of Transport Studies, University of Leeds Working Paper No 184.

Ogus, A. 2006. *Costs and Cautionary Tales: Economic Insights for the Law.* Oxford: Hart.

Ogus, A. 2009. Criminal Law and Regulation. In Garoupa, N. (ed.) *Criminal Law and Economics.* pp. 90–110. Cheltenham: Elgar.

Olson, M. 1965. *The Logic of Collective Action.* Cambridge, MA: Harvard University Press.

Polinsky, A.M. and S. Shavell. 1979. The Optimal Tradeoff between the Probability and Magnitude of Fine. *American Economic Review* 69, 880–891.

Polinsky, A.M. and S. Shavell. 2000. The Economic Theory of Public Enforcement of Law. *Journal of Economic Literature 38,* 45–77.

Smith, J. 1992. Controlling Parking: Experience in the United Kingdom, Study for Transport Research Laboratory. http://popcenter.org/Library/CrimePrevention/Volume%2002/03smith.pdf

Utset, M.A. 2005. A Model of Time-Inconsistent Misconduct: The Case of Lawyer Misconduct. *Fordham Law Review* 74, 1319–1352.

Clearance Rates: Indicators of Certainty of Punishment or Marginal Utility of Police Investigation?

Leif Petter Olaussen

Introduction

According to the general theory of deterrence (or prevention) the efficiency of punishment as an instrument to combat crime depends on certainty, severity and celerity of punishment. I will only focus on certainty because this is the factor which has attracted most empirical research, and in many reports the author(s) conclude that certainty of punishment has an impact on crime. This is especially true for research built on aggregate data analysed by econometric regression techniques; for recent reviews see Nagin (1998) and Eide et al. (2006). In Norway Eide (1994) is an outstanding example of the econometric approach in studies of deterrence effects. His interest in deterrence research since 1981 has stimulated me to try to understand the econometric approach which I first met in Andenæs (1975), and the many limitations and problems of this approach, highlighted by the US panel of researchers convened to assess the validity of evidence for deterrence effects; see Blumstein et al. (1978). I must admit that the panel's report and the many obstacles to deterrence research taken up both by Andenæs (1975) and Gibbs (1975) made me very sceptical to the validity of assertions about empirical evidence for deterrent effects. Because of this I am one of the criminologists in the Nordic countries who was asked by Eide (1999) why we have neither invested energy in deterrence research nor advocated conclusions in econometric deterrence studies. In this paper I will try to give a more specific answer to Eide's question by focusing on a few crucial problems in the most prevalent design in econometric deterrence studies – cross-sectional studies – which represent the main bulk of studies claimed to sustain the hypothesis that certainty of punishment influences the level of crime.

Deterrence theory – field of tenability and testability

The general theory of deterrence is a theory about individuals, how they probably respond to threats of formal punishments inflicted by penal authorities. The most important scientific question is whether the theory is tenable, but testing of deterrence theory is not a straightforward task.

Despite we all know that a valid test of a theory must be conducted within the theory's field of tenability, Galtung's remark that a "cardinal sin in social science research is precisely the failure to specify the conditions of assumed validity" (Galtung 1970: 316) is a relevant reminder also for research and discussions of deterrence theory. It is frequently called general deterrence (or prevention) theory, and this designation connotes that it is a theory about how the behaviour of people in general – *everybody* – is influenced by threats of formal penal sanctions. But this assertion would be an extension of the theory's field of tenability. The Norwegian professor in penal law, Johannes Andenæs, a lifelong advocate for general prevention theory, stated explicitly that the theory is tenable only for a *subsection* of the general population:

> The threat of punishment is directed to all of us, but it affects us differently. With regard to a certain kind of criminal conduct, the population could be divided into three groups: (a) the law-abiding man, who does not need the threat of law to keep him on the right path; (b) the potential criminal, who would have broken the law if it had not been for the threat of punishment; and (c) the criminal, who may well fear the law but not enough to keep him from breaking it. It is in the intermediate group, the potential criminal, that the deterrent effect of punishment is at work. (Andenæs 1974:111–112)

Likewise Stephen D. Webb (referring to Jackson (1964), Grasmick and MaLaughlin (1978), and Zimring and Hawkins (1968)), wrote:

> What keep most people law abiding are the prescriptions and proscriptions for conduct that are internalized in the socialization process – not the written law and its

> sanctions. Thus only the "inadequately" or "abnormally" socialized individual fits the model of classical criminology and is deterred from expressing deviant impulses by a nice calculation of pleasures and punishment. This, of course is impossible to document but it does point to the likelihood that most persons need not be deterred from serious criminal activities (Webb 1980, p. 24)

Because the theory's field of tenability is limited to "potential criminals" one is immediately faced with the question: How to proceed to find a representative group or sample of them? If we cannot, a valid test of the theory will be difficult to carry out because its tenability can neither be tested on a random sample of the population nor on known criminals. Maybe Andenæs was not aware of the consequences of this problem when he noted about categories of people within the population mentioned above that:

> We do not know the proportions of persons in these categories, but they will obviously vary by offence and even by geographical area. Nor do we have any easy means of identifying the citizens who belong to the different groups. Moreover, the groups are not static but change with changing conditions. Under exceptional condition, e.g., war or other serious crises, the number of actual as well as potential offenders may increase many times. (Andenæs 1974:112)

This is an honest observation, but the fact it imparts is a formidable obstacle against serious tests of deterrence theory based on individual data. But econometric studies using aggregate data will also have to face this problem even if they are less concerned with the question of the truth of deterrence theory than estimation of deterrence effects.

Gary Becker and Isaac Ehrlich who initiated the interest in deterrence research among economists begged the question of truth of deterrence theory. They used fundamental theoretical assumptions in deterrence theory as a trustworthy foundation for construction of models of behaviour (successfully used in economics) to *estimate deterrent effects* of probability and severity of punishment, taking for granted that deterrence theory is tenable. None of them discussed the truth of deterrence theory, and Becker wrote in a sweeping statement that there is unanimous agreement on this:

> Practically all the diverse theories [about causes of crime], agree, however, that when other variables are held constant, an increase in a person's probability of conviction or punishment if convicted would generally decrease, perhaps substantially, perhaps negligibly, the number of offences he commits. In addition, a common generalization by persons with judicial experience is that a change in the probability has a greater effect on the number of offences than a change in the punishment, although, as far as I can tell, none of the prominent theories shed any light on this relation. (Becker 1968: 176)

Becker immediately saw that deterrence theory fit like a hand in a glove into

> . . . the economists' usual analysis of choice and assumes that a person commits an offence if the expected utility to him exceeds the utility he could get by using his time and other resources at other activities. Some persons become "criminals", therefore, not because their basic motivation differs from that of other persons, but because their benefits and costs differ." (ibid.)

He then devoted his efforts to construct a theoretical model which would make it possible to answer the normative question "how many resources and how much punishment *should* be used to enforce different kinds of legislation" (Becker 1968: 170). He was explicitly concerned with estimation of *optimal* law enforcement not with testing the truth of deterrence theory. Isaac Ehrlich went beyond Becker's theory by including both punishment and rewards in his concept of "opportunities", and linked his theory of participation in illegitimate activities with the general theory of occupational choices by presenting the offender's decision problem as one of an optimal allocation of resources under uncertainty (Ehrlich 1973: 522; see also p. 524). But nor did he question the tenability of deterrence theory. He too implicitly supposed that it would be properly tested when parameters in econometric models of crime are estimated. Since then it seems to have been taken for granted that model estimates which show negative statistical associations in cross sectional statistical data between crime and apprehension, conviction or time served in prison, are valid corroborations of deterrence effects. In the next section I will argue that there are several reasons to doubt the validity of this conclusion.

Feasibility of cross sectional analysis of aggregate data

Although everyone knows that deterrence theory is about *individuals* the most prevalent approach in econometric studies of general deterrence, is to use *aggregate data* in cross sectional (or sometimes longitudinal) studies (Eide et al. 2006). In cross sectional studies built on US data, the states normally are the units of analysis, and in Eide (1994) models were estimated on data for the 53 Norwegian police districts.

My first objection to this approach is that use of aggregate data for states or police districts represents a *logical* fallacy because the theory is about individuals, not administrative or geographical areas. (There is no plausible reason to believe that such areas have the capacity to be deterred.) And because it is a logical fallacy it cannot plausibly be rectified by any statistical procedure.

Eide agrees with Andenæs and Webb that the theory's field of tenability is restricted to a subgroup:

> A decrease in actual probability or severity of punishment, actually observed by everybody, will make crime more attractive. The change will not necessarily change the behaviour of a given individual, perhaps not even a majority of individuals: the change may just not be enough to substitute an illegal activity for a legal one, or the person has already specialized in legal activities. (…) In a large population, however, it is highly probable that at least some individuals are just on the brink of committing an illegal act before the decrease in punishment, and the decrease is just sufficient for it to happen. Gradual decreases in punishment will thus produce changes here and there in the population, and a noticeable change in the aggregate crime will take place. (Eide 1994:91)

My second objection to a test using aggregate data is that it is far from obvious *why* a valid test of deterrence theory can use aggregate data for *large groups* of people (like US states or Norwegian police districts) to check if a *minority* ("some individuals") within each group behave according to deterrence theory. It is difficult to see why it is plausible to assume that estimates of statistical parameters for relationships in data covering a whole nation will yield valid estimates for a minority group like potential criminals, who's proportion "will obviously vary by offence and by geographical area" (Andenæs, above). And how will the estimates be influenced by crimes committed by criminals who may well fear the law but not enough to keep them from breaking it? (cf. Andenæs, above).

A possible reply to this objection might be that econometric studies correct for variations in size of the group of potential criminals in different areas because the models used in such studies have included criminological theories and data which estimate cross sectional variations in number of potential criminals. Eide's (1994) theoretical approach to crime, his "model of norm-guided rational behaviour", is a prominent example illustrating that economists think that much more than people's rational considerations of penal threats might influence an individual's choice between legal and illegal activities. In accordance with lots of criminological studies, in his theoretical model the individual's choice

> . . . depends on his norms and wants, his abilities, the situation or environment in which he lives, and his beliefs about the achievable outcomes and about the satisfaction produced by the various acts and outcomes. Differences in one of these factors between any two individuals may, cet. par., make one person law-abiding, and the other not. Better opportunities for theft for the latter may be sufficient to make the difference; or perhaps not, if norms or other factors are strong enough to prevent it. For whole regions or countries one may presume that if the opportunities of theft are better in one population than in another, the number of thefts will, cet. par., be higher in the first one. Some of those who are on the brink of stealing, will become thieves because of better opportunities. (Eide 1994:103)

I don't know of any econometric study advancing a more convincing theoretical model. But Eide's conclusions and estimates of deterrence effects as well as other effects are based on a rather narrow set of socioeconomic and demographic variables (specified in Eide 1994: 262), because there are not available data for many of the factors considered as relevant and important enough to be included in the theoretical model. In other words: lack of relevant and important data – which is a common problem for econometric studies (Eide 1994:174-175) – and different problems with models specifications and identification[1] problems in parameter estimations, render it possible that the parameter estimates built on a meagre set

1 Fischer and Nagin (1978) is still a very good introduction to these problems in deterrence research.

of indicators might be completely wrong. This should be a good reason to exercise scientific caution in interpretations and conclusions.

Also my third objection is related to mismatch between theoretical and empirical units. In cross sectional deterrence studies it is supposed that variations across areas in percent of criminal cases cleared-up (or apprehension per crime, or some other more or less equivalent measurement) are valid measurements of variations in individual (subjective) perceptions of probability of apprehension (or of "certainty of punishment", which is the theoretical construct in deterrence theory). If the percent cleared-up is 47 percent in area A and 22 percent in area B it is believed that these figures represent valid[2] measurements of subjective perceptions of risk of apprehension among potential criminals in the two areas. However, I have never come across any study which explains *why* it is plausible to assume that percent of solved cases in an area is a valid measure of *subjective* probability of punishment among people is a certain section of the population living in the area. Eide (1999:86-87) touches on this question, and answers it by an example where he uses consumption theory: according to economic theory of consumer's conduct total consumption of bananas depends on price of bananas and of comparable products, even if everybody does not know the exact price of or buy or eat bananas. I don't hesitate to accept that total consumption of a commodity partly depends on prices if the commodity has an observable price on the market, and if there also is available information about the price for comparable products. I find it plausible because there is a specified *mechanism* – information about market prices – in consumption theory, but because there is no "market" for crimes where anyone can observe the probability of punishment for any crime and compare the costs of crime with the costs of alternative actions, I don't see any reason to assume an analogy in mechanisms between total consumption of bananas and total number of crime. Accordingly, my third objection is that econometric cross sectional studies of crime are lacking a substantial explanation which specifies *mechanism(s)* which make it plausible to assume that clearance rate will be positively correlated with subjective perceptions of certainty of punishment among potential criminals. I also join Andenæs (1975) and Gibbs (1975) who noted that there is a need to examine the asserted link between percent cleared-up and cognitive states among potential criminals, which we according to

2 An empirical variable measuring a theoretical property (construct) is valid if any difference in measurements reflects a difference in the theoretical property – and nothing else.

Nagin (1998:15–19) still don't know very much about. Promotion of deterrence theory should be very cautious until we both have specified mechanism(s) and empirical research which corroborates the tenability of this link.

My forth objection is connected to the first. Whenever aggregate data is used in cross sectional studies to test individual theory or to estimate parameters describing relations on the individual level (i.e. units on a lower level than the aggregate) we know from Robinson's (1950) seminal article that a parameter estimate based on aggregate data will probably not be a valid estimate for relations on individual level. He exemplified and proved mathematically that ecological correlation coefficients based on aggregate data will yield unbiased[3] estimates for individual level correlations only under conditions which ordinarily are not encountered in sociological data (p. 357). Some years later Goodman (1953 and 1959) showed that unstandardized regression coefficients computed on aggregate data do not always yield biased estimates of individual-level relations. In a carefully designed criminological study Slatin (1969) confirmed Robinson's and Goodman's conclusions. Later Hammond (1973) and Firebaugh (1978) tried to specify sociological sources of errors in cross-level estimation to find conditions under which aggregate-level data provide unbiased estimates of individual-level regression coefficients. Firebaugh concluded (p. 569) that aggregate-level regression coefficients will only give unbiased estimates of individual-level effects if one can rule out any possibility of an independent structural or group effect on the dependent variable. An independent effect will be present if the independent variable regressed on the dependent variable is a measure of two (or more) different constructs, or if the independent variable influences the dependent one directly. I think this often is the case in econometric cross sectional deterrence studies based on crime statistics[4]. It is assumed that the percent of crimes cleared-up (X) is a valid measure of "objective certainty" of punishment, which (through unknown mechanism(s)) will influence the individual's "subjective certainty" of punishment. If true, this would not in itself guarantee unbiased esti-

3 Cross-level bias is present if there is a difference between obtained aggregate level coefficients and individual-level coefficients.

4 Hakim (1994:37) emphasizes that economists often display little concern for quality and limitations, important for validity, when they use data from administrative systems as research data. The methodological problems mentioned in this section seem to be unknown or neglected in econometric deterrence studies.

mates from aggregate data. If the figures for clearance rate (X) also (or instead) are a measure of something else, i.e. the *proportion of reported cases with clues* which will help the police to clear-up the case (this possibility will be developed below), the aggregate-level estimates of regression coefficients would be a biased estimate for individual-level relationships, even if there happens to be a link between measured clearance rate and individual risk perceptions among potential criminals. The aggregate estimate would also be biased if the percent of cases cleared-up is a measure of overburdening of or lack of capacity[5] in the criminal justice system, or fear of social reprobation (Andenæs 1974:16) which is often conjectured in deterrence research. Since one cannot rule out the possibility that the clearance rate is a conflated measurement of several completely different constructs, the possibility that clearance rate yields biased estimates of deterrence effects cannot be ruled out either.

Varying marginal utility of police investigation

Even if we knew for sure that potential criminal's perceptions of risk of apprehension is strongly influenced by the percent of crimes cleared-up, we could not safely assume that the theory of deterrence is a valuable theory for crime policy. In my view Gary Becker, Isaac Ehrlich and many of the economists they inspired to conduct deterrence research, have not paid due attention to another important empirical[6] question: Is it true that there are readily available means which could be employed to increase significantly the percent of crimes cleared-up? An answer which seems to be implied in deterrence studies is that more policemen will be an efficient measure. But do we *know* that this is true?

In an interview many years ago I asked an experienced Norwegian police detective what a police detective's work is about. He immediately quoted a phrase[7] he had been taught at the police school: "To discover, protect, and collect clues

5 This conjecture is also called the system capacity hypothesis.

6 Use of the theory in crime policy would of course also make it necessary to consider many ethical questions which I leave out here.

7 Among Norwegian police detectives it was called the S-rule because all words in the phrase start with S: *"Søke, sikre, samle spor som samlet sannsynliggjør sakens sanne sammenheng, siktedes skyld så vel som skyldfrihet."*

which together probably tell what truly happened, if a suspect is guilty or if he is not." This condensed expression of practise-based police knowledge sums up nicely the key importance of *clues* for clearance of crimes (see also Guyot 1991:97), if the perpetrator is not taken red-handed, which does not happen very frequently in many crime categories. No doubt police eyes, hands, knowledge, and intuition are necessary to find, secure, collect and analyse clues to solve crimes. But to have success in this work police often depend on luck and information mainly from two sources of knowledge.

Firstly, police may have some knowledge of criminals who live in their area, especially of many of the recidivists. The modus operandi of "their own" criminal's might be known, and the police may know which criminals are out of jail, who are friends with whom, who might be accomplices or willing to inform the police about other criminal's activities, etc. This kind of police knowledge about "their own" local criminals is often of crucial importance to be able to solve cases. The amount and quality of this kind of knowledge will, however, differ across police forces, and almost certainly along an urban-rural axis. In highly urban areas there will tend to be too much crime and too many criminals (both belonging there and migrating there) for the police to be able to have as good and updated knowledge as will be possible for their colleagues in rural areas. Because of this I would expect that the clearance rate will tend to be highest in rural areas where surroundings facilitate a richer body of knowledge about the whereabouts of active criminals than in urban surroundings.

Secondly, police will depend on knowledge from the public. Ordinary people who have seen or heard or found something, or who know who are together with whom, who wear this or that type of clothing, drive or own a car of this or that type, etc., will quite often be the ones who supply the police with clues or information which makes sense of a clue police already have, and make it possible for police to identify a perpetrator. Without clues or information from the public even active police will often be unable to clear-up many cases. However, people will not always be able to be of much help to police in their work to solve crimes, and I hypothesise that people in urban areas are more handicapped than rural dwellers. In urban areas people generally don't know each other and each other's belongings, and it can be difficult to know if an observed person is "in a wrong place at a wrong time" and therefore is perceived as a suspect or criminal. Separation of living areas, business areas and entertainment areas in cities reduces the capacity for social control in everyday life. And even if victims, neighbours or bystanders are able to give police accurate descriptions (sex, age, clothes, hair colour, etc.) of an observed criminal in an urban context, there will frequently be so many potential persons who fit the observations (even among criminals known to police) that even very good observations may be of little help to police. Most of this will be different in rural areas where people tend to know each other, and some of each other's belongings (bicycles, cars, boats, etc.) much better. Because of these urban-rural differences in *anonymity* I hypothesise that both quality and number of clues in cases reported to police will depend on degree of urbanization and facilitate a higher clearance rate in rural than in urban areas.

A Swedish study of variations in clearance rates in 118 Swedish police districts by Ahlberg and Knutsson (1987:83) lends some empirical support to my suggestions above. Their main conclusion was that differences in the composition of crime (crime-mix) and the number of crimes per person charged explained half of the variance in clearance rate. Crime-mix is a significant factor because the proportion of cases which is cleared-up at the moment of reporting (self-cleared-up cases), differ greatly between crime categories. Drug cases and shoplifting are numerically important categories with a high portion of self-cleared-up cases, while this portion is very low for burglary. But Ahlberg and Knutsson also found a negative urbanization effect: the higher the number of inhabitants in the main town in the police district, the lower was the clearance rate (pp. 84-85). Their suggested explanation is that high degree of anonymity in urban areas has a restraining effect on police detection of crimes because anonymity is both restraining police knowledge of the whereabouts of criminals operating in urban areas and the public's possibility to help the police to clear the crimes. In their study differences in police resources across police districts had no systematic effects on clearance rates.

These thoughts and observations corroborate another possible interpretation of the clearance rate: the percent of crimes cleared-up in an area is a measurement of *local marginal utility of police investigations* of cases without specific clues which i) characterize one or a few known criminals, or ii) might release information from people which clear the case. In urban areas the marginal utility will be *low* because there will tend to be a low portion of not cleared-up cases *with clues* which could solve the case if police investigations were instigated (or intensified). In rural areas the marginal utility will be higher because the portion of not cleared-up cases *with clues* which could solve the case will tend to be higher.

This suggested interpretation will also have implications for specifications of causal connections between the three variables crime level (C), percent of cases cleared-up (P), and degree of urbanization (U). Leaving out the possibility of recursive relationships (C ↔ P), specifications of relations according to deterrence theory would either be Model A or B:

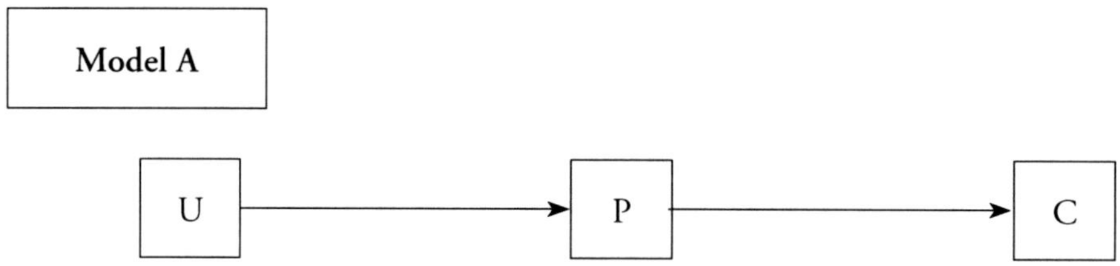

Degree of urbanization (U) is supposed to influence percent of cleared-up cases (P) because anonymity is positively connected to degree of urbanization: high degree of urbanization gives a high level of anonymity, and anonymity is negatively connected to probability of clearing crimes: high degree of anonymity gives low probability of clearance because anonymity is unfavourable for observations and other clues which might lead to clearance of crimes. In accordance with deterrence theory it is supposed in Model A that the level of P will influence the crime level (negatively and) directly.

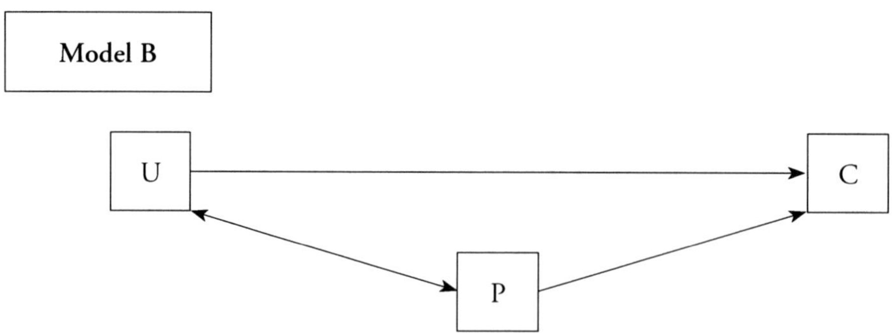

Model B is very much the same as Model A (see above). In addition it is supposed in Model B that degree of urbanization directly influences the level of crime: high level of urbanization is supposed to be favourable for crime because of a higher number of objects (bikes, cars, shops, flats, etc.) which may be attractive to criminals – and a higher number of motivated criminals, than there are in more rural areas.

My alternative hypothesis – that P is a measurement of (local) marginal utility of police investigation of cases with none or scanty clues – would rather suggest Model C and D:

Model C

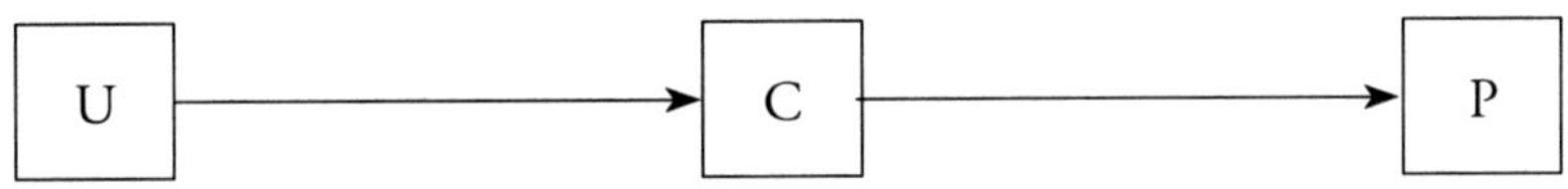

It is supposed that degree of urbanization directly influences the level of crime: high level of urbanization is supposed to be favourable for crime because of a higher number of objects (bikes, cars, shops, flats, etc.) which may be attractive to criminals – and a higher number of motivated criminals, than there are in more rural areas. The volume of crime is supposed to influence (negatively and) directly the percent of cleared-up crimes: high volume of crime gives low clearance rate because there will (rarely) be enough police because the marginal utility of police detective work is (very) low.

Model D

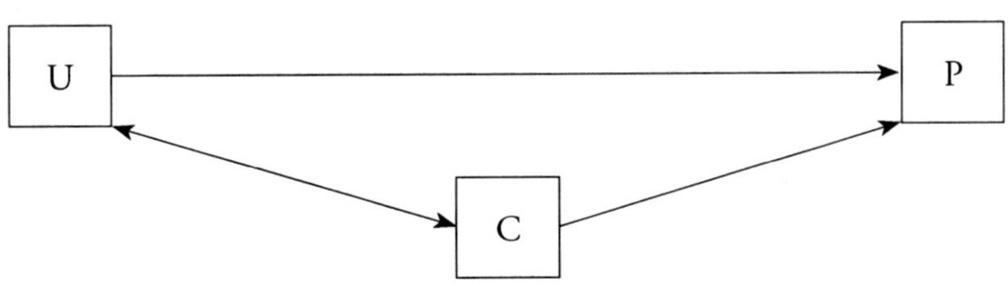

Model D is very much the same as Model C (see above). In addition it is supposed in Model D that degree of urbanization directly influences the percent crimes cleared up: high degree of urbanization gives a high level of anonymity which is negatively connected to probability of clearing crimes: high degree of anonymity gives low probability of clearance because anonymity is unfavourable both for people's capacity to help the police with observations and other clues which might lead to clearance of crimes and for police force's capacity to be updated on relevant information about known criminals and modus operandi, thus directly reducing the marginal utility of police investigations.

I have performed a *provisional* test of the feasibility of these models on Norwegian data for 1970 and 1990 for the 19 counties in Norway. Data for C is number of crimes investigated by the police per 1000 inhabitants, P is percent of crimes cleared-up, and U is percent of inhabitants living in villages/towns/cities with at least 2000 inhabitants. All data are from publications by Norwegian Statistics.

1970				1990			
	C	P	U		C	P	U
C	-	-.777	0.892	C	-	-.493	0.871
P		-	-0.778	P		-	-.502
U			-	U			-

Table 1: Pearson correlation between crime level (C), percent of cleared crimes (P), and degree of urbanization (U) in Norwegian counties in 1970 and 1990.

Correlation coefficients in Table 1 show the statistical associations in data for both years. All coefficients are in the expected direction (independent of which of the models A-D above one thinks is feasible) and coefficients are fairly high, especially between degree of urbanization and level of crime, 0.892 in 1970 and 0.871 in 1990. In data for 1970 the correlations between urbanization and percent of cleared-up cases is -0.778, but decreased to -0.502 in 1990. The correlation between percent cleared-up and crime level decreased from -0.777 in 1970 to -0.493 in 1990. Both decreases are due to reduced variation in clearance rate in 1990. From 1970 to 1990 the percent of cleared-up cases decreased significantly in counties with a low level of urbanization in 1970. I guess that there are three important reasons for this. One is that statistical registration of reported crimes was most affected in these counties during the 1980s when a computer-based case system (STRASAK) was gradually introduced in the police. Another is that increasing mobility (also) among criminals across police district borders (even in rural areas) has made it far more difficult for police even in the least urbanized counties to have more than fragmentary knowledge about possible perpetrators. Thirdly, the population's capacity to help police clear-up crimes has decreased even in the least urban areas because informal social control has decreased due to increasing participation of females in the work force, and a generally increased mobility.

Assuming that there are no significant recursive connections between crime and clearance rate, correlation coefficients in Table 1 can be used as a *tentative* check if any of the four specified models fits the correlation matrixes in the table 1. If *Model A* fits the data reasonably well, then $r_{UC} = r_{PC} \cdot r_{UP}$, or :

(1) $$r_{UC} - r_{PC} \cdot r_{UP} = 0.$$

Entering figures from the correlation matrix above into (1) we get:

For 1970: $r_{UC} - r_{PC} \cdot r_{UP} = \underline{0.287}$; For 1990: $r_{UC} - r_{PC} \cdot r_{UP} = \underline{0.624}$

This does not meet the requirement in equation (1), and indicate that *Model A* does not fit the data. If *Model B* fits the data reasonably well, then r_{UP} would be *equal* to the partial correlation, $r_{UP \cdot C}$, or:

(2) $$r_{UC} - r_{UP \cdot C} = 0.$$

According to Blalock (1979: 459) the (first order) partial correlation in a three variable model, like the one between urbanization (U) and percent of crimes cleared-up (P) – controlled for level of crime (C) – can be calculated using the formula (3):

(3) $$r_{UP \cdot C} = \frac{r_{PU} - r_{PC} \cdot r_{UC}}{\sqrt{1 - r^2_{PC}} \sqrt{\cdot\, 1 - r^2_{UC}}}$$

Calculations for 1970 give $r_{UP \cdot C}$ = -0.298 and for 1990 $r_{UP \cdot C}$ = -0.170. Using equation (2) give:

1970: $r_{UP} - r_{UP \cdot C} = - \underline{0.480}$; 1990: $r_{UP} - r_{UP \cdot C} = - \underline{0.332}$.

These results do not meet the requirement in equation (2), and indicate that *Model B* does not fit the data. Data do not fit the two models which are in agreement with deterrence theory.

What about the other two models, C and D, where it is supposed that the clearance rate measure marginal utility of police investigations? If *Model C* fits the data reasonably well, then $r_{UP} = r_{UC} \cdot r_{CP}$, or:

(4) $r_{UP} - r_{UC} \cdot r_{CP} = 0.$

If we enter figures from the correlation matrix into (4) we get:

For 1970: $r_{UP} - r_{UC} \cdot r_{CP} = \underline{0.0849}$; For 1990: $r_{UP} - r_{UC} \cdot r_{CP} = \underline{0.0726}$

None of the figures equals zero, but they are not very far from it – which indicates that *Model C* fits the data pretty well, or at least better than *Model A* did.

If *Model D* fits the data, then r_{UP} would be *equal* to the partial correlation, $r_{UP \cdot C}$, or:

(5) $r_{UP} - r_{UP \cdot C} = 0.$

Applying the same general formula for (first order) partial correlation as above, partial correlation between urbanization (U) and level of crime (C) controlling for percent of crimes cleared (P), can be calculated using the formula (6):

(6) $$r_{UC \cdot P} = \frac{r_{UC} - r_{UP} \cdot r_{cp}}{\sqrt{1 - r^2_{UP}} \sqrt{\cdot\ 1 - r^2_{UP}}}$$

Calculations for 1970 give $r_{UC \cdot P} = 0.727$ and for 1990 $r_{UC \cdot P} = 0.827$. Using equation (5) give:

1970: $r_{UP} - r_{UP \cdot C} = \underline{0.165}$; 1990: $r_{UP} - r_{UP \cdot C} = \underline{0.044}$;

These results do not comply fully with the requirement in equation (5), but the figure for 1990 is close to zero. I think that the results indicate that *Model D* also fits the data for1990 reasonably well. In sum, these very *tentative* checks indicate that *models C and D* fit the data well enough to stimulate research which could check out more directly if the key assumption underlying them is correct, i.e. if marginal utility of police work is negatively correlated with degree of urbanization. If this is true more police will *neither* be a very efficient means to increase the clearance rate – *nor* the perceived certainty of arrest – in areas where it is most needed, in urban high crime areas.

Conclusions

In my view cross sectional deterrence studies suffer from three major problems. Firstly, we don't know anything about links between clearance rates and subjective perceptions of punishment. Secondly, regression coefficient computed on aggregate data will only yield unbiased estimates for individual level deterrence effects if clearance rates *only* measure "objective certainty" of punishment, which I think is a highly improbable condition. Most certainly, the rates (also) measure marginal utility of police investigations, system capacities and/or fear of social reprobation. Thirdly, for deterrence to be a practical tool in criminal policy one needs a means to increase "objective certainty" of punishment. It is, however, far from sure that there are any efficient means available.

To me it seems to be very difficult to find an appropriate research design to test if perceptions of certainty of punishment are influenced by percent of cases cleared up, first and foremost because the theory lacks a mechanism which specifies how clearance rate will influence perceptions of certainty of punishment. In addition, it is difficult to find a sample of "potential criminals" who, according to deterrence theory, constitute the field of tenability.

The frequently observed statistical association in cross sectional studies between level of crime and percent cleared-up may be explained by an alternative interpretation of the clearance rate: it is a function of marginal utility of police investigations, the size of which is a function of (i) the public's ability to supply the police with clues or otherwise help the police to clear-up crimes; and (ii) the ability of the police to build up and act upon updated knowledge about the whereabouts of criminals operating locally. I suggest that both abilities are negatively associated with level of anonymity and therefore with level of urbanization, producing frequently observed negative associations in cross sectional studies.

If my suggested assumption is wrong it would be relatively easy to falsify it by empirical research which checks if it is true that the proportion of cases *which is not cleared-up*, but which *has clues* that could make it possible to solve the case, is negatively associated with level of urbanization. In a connected study one could estimate the costs involved to increase the clearance rate with x percent in police districts with different levels of urbanization. Such studies would be very informative whether one believes in deterrence theory or not, because they would inform us whether police manpower could be a viable measure to increase the clearance rate significantly.

References

Ahlberg, J. and J. Knutsson. 1987. *Varför varierar uppklaringsprosenten?* Stockholm: BRÅ Forskning 1987:1.

Andenæs, J. 1974. *Punishment and Deterrence.* Ann Arbor: The University of Ann Arbor Press.

Andenæs, J. 1975. General Prevension revisited: research and policy implications. *Journal of Criminal Law and Criminology*, vol. 66, pp. 338–365.

Becker, G.S. 1968. Crime and Punishment: An Economic Approach. *Journal of Political Economy,* Vol. 76 (2), pp. 169–217.

Blalock Jr., H.M. 1979. *Social Statistics.* Revised 2nd Edition. New York: McGraw-Hill Book Company.

Blumstein, A.J. Cohen and Daniel Nagin (eds.). 1978. *Deterrence and Incapacitation: Estimating the Effects of Criminal Sanctions on Crime Rates.* Washington DC: National Academy of Sciences.

Ehrlich, I. 1973. Participation in Illegitimate Activities: A Theoretical and Empirical Investigation. *Journal of Political Economy,* Vol. 81 (May-June), pp. 521–565.

Eide, E. 1994. (in cooperation with J. Aasness and T. Skjerpen) *Economics of Crime. Deterrence and the Rational Offender.* North-Holland: Amsterdam, Lausanne, New York, Oxford, Shannon and Tokyo.

Eide, E. 1999. Kriminaløkonomi. De ukjente studier av almenprevensjon. *Tidsskrift for rettsvitenskap*, pp. 77–119.

Eide, E., P.H. Rubin and J.M. Shepherd. 2006. *Economics of Crime.* Hanover, MA: Publishers Inc. (A reprint from: *Foundations and Trends in Microeconomics*, vol. 2(3) 2006.)

Firebaugh, G. 1978. A Rule for Inferring Individual-Level Relationships from Aggregate Data. *American Sociological Review*, vol. 43(4) 1978, pp. 557–572.

Fischer, F.N. and D. Nagin. 1978. On the Feasibility of Identifying the Crime-function in a Simultaneous Model of Crime Rates and Sanction Levels, p. 361–399 in Blumstein et al. (1978).

Galtung, J. 1970. *Theory and Methods of Social Research*. Oslo, Bergen, Tromsø: Universitetsforlaget.

Gibbs, Jack P. 1975. *CRIME, PUNISHMENT and DETERRENCE*. New York, Oxford, Amsterdam: Elsevier.

Goodman, Leo. 1953. Ecological Regressions and Behavior of Individuals. *American Sociological Review*, vol. 18, pp. 663–664.

Goodman, Leo. 1959. Some Alternatives to Ecological Correlation. *American Journal of Sociology*, vol. 64 (May) 1959, pp. 610–625.

Grasmick, H.G. and S.D. MaLaughlin. 1978. Deterrence and Social Control. *American Sociological Review*, vol. 43 (April) pp. 272–278.

Guyot, D. 1991. *Policing as though People Matter*. Philadelphia: Temple University Press.

Hakim, C. 1994. *Research Design. Strategies and Choices in the Design of Social Research*. London and New York: Routledge.

Hammond, J.L. 1973. Two sources of Error in Ecological Correlations. *American Sociological Review*, vol. 38 (December) pp. 764–777.

Jackson, T. 1964. Is Punishment Necessary? *Journal of Criminology, Criminal Law and Police Science*, vol. 55 (September) 1964, pp. 332–337.

Nagin, D.S. 1998. Criminal Deterrence Research at the Outset of the Twenty-First Century, pp. 1-42, in Michael Tonry (ed.), *Crime and Justice. A Review of Research*. Vol. 23. Chicago and London: The University of Chicago Press.

Robinson, W.S. 1950. Ecological Correlations and the Behaviour of Individuals. *American Sociological Review*, vol. 15 (June), pp. 351–357.

Slatin, G.T. 1969. Ecological analysis of Delinquency: Aggregation Effects. *American Sociological Review*, vol. 34 (6), pp. 894–907.

Webb, S.D. 1980. Deterrence Theory: A Reconceptualization. *Canadian Journal of Criminology*, vol. 22(1), 1980, pp. 23–35.

Zimring, F. and G. Hawkins. 1968. Deterrence and Marginal Groups. *Journal of Research in Crime and Delinquency*, vol. 5(2), 1968, pp. 100–114.

Joint and Several Liabilities in Bankruptcy Revisited

Erik Røsæg

1 Introduction

When more than one person is liable for the same debt, they are jointly liable. If claims can be made to each of them for the whole unpaid amount, they are also severally liable. In continental terminology, joint and several liabilities correspond to "solidaric" liabilities.

In bankruptcy, joint and several liabilities are treated at the outset like any other liabilities. The creditor makes claim for the full unpaid amount, and gets payment – dividends – on a *pro rata* basis.

In principle, all creditors are supposed to get the same percentage of their claims covered.[1] However, there are many exceptions. Some are based on the desire to encourage lenders. This is the reason why mortgagees have a preferential status.[2] Some are based on the special needs of the claimant, such as maritime liens for wages and personal injury claims,[3] and preferential rights of dividends for salaries.[4] Others are based on various conceptions of a special duty to pay, such as maritime liens for port dues and salvage,[5] and preferential rights of dividends for taxes and funeral expenses.[6]

1 Norwegian Act No. 59/1984 relating to Creditors' Rights to Satisfaction of Claims (Satisfaction of Claims Act), Sec. 9-6.

2 Jens Edvin A. Skoghøy, *Panterett* (2nd ed., Oslo 2008) p. 26 *et seq.*

3 Norwegian Maritime Code, 1994, as amended, Sec. 51.

4 Satisfaction of Claims Act, Sec. 9-3.

5 Norwegian Maritime Code, 1994, Sec. 51.

6 Satisfaction of Claims Act, Sec. 9-2.

The rationale of some privileged rights is not altogether clear, such as the right of set off in bankruptcy.[7]

There is, however, no really coherent system in this, neither in Norway nor, as far as I know, in any other jurisdiction. The prime example of anomalies is non-maritime personal injury claims, which do not enjoy a preferred status in bankruptcy, but for which a preferred status could easily have been defended.

For the unfortunate non-preferred creditors, one usually refers to the prosaic fact that there is not enough in the estate for all creditors – that is why the debtor was declared bankrupt in the first place – and that all creditors are treated equally. However, this is not very comforting when some creditors are apparently more equal than others.

Joint and several liabilities also enjoy a certain preferential status in many legal systems.[8] Dividends are payable not only on the basis of the outstanding debt, but also on the basis of parts of the debts already paid by others of the jointly and severally liable co-debtors. This preferential status is unique in two ways. First, the preference is not for the full debt, but depends on actions of others at the time of bankruptcy. And second, the rationale of the rule is entirely technical; the idea is, as we shall see, that the bankruptcy machinery will work smoother with this rule than without it.

It is, of course, always possible to find other rationales. But none of them are really convincing, at least for a general rule of this kind:

- One can say, of course, that a person who is in the good position of having more than one debtor from whom he can recover his claims also deserves the additional benefit of some extra dividends.[9]
- One can say, of course, that the rule gives debtors who can offer sureties an extra negotiation chip in the negotiations with lenders.
- One can say, of course, that claimants against joint tortfeasors, who do not enjoy preferential positions in bankruptcy (see above), should at least have this benefit.[10]

---

7 The rules on set off in bankruptcy are found in Satisfaction of Claims Act Sec. 8-1 *et seq*. For a discussion *de lege ferenda*, see Sjur Brækhus, *Konkursrett utvalgte emner (Bankruptcy Law, Selected Topics)* (Oslo 1970; 3rd printing 1975) p. 192 *et seq*.

8 See, *e.g.*, the German *Insolvenzordnung* (InsO), 1994 (BGBl. I p. 2866), sec. 43-44.

9 "For everyone who has will be given more ..." (Matthew 25:29, New International Version).

10 Joint tortfeasors are jointly and severally liable; see Norwegian Act No. 26/1969 on Compensation for Torts (Torts Act), Sec. 5-3.

In the following, the rule on dividends in bankruptcy in respect of joint and several liabilities will be discussed in its Norwegian version.

2 Satisfaction of Claims Act – the basic rules

The main rule concerning the dividends in the bankruptcy estate of one of a number of co-debtors is the Satisfaction of Claims Act, 1984, Sec. 8-7:[11]

> Sec. 8-7 Right to dividends in cases of joint and several liability
> If a number of debtors are jointly and severally liable, the right of the creditor to dividends from the bankruptcy estate of the debtor shall not be reduced by:
> 1) part payments from a co-debtor who had the right to reclaim what was paid from the debtor
> 2) part payments by dividends from the estate of a co-debtor
> 3) part payments that the creditor has received from a co-debtor later than three months before the date of the filing for bankruptcy.[12]
>
> However, the part payment does not reduce the right of the creditor to dividends to the extent that the co-debtor has got satisfaction for his or her recourse claim from the debtor, provided that the satisfaction is not void in bankruptcy.

The section contains two distinct rules, one expressed in number 1 and one in numbers 2 and 3. The similarity between the two rules is that they both concern the calculation of dividends when the debtor in bankruptcy has co-debtors.

Nos. 2 and 3 are relevant in this context because they list instances when the creditor with more than one debtor gets a greater share. No. 1 is irrelevant, because it is a rule on distribution of the dividends attributable to a claim, without putting the creditor of that claim in a more favorable position than others. This calls for some further explanation.

No. 1 deals with the situation when the co-debtor of the bankrupt party has a recourse claim against him for what he has paid. Typically, this is so when the co-debtor is a surety. Whatever the surety pays the creditor can be claimed back

11 Translated by the author.

12 Literally, "time limit day" (for calculating time limits in connection with the bankruptcy); see the definition in the Satisfaction of Claims Act, ch. 1.

from the bankrupt, the main debtor. Such co-debtors will be referred to as sureties in the following.

In such cases, it is clear that dividends are not payable both on the basis of the claim of the main creditor and the basis of the recourse claim of the surety. The surety shall have no dividends unless the creditor has been satisfied in full. This follows from an express provision of the Satisfaction of Claims Act, Sec. 8-9. If the bankrupt debtor owes 100, dividends are to be calculated on the basis of 100, even if there is also a potential recourse claim for the same amount from the surety. This is an exception from the main rule that the potential recourse claim shall qualify as a bankruptcy claim.[13]

The Satisfaction of Claims Act Sec. 8-7 No. 1 is just a reflection of this principle: when the surety makes a part payment, his claim for dividends for the recourse claim would increase as much as the main creditor's claim for dividends would diminish had the part payment not been ignored. Because the main creditor is to be granted priority over the surety, it is better to let the claim for dividends remain with the main creditor.

The other creditors are not affected by this. Even if there is a surety, dividends will be paid on the basis of the claim only once.

This is different in respect of the Satisfaction of Claims Act, Sec. 8-7 **Nos. 2 and 3**. In these cases, dividends are payable by more than the outstanding amount. While the main rule is that dividends are payable on the basis of the outstanding amount at the commencement of the bankruptcy less subsequent payments,[14] Nos. 2 and 3 make exceptions to this:

- No. 2 provides that payments in the form of dividends from a co-debtor (that is, typically, when the co-debtor is bankrupt as well) shall be ignored, even if the basis for calculation of dividends in "our" bankruptcy then will be higher than the unpaid debt at the commencement of the bankruptcy and later.
- No. 3 extends this rule to apply even to payments not by dividends, if the payments are made just before the bankruptcy or during the bankruptcy period. (Also the period after the filing for bankruptcy and the commencement of it are "later than three months before the date of the filing for bankruptcy".)

---

13 Satisfaction of Claims Act, ch. 6.

14 *Ibid.*

The rules in Nos. 2 and 3 mean that the creditor with co-debtors can get more than his share of the dividends; he can get dividends on the basis of more than his actual claim. This is the rule that shall be further discussed in the following, and it will be referred to as the **part payment rule**.

The situations addressed in No. 1 – part payment by sureties – will not be addressed in the following. It is perhaps worth mentioning that one of the situations that will be discussed, as Nos. 2 and 3 apply, is when the issue is whether a part payment *by the main debtor* is relevant for the calculation of dividends in the *bankruptcy of the surety*. The main debtor has no recourse to the surety, so that No. 1 does not apply.

3 The traditional rationale for the part payment rule

In the following, the rationale for the part payment rule, as outlined above, will be discussed. Initially, we assume that all co-debtors are bankrupt.

3.1 The information problem

The rule that payments made from the bankruptcy estate of one co-debtor do not have to be taken into account in the bankruptcy estates of the others is obviously convenient for the trustees in bankruptcy.[15] Indeed, the problems of keeping track of what other trustees did may have sufficed to justify the part payment rule in the 19th century, when it was established in the Norwegian courts.[16] Today, however, the situation is different. Information about each bankruptcy estate is available on the Internet,[17] and electronic communication makes updating easy. The information problem can no longer justify the part payment rule.

3.2 The recalculation problem

Without the part payment rule, a trustee in bankruptcy may have to recalculate the dividends when a part payment is made from the estate of a co-debtor. This

15 Brækhus (1970) p. 225.

16 Rt. 1851.817 (which however relates to a part payment by a debtor with a right of recourse).

17 See Konkursregisteret <http://www.brreg.no/registrene/konkurs/>.

may have been a problem at the time when the part payment rule was established, because recalculation meant new, endless columns filled in with pen and ink. The need to avoid such exercises could in itself suffice to justify the rule.

I am not sure that this ever has been true. There are often some movements in the claims for other reasons than part payment, for example, because the losses of claimants who claim compensation are ascertained. Thus, the part payment rule cannot entirely eliminate the recalculation problem.

But again, the technology has in any event changed the premises. The invention of the spreadsheet – which has been in general use for less than a decade – has made recalculation an easy task. Even deductions for advance payments to creditors calculated on the basis of the old rate can be easily managed in a spreadsheet. The recalculation problem is no longer a problem that can justify the part payment rule.

3.3 Dependent dividends and the delay problem

A more complicated problem which can be avoided by the part payment rule concerns the interdependency of the dividends in the bankruptcies of co-debtors. Whatever is payable from one of the bankruptcy estates influences what is payable from the other, and *vice versa*.

There are two strategies to deal with this problem other than the part payment rule. The issue is whether the disadvantages of these strategies can justify that some creditors get more than their proportional share by means of the part payment rule.

The first strategy is to attempt to calculate the dividends in each bankruptcy estate taking into account the proceeds from the bankruptcies of the co-debtors. Can the problems of this strategy justify the part payment rule?

We name the following parameters in a situation with two co-debtors and one claim for which they are jointly and severally liable:

	Estate of co-debtor 1	Estate of co-debtor 2
Assets	A	a
Debts except the joint liability	D	d
Joint and several liability	J	
Dividends expressed as a fraction	X	y

In that case, the dividends in the two estates could be determined by resolving the following system of equations: [18]

$$A=DX+JX(1-y)$$
$$a=dy+Jy(1-X)$$

This would perhaps be manageable. But the complexity increases drastically if there are a number of joint and several liabilities with different sets of co-debtors, and perhaps also more than two co-debtors for each of these liabilities. In addition, practical problems arise if one does not have the full overview of all the involved estates simultaneously, which would typically be the case if one bankruptcy is opened long after the others. Thus, the final payment from the bankruptcies first opened could be delayed.[19]

The practical problems and complexity of this strategy make it unattractive in its pure form; so unattractive that it could warrant a preference for the part payment rule. However, there is a question as to whether this mathematical approach is too ambitious. Rather than giving some creditors too much because one cannot easily calculate the exact dividends, one could open up for more pragmatic solutions for determining the dividends on an estimate basis, either on the basis of rougher formulas than equations such as those above or on the basis of a competence *ex lege* for trustees in bankruptcy to make agreements of this type.

18 The equations are taken from Brækhus (1970) p. 224.

19 There are liberal rules for advance payment in Norwegian law that would take care of the substantive parts of the payments; see Norwegian Act No. 58/1984 relating to Bankruptcy (Bankruptcy Act), ch. XV.

The alternative strategy would be to calculate the dividends on the basis of payments actually received from the estates of co-debtors. The calculations would then be easy. However, this would have the unfortunate effect that the creditors of the co-debtor whose estate made the later payment would end up with an advantage. Without the part payment rule, they would not have to pay dividends from the part of the debt paid in the first bankruptcy.

This incentive to delay could be unfortunate. It could again motivate the creditors in all the co-debtors' bankruptcies to slow down the process and postpone payments and the finalization of the bankruptcy. The part payment rule would remove this incentive.

3.4 Extension of the delay principle

The prevailing idea behind the part payment rule in current Norwegian bankruptcy law has been to remove the incentives to slow down bankruptcy proceedings.[20] Quite logically this has led to an extension of the rule.

Thus, there is no requirement that all co-debtors shall be bankrupt at the same time, or even that the bankruptcy of the other co-debtors shall be formalized. All payments from co-debtors are subject to the part payment rule, even if the payment has been made after a composition agreement among creditors or in proceedings which are finalized long before the opening of the bankruptcy in which the issue of the application of the part payment rule arises. All "part payments by dividends" are subject to the rule.[21]

The idea is that, had the part payment rule not applied here, the creditors of the co-debtor claimed first would have a motive to instigate a formal bankruptcy running simultaneously with that of other co-debtors. This could be a disincentive to the fast and smooth finalization of the insolvency dealings in respect of the first co-debtor.

In this way, the delay principle is the main rationale behind the rule in the Satisfaction of Claims Act, Sec. 8-7 No. 2, applying the part payment rule in simultaneous as well as successive bankruptcy proceedings, and in formal as well as informal creditor settlements.

20 Brækhus (1970) p. 226.

21 Satisfaction of Claims Act, Sec. 8-7.

3.5 Order for payment should not be of consequence

In the extension of the delay principle, it has been submitted that it is unfair that the position of the creditor with co-debtors is influenced by a random event such as the order of payment from the two bankruptcy estates.[22] For my part, I am not sure whether it is a bad thing that also random events have certain legal effects, and there are certainly several examples of this. But whatever the case may be, I feel it is difficult to use this anomaly to justify creating yet another, that is, to give creditors with two debtors more than their pro rate share. One anomaly is hardly better than the other.

3.6 Facilitation of part payment

The extension of the part payment rule in the Satisfaction of Claims Act, Sec. 8-7 No. 3 is motivated by a desire to facilitate part payments.[23] If the part payment is in the form of dividends, the part payment rule follows from No. 2, which is discussed separately. The point of No. 3 is therefore to facilitate part payment from a solvent co-debtor.

If the part payment rule did not apply to such payments, it would hardly matter: without the part payment rule, the creditor may perhaps have a certain desire to delay the payment from co-debtor A until after the opening of the bankruptcy in the estate of co-debtor B, which he may see coming. In that way, the part payment rule would apply, and he would get more dividends from the estate of co-debtor B.

However, if the creditor first foresees the bankruptcy of one co-debtor, he would be foolish not to accept whatever he can get from another.[24] Applying the part payment rule to part payments from a solvent co-debtor in the period just prior to the bankruptcy of another therefore does not speed up things, and therefore does not make much sense.

Legally, the creditor may refuse part payment in these cases.[25] But my point is that he most likely would not wish to refuse a safe part payment for the unsafe

---

22 Brækhus (1970) p. 225.

23 NOU 1972: 20 *Gjeldsforhandling og konkurs (Debt Settlement Proceedings and Bankruptcy)*, Oslo 1972, p. 337.

24 Brækhus (1970) p. 226.

25 Viggo Hagstrøm, *Obligasjonsrett,* Oslo 2003, p. 198.

prospects of a later part payment and an even unsafer prospect of marginally higher dividends in the co-debtor's bankruptcy. In any event, if the legal right to refuse part payment is a problem, then perhaps this rule should be altered rather than extending the part payment rule to these situations.

4 A closer look at the delay problem

After having had a look at the traditional rationale for the part payment rule, I will now have a closer look at the delay problem. As we have seen, this was the idea behind the Satisfaction of Claims Act, Sec. 8-7 No. 2. The quintessence was that the part payment rule should remove an incentive to delay in insolvency dealings. But how sound is this rationale?

There are several situations where one can do just as well without the part payment rule, because it is unlikely that delay will be caused in any event.

Obviously, this is the case when dividends are (expected to be) low. In these cases, all creditors would just like to get it over with, and will not bother to cause delay in order to get a marginal increase of dividends.

It is likely that dividends must be quite substantial in order to motivate actions that can cause delay. This is so because the delay is costly for the creditors, too, because more administrative costs will be deducted from the estate[26] and because for all practical purposes, no interest is accrued in the course of the insolvency proceedings.[27]

Low dividends are quite common. However, it also happens that dividends are high enough to be an incentive for creditors to cause delay.[28] In these cases, however, another mechanism may come into play: the creditor with co-debtors may have a motive and sufficient influence to prevent delay.

The creditor has a **motive** to prevent delay if there is a significant difference between the expected dividends in the estates of the co-debtors. In these cases, he would (without the part payment rule) prefer that payments were first made

---

26 Satisfaction of Claims Act, Sec. 9-2.

27 *Ibid.*, Sec. 9-7.

28 Konkursrådet, *Konkursbobehandling – Resultater og myter (Estate Bankruptcy Administration – Results and Myths)*, 2 October 2000, <http://www.konkursradet.no/Nyheter/Konkursbobehandling-Resultater-og-myter-173/#soketreff>.

from the estate with the greater dividends expectation (co-debtor A), and not in the estate with the lower dividends expectation (co-debtor B). He must make sure that the highest percentage of dividends is applied to the highest claim, which is the claim in the first bankruptcy.

Although this is quite straightforward in principle, the picture can be somewhat blurred if A and B's creditor also has other claims in the estate with the higher dividends expectation (co-debtor A). Whatever that creditor loses on the claim for which A and B are jointly and severally liable, if payments from the estates are made in the wrong order, might be able to be recovered because of the increase in the dividends from estate A that follows. This may be the case if the creditor's claims solely against debtor A are greater than the claim he has against A and B severally as well as the claims of other creditors in estate A.

This mechanism is quite plain: whatever the creditor gains or loses on his claim against the co-debtors, because of the order of payment from the estates, has to be paid to or covered by the other claims in that estate. If the creditor of A and B has a large part of these other claims, the creditor, for example a bank, had better concentrate on getting the most out of these rather than on the claim against A and B.

Whatever the case may be, the creditor of A and B may very well see that his interests are better served by payments from the estate of co-debtor A first and from the estate of co-debtor B thereafter, or *vice versa.* In that case he will have a motive to break the deadlock situation in which all creditors want all payments to be the last. If he has the influence to make things happen accordingly, the part payment rule will not be needed in these cases.

Whether the **influence** of A and B's creditor is sufficiently strong to determine the order of payment for the estates of co-debtors A and B depends to some extent on negotiation skills and initiative. His voting power in the estates, however, is also significant. A majority creditor may very well influence the way the proceedings are handled.[29]

In this case, it is the relative strength that matters: What is the sum of this creditor's claims compared to the sum of the other creditors' claims? If the dividends are so high that it is worthwhile to influence the handling of the bankruptcy estate – as is the assumption here – the creditor can still have considerable relative strength if the assets are great. Again, one has to count the claim the

---

29 Voting power is by the amount of the claim; see Bankruptcy Act, Sec. 96.

creditor has against the co-debtors A and B together with the claim he has against A and B separately in their respective estates.

Altogether, the situations may vary. But it is likely that in a number of situations, one of the creditors has both the motive and the influence to make sure that one of the bankruptcy estates pays out before the other. In this way, the delay deadlock can be broken without the part payment rule.

5 Conclusion

The part payment rule is complicated, and the alleged rationale offered for it is even more complicated. Even worse, some of the rationale does not stand up to scrutiny.

To a certain extent the part payment rule can still be justified by the need to avoid incentives that make creditors delay bankruptcy proceedings. This may – or may not – be sufficient to justify such a complex rule, which departs from the *pro rata* principle in bankruptcy. We have, however, seen that even this justification has a very limited sphere of application. It is not relevant when the dividends are low or the creditor with co-debtors has a motive and the influence to prevent the delay. For my part, I do not think the very few remaining situations in which there is a possibility for delay can justify the rule.

More than Meets the Eye

Law and Economics in Modern Company Law

Beate Sjåfjell[1]

The Position of Law and Economics in Modern Company Law

The Significance of Law and Economics

Law and economics, or legal-economics, is the field of science that introduces economic theory into legal theory and enriches them both: "Legal economics may be characterized as applied economics, but applied legal economics is law".[2] The rise of law and economics within company law[3] is significant in at least three ways. Firstly, law and economics may contribute to the structuring of analytical issues and provide valuable insights both through theoretical contributions and empirical studies. Secondly, company law legislation and academic debate are increasingly based on legal-economic theory or at least sought substantiated with reference to legal-economic terms.[4] Thirdly, and accordingly, the legal-economic assumptions that form the basis for legislation and for positions in the academic debate need to assessed.

---

1 I am grateful to Erik Røsæg and Endre Stavang for each in their own way introducing me years ago to law and economics, to Erling Eide for his patient guidance in the early days and to Jukka Mähönen for being an inspiring discussion partner. My thanks also to Erling Hjelmeng, for his reflections on the significance of the alternative analytical structure presented here. The usual disclaimer applies.

2 Eide and Stavang (2008) p. 606 (translated by the current author).

3 See Hopt (2006) pp. 1184–1186.

4 See also Mähönen (2009).

This article concentrates on the first topic: the use of law and economics to structure a legal analysis.[5]

The Perceived Limitation of Law and Economics

Legal-economics is often perceived today as identical with only one or a very limited number of legal-economic theories and is understood as not only descriptive theories but also as normative imperatives.[6] A discussion of whether shareholder primacy is a suitable guideline for law-making in the regulation of companies, or of whether shareholder profit maximization is a good guideline for decision-making in companies, is therefore often seen as a debate for and against law and economics. The contribution of legal economics in vital legal debates is thereby unduly limited. The fact that legal-economists themselves are much to blame for this too narrow perception of the field is acknowledged by the authors of *The Anatomy of Corporate Law,* who use *functional* rather than *economic* in their title, to avoid association with

> . . . the sometimes tendentious use of economic argumentation to support particular (generally laissez-faire) policy positions, as well as the tendency in economic analysis to neglect non-pecuniary motivations or assume an unrealistic degree of rationality in human action.[7]

This limitation needs to be addressed on two grounds. Firstly, there are a number of legal economic theories relevant to company law beyond that of agency theory.[8] Secondly, it is perfectly possible to discuss and even apply legal economics with agency theory as the starting point, without taking the normative standpoint that shareholders should be given primacy.[9] As agency theory is regarded as the dominant mainstream legal-economic theory in company law, an illustration of this may

5 As concerns the second and third aspect, a critical perspective on the mainstream use of law and economics forms an integrated aspect in the analysis of the underlying issues and legislative objectives of EU company and securities law in Sjåfjell (2009) Parts II–III.

6 See also ibid. Sect. 3.2.3.

7 Kraakman et al. (2009), p. 4.

8 See e.g. Blair and Stout (1999), pp. 247–328.

9 The discussion in *The Anatomy of Corporate Law* illustrates this, although their conclusions tend to be in favour of shareholder primacy.

be of interest in the general company law debate. *The Anatomy of Corporate Law* has deservedly received acclaim for the insightful and thought-provoking structuring of company law issues in a cross-jurisdictional perspective. It is therefore a privilege to have this opportunity to confront the overly shareholder-focused perspective of *The Anatomy*, and use the book as a basis for showing that an alternative structure is possible to develop. After a brief introduction of agency theory and *The Anatomy's* shareholder focus, I will show how an alternative analytical structure may be developed based on the principles of agency theory.[10]

Agency Theory and the Dominant Shareholder Focus

Agency Theory in a Nutshell

The two important keywords for understanding the basics of agency theory are information and incentives.[11] A crucial element of agency theory is the costs incurred as a result of the agent/principal relationship. From the perspective of company law, the persons actually controlling the company – whether this is the day-to-day management, the directors of the board or a large and active shareholder – can be seen as agents for other parties that are affected by the actions of the firm. These other parties – the principals – may, for example, be the (other) employees at the firm, or the (other) shareholders of the firm, who are affected by the agent's decision. The principal may not have the same information as the agent, and may be unable to monitor the agent's actions without incurring excessive costs, and must therefore try to find the right incentives to make the agent act in the principal's interest. Or, from a legislator's point of view, someone else might consider finding or creating those incentives. The description of legal strategies in *The Anatomy* aims to cover the options at the legislature's disposal when dealing with agency issues.[12]

---

10 This is based on the more extensive discussion in Sjåfjell (2009) Part IV, where I developed the analytical tool that I used in Part V for an analysis of the Directive 2004/25/EC on takeover bids (OJ 2004 L 142/12–23, the Takeover Directive).

11 Pratt and Zeckhauser (1991) p. 1.

12 See the overview of the main legal strategies (sub-divided into regulatory and governance strategies) that the legislature has at its disposal to handle conflicts of interests (denoted "agency issues" in the terminology of *The Anatomy*), Kraakman et al. (2009) pp. 37–45.

Agency issues in company law are the conflicts of interests that exist in this area. One of the functions of company law is the regulation of such conflicts to the extent deemed necessary. Agency theory offers a way to identify and understand these conflicts of interest and the mechanisms that govern them. Agency theory may therefore help us to discern the effects of any given regulatory effort (including deregulation). To explain agency theory from another angle relevant to company law, it can be seen as an attempt to structure the discussion of two fundamental questions: Who makes the decisions? What are the costs (or, more broadly, the consequences)? Analysis of the agency problem may pinpoint who is dependent on whose decision, which will in turn indicate who is in a position to exploit or take advantage of whom (i.e. to put their own interests ahead of others'). It may also shed light on the costs of trying to alleviate or hinder such potential negative effects.

The costs of these alternative methods are known as agency costs. The term costs does not (necessarily) mean that money is directly involved, it means costs in the broadest sense of the word; consider, for instance, the situation where a board of directors is checking on managers at all times to make sure they are acting in accordance with directives from the board. Nor does the term imply that a figure has to be attributed to the cost – often we will not have the information required to do this, so we must try intuitively to assess whether the costs, or more generally the disadvantages, are, for example, excessive, tolerable or negligible.

Agency costs can be divided into three main categories: the expense of monitoring the agent; so-called bonding expenses (simply put, expenses incurred, typically by the agent, through actions that aim to satisfy the principal's need to know, e.g. obtaining external auditing); and the loss that the principal suffers due to the divergence between the agent's and the principal's interests.[13] The lower the costs, the better the result for all involved. In complex relationships, the trade-offs between the different agency issues must be considered. To identify the principals and the agents, we apply a mix of common sense, factual and legal information and an analytical mind.[14]

---

13 Jensen and Meckling (1976), pp. 305–360 pp. 308 and 339–339.

14 See for a further down-to-earth explanation, Posner (2000).

The Dominant Shareholder Focus

Early work on agency theory within company law concentrated on a single agency issue, that is, the shareholders (as principals) vs. the managers (as agents).[15] The modern version of agency theory, as set out notably in *The Anatomy of Corporate Law,* takes in other parties and also describes other conflicts of interest (agency issues). However, from a wider perspective, which recognizes a complexity of involved parties and affected interests in company law,[16] we see that also the approach of *The Anatomy* is overly restricted to the shareholders. The three general agency issues in company law described by *The Anatomy* are the "firm's owners" (i.e. the shareholders) vs. "hired managers"; controlling vs. non-controlling "owners"; and "the firm itself – including, particularly, its owners" vs. contractual parties, referred to otherwise in the book as non-shareholders.[17] Although *The Anatomy* seems to indicate quite a wide interpretation of the term "non-shareholder" in its description of the normative goal of company law,[18] the discussion of "non-shareholders" in the substantive chapters of the book is mainly limited to creditors and employees, and the general focus seems to be on the shareholders' interests. In the chapter on control transactions, for example, three issues, roughly speaking, are discussed: two main issues encompassing agency issues between target shareholders and board, controlling and non-controlling target shareholders, and bidder and (especially the non-controlling) minority target shareholders, with the focus consistently on the interests of the target shareholders, and one minor issue, namely that of the protection of the "non-shareholders".[19]

The combination of calling shareholders "owners"[20] and, rather symptomati-

---

15 Although other agency issues than that of shareholder-manager were recognised; Jensen and Meckling (1976) on p. 310: "Contractual relations are the essence of the firm, not only with employees but with suppliers, customers, creditors, etc. The problem of agency costs (…) exists for all of these contracts (…)".

16 See Sjåfjell (2009) Ch. 3 and 4.

17 Kraakman et al. (2009) p. 35 and *inter alia* p. 89.

18 Employees, creditors and customers ("contractual parties") according to ibid. p. 35, and in the discussion of the normative goals of company law, even recognising the interests of "local communities and beneficiaries of the natural environment", see p. 28.

19 Ibid. Ch. 8.

20 On the positive side, the authors define what they mean by referring to the shareholders as owners, see ibid. p. 14: "There are two key elements in the ownership of a firm, as we use the term 'ownership' here: the right to control the firm, and the right to receive the firm's net earnings." For a discussion of the ownership term, see Sjåfjell (2009) Sect. 3.3.3 and 4.3.4.3.

cally for the focus of the discussion, using the term non-shareholders for everybody but shareholders (and managers), as well as a tendency to identify the company with the shareholders,[21] sets the stage for an analysis that is too narrow in its focus.

An inherent limitation in the agency theory's structure, whereby conflicts of interest are paired, seems to be a lack of an overall assessment of the trade-offs between the various issues.[22]

Further, the structural diversity allowed for in modern agency theory seems limited to a differentiation between dispersed shareholdings and block-held shareholdings, depicted as the Anglo-American and European models respectively. Basing the analytical tool solely on a differentiation as to whether the shareholding is dispersed or block-held is illustrative of the tendency of the agency theory (as depicted in *The Anatomy*) to focus strongly on shareholders. Even with a primary focus on shareholders, there may be reason to question whether this is really a satisfactory basis for considering the real-life variety of control structures.[23]

An Alternative Analytical Structure

The Company, Involved Parties and Affected Interests

The starting point for the structure here is a perception of the relationship between the company itself, its involved parties and affected interests, that takes the company as a real-life entity as a starting point.[24] This gives us three

21 As illustrated by this quote: "the firm itself – including, particularly, its owners", Kraakman et al. (2009) p. 35.

22 The significance of considering the trade-offs is also pointed out in Kraakman et al. (2004) p. 223.

23 Of which an overview is given in Sjåfjell (2009) Sect. 12.4. Considering the goal of Kraakman et al. (2009), which is to present an analytical tool for a very wide range of subjects in an "international", "functional" and "short" manner, the limitation as to control structures is nevertheless understandable – albeit that the focus on shareholders may clash somewhat with their fourth aim of doing this in a "neutral" manner (all quotes from the Preface to *The Anatomy of Corporate Law*).

24 Sjåfjell (2009), Ch. 4, bearing in mind the variety of European control structures indicated in Sect. 12.4.

sets of potential conflicts of interests,[25] which are of a general, company law nature.

The first set of potential conflicts of interest lies within the company. I have defined the groups within the company as the employees, including top management, and the board.[26]

The second set concerns the company's relationship with, and the relationships between, contractual parties. Contractual parties are here defined as being all parties outside the company but having some kind of contractual relationship – in the wide sense of the term – with it. This group includes customers (whether ordinary shop customers, patients or clients), retailers, suppliers, banks, bondholders and other creditors, as well as shareholders and, possibly, local or national authorities.[27]

The third set concerns other affected interests, notably the local communities and the objective of global sustainable development.[28] Although the extent to which other affected interests are recognised as relevant in a company law setting will vary, this third set is important to include. This is based on the aggregated economic, environmental and social significance of companies, which renders societal attempts to deal with environmental, societal or human rights issues insufficient without the willing, or compulsory, collaboration of companies.[29] The recognition that there may be a conflict between these societal interests and hard-core company interests is then necessary for a debate on the way forward.

As this analytical structure originally was developed with the analysis of the Takeover Directive in mind, a fourth set, particular to takeovers, is included. This involves the potential acquirer directly and describes potential conflicts of interest between the acquirer and the other groups.

25 Just as the term "agent" in agency theory is not meant to invoke thoughts of the law of agency, the term "conflicts of interests" is not to be understood in the legal sense as, for example, a situation whereby a person is disqualified from holding a position because of a "conflict of interest". Rather it is used synonymously with "agency issue", namely, that there is a potential for conflicting interests where a person, group or entity is in a position to affect other persons, entities or interests.

26 Sjåfjell (2009) Sect. 4.2.

27 Ibid. Sect. 4.3.

28 Ibid. Sect. 4.4.

29 The extent to which this responsibility follows from enforceable law, soft law, social norms, etc. will obviously vary between jurisdictions and – not least – across time. Concerning the status in EU law, see ibid. Ch. 10 and 11.

Based on all the potential conflicts of interest within the above-mentioned sets, a selection of analytical issues was made that formed the structure of the analysis and evaluation of the Takeover Directive. Some of the issues described in the systematic overview below were combined in the final selection. The alternative to combining several issues concerning conflicts of interest would be to assess a larger number of separate conflicts – paired together as in agency theory. The formulation of larger analytical issues in the final selection was intended to overcome the limitation inherent in this system of pairing. This does not, however, remove the need for an overall assessment.[30]

Obviously there may also be potential conflicts of interest within any of the groups mentioned below, such as the board, the employees or the creditors. If we are to create a manageable analytical structure, however, there is a limit as to how far we can go into such sub-issues. As a general rule, therefore, each group will be dealt with as being relatively homogenous, except where it is deemed necessary to differentiate, for example, between controlling and non-controlling shareholders, or between board members representing different interests, although the heterogeneity within the groups will be indicated whenever especially relevant. This approach should not be perceived as one that ignores the potential of conflicts of interest within the individual groups, but merely as the inevitable consequence of constraints on time and space.

Conflicts of Interest Within the Company

Depending on the jurisdiction, the role of the board may be perceived as being either more or less shareholder-oriented. Even where the board's main task is seen as being the maximisation of shareholder profit, the board has to balance and consider the variety of interests involved in the running of the company.[31] It is in this light that the board in agency theory is seen as an organ that deals not only with the original agency issue – that of shareholders vs. managers, but also with those of controlling shareholders vs. non-controlling shareholders and the com-

30 Which was carried out at the end of ibid. Part V.

31 See, *inter alia,* Hertig (2005), pp. 269–282 p. 270 describing the board's "multiple functions: crisis management, regulatory compliance, management monitoring, strategy setting, and mediation of conflicts of interests".

pany vs., for example, its creditors and employees.[32] The board must – in any jurisdiction – ensure that the company is well run, that its contractual and legal obligations are met and that its future is ensured.[33] The focus on shareholder profit, which to a large extent is more a matter of culture and market pressure than a matter of law, is just one aspect of what the board has to consider.[34]

The complex and unique position of the board, as the organ whose sole function is to ensure that the company is properly run, taking into account all involved parties and affected interests, gives rise to the issue of the potential for conflicts of interest within the board itself. Even in boards with an apparently homogenous composition, the priorities of the individual members may differ, even though they are offered the same incentives. Individual board members may react differently to so-called high-powered pecuniary incentives and so-called low-powered non-pecuniary incentives (moral standards, reputation and professional pride) which will not necessarily always lead different people to take the same actions.[35] On the other hand, the psychological mechanisms that operate in a group working together may unite an apparently divided group.[36] But if the divisions between groups of board members are too strong, the real deliberations and decision-making may (to the greatest extent possible) take place outside formal meetings.

Top management has to execute the guidelines and decisions of the board and seek its advice. The composition and functioning of the board may strongly influence its relationship with top management. Where the board has a high proportion of members independent of the management and where it focuses strongly on its monitoring role, the quality of its advice to management may suffer, both through a lack of insider knowledge and because the management's fears of the board's monitoring role may make it reticent in providing the information

32 As indicated by Kraakman et al. (2009) p. 14, and discussed further in Ch. 3 and 4.

33 Or to take the relevant steps if the company is deemed not to have a future.

34 Overview and discussion in Sjåfjell (2009) Part II, notably Sect. 4.2.2.

35 The use of the terms "high-powered" and "low-powered" incentives is inspired by Kraakman et al. (2009) p. 43.

36 Even so far as to represent a problem for the fulfilment of the role of the board: "The most significant group bias for our purposes, however, is the 'groupthink' phenomenon. Highly cohesive groups with strong civility and cooperation norms value consensus more than they do a realistic appraisal of alternatives", Bainbridge (2002), pp. 1–55 p. 32.

the board needs to give good advice.[37] On the other hand, if there are very close ties between board and management, the board's advice may be better informed, while its monitoring role may suffer.

The job of the employees in general is to follow up and execute the directives of the board, as conveyed by the top management. Of course, the employees as a group may not be homogenous in their interests either: they may have diverging priorities based on their individual situations and future prospects and wishes.

There may be several potential conflicts of interest between the groups within the company. The directors of the board and top management may pursue priorities that differ from those of the rank-and-file employees, concentrating on showing good results for the company as opposed to job safety or relocation rather than keeping the company in the same area (although top management may side with the other employees on both of these issues, rather than with the board). The employees (including or excluding top management) may be more interested in having an easy time at work than in achieving the best results for the company. Top management may be more interested in procuring benefits for themselves than carrying out the directives of the board. The situation may also be reversed, with employees, including top management, diligently and loyally working in the company's best interests, while board members shirk their responsibilities and focus on the social status of board membership and the pecuniary benefits.

In the context of a takeover, the directors of the board, the top management and the rest of the employees could all be on the same side – all afraid of losing their positions if the takeover is successful. However, there are potential conflicts of interest: the positions of the board directors and top management may be in danger if there is a takeover, while the job security of (most) rank-and-file employees may be unaffected. It may even be that a takeover and a new, improved board and top management are deemed necessary to save the company and secure jobs. This kind of potential conflict in the takeover process could also take the form of top management securing themselves golden parachutes, leaving the rest of the employees to face possible restructurings, or even shut-downs, without any company-provided safety net. These potentials for conflict of interest within the company in a takeover situation may be split into three issues: whether the board (and top management) will take care of the interests of the company itself (as in

37 Adams and Ferreira (2007), pp. 217–250.

the interests of the enterprise);[38] whether (and in what manner) the board will take care of the interests of all the employees; and whether the top management will take care of the interests of the rest of the employees.

Conflicts of Interest Involving Contractual Parties

The company may have other interests (the continued life and development of the company and, from the perspective of those within the company, staying in the same location, high wages or fees, job-related perks, etc.) than prioritizing the best interests of its contractual parties (be that high-risk maximization of profits or merely having its obligations met on a regular basis). Of course, seen from the other side, there may be a conflict between the interests of the contractual parties and those of the company: the contractual parties may be more interested in short-term profit and less in the continued life of the company and wage increases for its employees, etc., while, in the case of long-term contractors, the interests may – but not necessarily always – be aligned.[39]

With regard to all issues, the company (i.e. the people within it: the board and the employees, including top management) may not necessarily be of one mind. We could therefore further sub-divide the conflicts of interest, with one subset consisting of conflicts between the board and the different groups of contractual parties, a second subset of those between the top management and the different groups of contractual parties, and the third of those between the rank-and-file employees and the different contractual parties. This will be done where necessary in our context but, as a starting point, we will here deal with the potential conflicts of interest as between the company as a whole, on the one hand, and the contractual parties, on the other.

In the context of a takeover, these issues may come to a head in several ways. Significantly, there may be a conflict of interest between the company and the shareholders of the company, as the shareholders may be more interested in making a profit by accepting the takeover bid than in taking care of the long-term

38 On the interests of the company, see Sjåfjell (2009) Sect. 4.2.2.3 and 5.2.2, and in the context of the directive, Sect. 16.3.1.

39 Recent history has amply illustrated the danger of attempting to mitigate the conflicts of interests between shareholders and board and management by aligning their incentives through option packages: Hill (2004) p. 266.

interests of the company. On the other hand – with regard to those shareholders who choose not sell to the acquirer – the shareholders may welcome an acquirer with plans to replace the board and top management and restructure, and possibly to relocate the company, while the board, the management and the employees may prioritize (apparent) security above change. In such a case, it may be the shareholders who attend to the company interest, in the sense of the interest of the enterprise. These potential conflicts may take on different forms depending on the shareholding structure – whether we are dealing with a totally dispersed shareholding (typically associated with the US, but also characteristic of individual European companies), the multiple block-holding structure typical in the UK, or the typical Continental European block-holding structure with one large shareholder, and on further considerations to do with the control structure and the actual decisional power of the shareholders, other involved parties and the board and management.

Two issues arise here: firstly, whether the board and/or the top management take the shareholder interests into account (to the extent the board/management are in a position to influence the takeover process) and secondly, whether the target shareholders (indirectly) take care of the interests of the company, including the employees.

Not all conflicts of interest within the scope of company and securities law directly involve the company, as defined above, especially not in a takeover situation, as the company itself is normally not a party to the control transaction(s). One issue of interest that is particularly relevant to a takeover is the potential conflict of interest between those shareholders with a majority or otherwise controlling holding, and the rest of the shareholders (the minority or otherwise non-controlling shareholders). Another issue is the potential for conflicts between the controlling shareholder(s) and other contractual parties.[40] Conflicts may also arise between contractual parties that are part shareholders and part debtholders and the "ordinary" shareholders, as well as between diversified institutional investors and shareholders who have all their investments in the shares of the one company. The latter may, for example, oppose a takeover or be in favour of a mandatory bid rule, while the former may be in favour of takeovers and against measures such as the mandatory bid rule, as this may prevent takeovers from taking place.

---

40 See e.g. the potential conflict between shareholders and bondholders, Cremers et al. (2007), pp. 1359–1388.

In a takeover situation, the target shareholders (or some of them) will be the recipients of the takeover bid, and therefore in a position to influence whether the takeover takes place (and, at least indirectly, on what terms). The actions of the target shareholders may affect the positions of the other contractual parties. Likewise, shareholders with controlling holdings may be in a position to affect the other shareholders.

Conflicts of Interest Involving Other Affected Interests

There is a potential conflict of interest between the company and the local communities and global community interest, including the objectives of sustainable development and adherence to human rights. The relevance of this in an analysis of a piece of EU legislation, such as the Takeover Directive, follows from the general objectives of the EU: any piece of legislation in any sector should ultimately contribute to – or at the very least not work against – the objective of sustainable development and the other general objectives.[41]

In the context of a takeover, this issue arises in the form of a question of whether the company, specifically the board and top management, in its reaction to the takeover bid takes sufficient care of the interests affected by the company as described above. An issue for possible assessment is the effect of the board/management's actions on the company's possibilities to internalize its normative responsibility for the local and global community interest and the board/management's possibilities and ability to take these interests into account. This is also a question of the extent to which the board/management can influence the takeover process.

Especially relevant here are the potential conflicts of interest between the shareholders and the other affected interests described above. There may, of course, also be a potential conflict of interest between other contractual parties, suppliers, other sources of finance, customers, etc., and these affected interests, but the other contractual parties are not directly in a position to influence the affected interests to the same extent as the shareholders. Generally these other contractual parties may be in such a position, but in a takeover context it is the shareholders – as recipients of the bid and prospective parties, to the takeover – that are the most powerful amongst the contractual parties, except for perhaps in exceptional circumstances where another party controls the takeover situation.

41 Sjåfjell (2009) Ch. 11, especially Sect. 11.2.

An issue therefore is whether the target shareholders, who may have the final say as to whether the takeover attempt succeeds, are in a position to do so in such a way that the affected interests described above are taken into account, and if so, whether the target shareholders take advantage of that opportunity.

Conflicts of Interest Involving the Potential Acquirer in a Takeover

Further sets of takeover-related potential conflicts of interest could be set up between the target company and the acquiring company and, of course, the acquiring company will be the venue for conflicts of interest similar to those outlined above in respect of the target company. In addition, potential cross-company conflicts of interest could be set up between the different groups (e.g. shareholders of the acquiring company vs. employees of the target company, and vice versa). However, in view of constraints on time and space, the discussion of issues will focus solely on the target company, its contractual parties and affected interests.[42] The acquirer will therefore only come into the picture where it is party to a potential conflict of interest with one of the groups in one of the three main sets of potential conflicts as defined here. In such cases, it will simply be viewed as the acquirer, with no differentiation as to whether we are dealing with a person or a company – and, in the latter context, whether the main actor is the board, the managers, or a controlling shareholder. The acquirer, of course, may also come into any of the potential conflicts of interest described above as an additional party on one side.

The potential conflicts of interest involving the acquirer include conflicts between the acquirer and the target company, as well as between the acquirer and the various contractual parties, and the affected interests, respectively.

The potential conflicts of interest between the acquirer and the company should be split into two: one involving the employees, including the top management, and the other involving the board of directors, as the board is meant to take all involved parties and affected interests into account.

There is a general potential for conflict of interests between the acquirer and the target company's contractual parties. We shall here focus on the possibility of

42 The target company is also the focus of the Takeover Directive, for which this analytical structure was developed.

conflict with the target shareholders, as they are party to the control transaction, taking into account the variety of European control structures.[43]

Where the target shareholders do not have effective (actual) control, possibly because effective control is in the hands of the board/management or another party, the issue may be between the acquirer and the target shareholders as a group, with the acquirer possibly taking advantage of the shareholders' inability to act together. On the other hand, that may be just as much a problem for the acquirer; consider the "free-rider" problem, which may lead to all the small shareholders holding out for a better offer.[44] If control is in the hands of the board/management, there may also be an issue between the acquirer and the board and/or the top management of the target company on the one hand and the target shareholders on the other.[45]

Similarly, it may be envisaged that the acquirer enters into a deal with another party controlling the company – for example a bank, or other influential source of finance (or exceptionally, the state), and conflicts of interest may then arise between the acquirer and this other party on the one hand, and (the rest of) the target shareholders on the other.

If the control rests with a block-holder, or a coalition of block-holders, the issue may be between the acquirer and the block-holder(s) on the one hand and the rest of the shareholders on the other hand.[46] The first issue mentioned above, between the acquirer and the company, may, of course, then also appear as an issue between the acquirer and the block-holder(s) on the one hand and the company, especially the employees, on the other.

Furthermore there may be potential conflicts of interest between the acquirer and other interests affected by the target company, for example the local communities or the global community interest.

Selection of Analytical Issues for the Takeover Directive

Based on the above discussion of potential conflicts of interest, I made a selection of analytical issues for the analysis of the Takeover Directive. The selection is

43 Indicated in Sjåfjell (2009) Sect. 12.4.

44 Burkart and Panunzi (2006), pp. 12–14 with further references.

45 See also Kraakman et al. (2009) Sect. 8.2.5.

46 See also ibid. Sect. 8.3.

included here as a significant part of the illustration of the development of an alternative analytical structure. Other purposes would, to a larger or smaller extent, require a different selection of analytical issues.

Decisive for the selection for the analysis of the Takeover Directive was the inclusion of the most central issues with regard to practical importance and the objectives of EU takeover law, both as actually stated in the Takeover Directive and in the context of its underlying objectives as a segment of EU company and securities law, which in turn is a sector of general EU law.[47] Three main issues, which are a combination of several mentioned above, were selected on that basis. The focus is on three significant interests – the company, the shareholders and the global community interest – and the directive's effect on these interests through the effect the directive has on three primary actors in takeovers: the board, the shareholders and the acquirer.

The focus on the company was chosen because ensuring the proper functioning of the company is vital to the viability of companies – to companies' possibility of fulfilling their economic and their wider societal role. Linked to this is the choice of the first of the three primary actors, which is one of the groups within the company: the board, chosen because of the significance of protecting the board's possibility and ability to fulfil its role.

The selection of shareholders, out of all the company's contractual parties, was based on shareholders' position as the recipients of the bid and the necessity to address the belief in shareholder primacy and the market for corporate control theory as a driver for economic development. This is especially relevant to the Takeover Directive, and to EU company and securities law in general. Choosing the shareholders as the second primary actors will particularly address the efficiency argument that underlies part of the shareholder primacy debate – namely the idea that letting shareholders decide will be for the overall good of society.[48]

If the selection of shareholders was easy on the grounds just mentioned, the same cannot be said of the decision to exclude other sources of finance, their relative position in the company, and the relationship between them and the shareholders and all the issues that this gives rise to. This decision was made solely because of necessary constraints on time and space.

---

47 Sjåfjell (2009) Ch. 11, on the core and contributory role, respectively, of company and securities law.

48 Shareholder primacy is discussed in ibid. Sect. 4.3.5.

The global community interest was included, as it relates to many of the general objectives of EU law to which all EU sector law ultimately should contribute: sustainable development, considered globally, and the adherence to human rights.[49] Including this interest is not merely a matter of law. From a normative perspective, global challenges necessitate the inclusion of this interest in any evaluation purporting to have a wide perspective.

The analytical question in relation to all these issues was the effect of the directive: What incentives, obligations or restrictions does the directive impose on the parties with respect to these issues? The legal strategies of *The Anatomy* were included in the analysis.[50]

The first main issue was that of the directive's effect on the target company in general and with special focus on the employees, to be analysed by reference to the three main actors in a takeover: the target company's board, the target shareholders and the potential acquirer. The effect on the company is relevant both with a view to European economic and social development and environmental protection. The latter was, however, mainly discussed under the third selected issue, concerning the global community interest.

The second main issue focused on the target shareholders and the directive's effect on the actions of the three main actors in a takeover and the influence of these actions on the interests of the shareholders. The main driver behind the directive's focus on the target shareholders is apparently a desire to facilitate takeovers which are intended to contribute to European economic development.[51] This issue will to a certain extent take on different forms, depending on which of the control structures, out of the variety offered by Europe, we are considering.

The third issue deals with sustainable development objective and the directive's influence on the three central actors in the takeover: the target board, the target shareholders and the potential acquirer.

The taking of broader issues as the basis for the analysis does not eliminate the

---

49 Ibid. Chap. 10 and 11.

50 Kraakman et al. (2009) pp. 37–45. For my use I have referred to them as strategies for dealing with conflicts of interests, rather than strategies for protecting principals – as a consequence of leaving the terminology of agency theory behind.

51 On the objectives of the directive, see Sjåfjell (2009) Sect. 9.3.5.

need for an overall assessment. The trade-offs between the resolution of the different issues must be taken into account.[52]

Law and Economics out of the Straightjacket

I hope that my alternative analytical structure inspired by agency theory will have illustrated how soft and hard values may be combined in a law and economics structure especially adapted to hard-core company and securities law. Such an alternative analytical structure could perhaps provide a meeting ground for shareholder primacy advocates and stakeholder proponents, allowing for a more nuanced discussion of the effect of the regulation of companies on the companies themselves, their employees, shareholders and other contractual parties, as well as on wider societal interests. If that is too utopian a vision, perhaps an alternative analytical structure that takes agency theory seriously, and leads to a dismantling of the related theory of the market for corporate control, could contribute to pricking the balloons of hot air that are created when legal-economic theories are used not as a starting point for a debate, but as the end of the argument; in short: as postulates.[53] Law and economics indubitably has a lot to offer the company law debate. Releasing law and economics from the straightjacket of shareholder fundamentalism would be a good start.

References

Adams, Renée B. and Daniel Ferreira. 2007. A Theory of Friendly Boards. *The Journal of Finance*, 62, pp. 217–250.

Bainbridge, Stephen M. 2002. Why a Board? Group Decisionmaking in Corporate Governance. *Vanderbilt Law Review*, 55, pp. 1–55.

Blair, Margaret M. and Lynn A. Stout. 1999. A Team Production Theory of Corporate Law. *Virginia Law Review*, 85, pp. 247–328.

52 The entire analysis of the directive, including its legal-economic basis (the theory of the market for corporate control), the analytical issues selected as shown here, and the overall assessment, may be found in ibid. Part V.

53 Which is how the market for corporate control has been used in relation to the Takeover Directive, see ibid. Ch. 15.

Burkart, Mike and Fausto Panunzi 2006. Takeovers (ECGI Working Paper Series in Finance, Paper No. 118/2006) <ssrn.com/abstract_id=884080> last visited 29 September 2007

Cremers, K.J. Martijn, Vinay B. Nair and Chenyang Wei. 2007. Governance Mechanisms and Bond Prices. *The Review of Financal Studies*, 20, pp. 1359–1388.

Eide, Erling and Endre Stavang. 2008. *Rettsøkonomi (Law and economics).* Oslo: Cappelen Akademisk Forlag.

Hertig, Gerard. 2005. On-Going Board Reforms: One Size Fits All and Regulatory Capture. *Oxford Review of Economic Policy*, 21, pp 269–282.

Hill, Jennifer. 2004. Corporate Scandals Across the Globe: Regulating the Role of the Director in Ferrarini, Guido, et al. (eds.), *Reforming Company and Takeover Law in Europe*, Oxford: Oxford University Press, pp. 225–266.

Hopt, Klaus J. 2006. Comparative Company Law in Reimann, Mathias and Reinhard Zimmermann (eds.),*The Oxford Handbook of Comparative Law*, Oxford: Oxford University Press, pp. 1161–1191.

Jensen, Michael C. and William H Meckling. 1976. Theory of the Firm: Managerial Behaviour, Agency Costs and Ownership Structure. *Journal of financial economics*, 3, pp. 305–360.

Kraakman, Reinier, et al. 2009. *The Anatomy of Corporate Law: A Comparative and Functional Approach.* 2nd ed. Oxford.

Kraakman, Reinier, et al. 2004. *The Anatomy of Corporate Law: A Comparative and Functional Approach.* 1st ed. Oxford.

Mähönen, Jukka. 2009. Do we need law and economics in company law? *Nordisk Tidsskrift for Selskabsret (Nordic Journal of Company Law)* pp. 146–157.

Posner, Eric A. 2000. Agency Models in Law and Economics (John M. Olin Law & Economics (University of Chicago Law School) Working Paper No 92/2000) <ssrn.com/abstract=204872> last visited 24 September 2007.

Pratt, John W. and Richard J. Zeckhauser. 1991. Principals and Agents: An Overview in Pratt, John W. and Richard J. Zeckhauser (eds.) *Principals and Agents: The Structure of Business*, (Repr. with new introd. orig. publ. 1985), Boston, MA: Harvard Business School Press, pp. 1–35.

Sjåfjell, Beate. 2009. *Towards a Sustainable European Company Law. A Normative Analysis of the Objectives of EU Law, with the Takeover Directive as a Test Case* (Alphen aan den Rijn, Kluwer Law International).

Some (In)consistencies in Environmental and Natural Resources Law

Endre Stavang

1. Introduction

My impression is that many legal scholars, including myself, often make appeals through use of the term (in)consistency. Thus, it seems to have normative force, or at least rhetorical power. I wonder: Is it a problem that we are not sufficiently aware of what it might mean? I don't know, but I think that the basic three meanings discussed in this article are at once clearly distinguishable and – at least *sometimes* – necessary to take into account simultaneously (if not always explicitly) in applied legal reasoning.[1]

A basic distinction in this article is between formal and substantive consistency, and I put almost all the emphasis on the latter.[2] This is partly because I choose to narrow my topic to be able to say something of interest, but also because I hope to counter what I perceive as a tendency to over-emphasize formal consistency at the expense of substantive consistency. The benefit of still taking both types of consistency into account is, at least, that it may be possible to discuss tensions or trade-offs between the two – which I would think is a requirement for both rationality and reasonableness.

Consistency involves a relationship between phenomena that are expected to be in concord with one another, for example words and actions. The taste for consistency can exist at the level of the individual as well as the level of some collective (or institution) making decisions. In psychology, for example, it is accepted

1 For other approaches, see Engel (2006) and Perez and Teubner (2006).

2 A related distinction is made with respect to analysis of individual (as opposed to collective) choice in Kahneman (1994) and this has been followed up in Hsee and Zhang (2004) p. 2.

that *individuals* have a need and desire for consistency. A famous example is the theory of cognitive dissonance, which concerns the psychological drive towards consistency and the distaste for experiencing inconsistencies, that is, the undesirable tensions that can arise between one's preferences and perception of reality.[3] These tensions can be perceived as inconsistencies, and individuals will try to diminish them because they are uncomfortable. If one fails to get an attractive job that one considers desirable because of its positive aspects, one will perhaps in retrospect convince oneself that the job wasn't really so attractive after all. It is like Aesop's fable, *The Fox and the Grapes:* "The grapes are sour, and not ripe as I thought".[4]

In economics, in parts of political science and within "rational choice sociology", consistency is a requirement for individual and collective rational choice. It is presumed, for example, that the individual's preferences are transitive: if A is preferred above B and B above C, then A is preferred above C. And if A is preferred above B in the absence of other alternatives, this order of preference prevails even if C becomes an option. A third type is dynamic consistency. This concept might be unfamiliar, so I will explain how I understand it.

The idea of dynamic consistency is probably rooted in common intuition, but in academic circles it was further developed by Thomas Schelling and is expressed in another generation's game theory of so-called dynamic interaction.[5] In 1977 Kydland and Prescott published an analysis of policy choices over time which further developed the theory and suggested applications to financial and monetary policies.[6] At its core, their finding was that many policy choices may be difficult to make in a dynamically consistent way. Assume that a rational and forward-looking authority chooses a schedule for its policy with a view to achieving the best possible outcome for the public in the period to which the policy applies. If the authority is given the opportunity to reassess and change the plan at a later date in the period, it is likely to do so because this will be the optimal approach for the period as a whole. But if people form expectations concerning the author-

3 See Festinger (1957) at pp. 2–3 where he substitutes dissonance for inconsistencies and consonance for consistency to reduce the logical connotations of the terminology and states the basic hypotheses.

4 For studies of public policy implications of inconsistencies at the level of individual decision-making, see e.g. Thaler and Sunstein (2008); Fennel (2009).

5 Schelling (1960).

6 Kydland and Prescott (1977).

ity's behaviour based on their experience at this later date, they may not have the incentive in the next period to do what was essentially the best thing from the start. Kydland and Prescott suggest that the authority can achieve more if their scope for weighing the advantages and disadvantages of the different alternatives for action in period 2 is limited and if this is announced in period 1.[7]

To illustrate how I understand the concept of dynamic consistency, I will point to the regulations prohibiting the erection of new buildings and the application of the authority to issue a demolition order, cf. the Neighbouring Properties Act *(Naboloven)*, Section 11, first paragraph:

> . . . If a building or other structure is unlawfully erected in such a way that part of the building stands on a neighbour's property, the neighbour is entitled to have it removed or modified. If as a result, expenses or losses incurred are so great as to be clearly disproportionate to the gain, and the owner of the building is not to blame to any appreciable extent, the owner may be awarded exemption from liability if the neighbour receives compensation in an amount that must not be set lower than the damage or inconvenience.

As we can see, the provision states that a building erected unlawfully on a neighbour's property shall be removed. However, the provision also states that the structure may remain standing if removal results in a waste of resources as assessed at the time of removal. Both lawyers and social scientists would probably say that the latter could easily undermine respect for the basic principle that buildings shall only be built on one's own property. From this perspective, the third rule in the provision should be noted: if the builder was negligent at the time of building, the building must be removed even though the cost at the time of removal seems excessive.

There is much to suggest that the reasoning behind Section 11, first paragraph of the Neighbouring Properties Act may be important for other parts of environmental and natural resources law. This should, however, be assessed for each of the three branches of government: the legislative, the executive and the judicial branch. In section 4, I will offer an example related to each type.

In one sense, one could say that consistency is what law is all about: to compare norms with other norms or with facts, and conclude whether there is con-

7 Kungl. Vetenskapsakademien (2004) pp. 2 and 5.

sistency or not. But for the purpose of conducting legal policy analysis (either *de lege ferenda* or *de sententia ferenda*), there are probably no clear conventions in *law* (understood here as a profession) for what consistency is accepted to be. However, it is possible to indicate certain basic judicial concepts that can quite naturally be associated with the term consistency. First of all, jurists and legislators often feel the need to base judicial behaviour generally on certain common principles across disciplines and specific issues. Secondly, there is a widespread judicial and political view that legal means by which to resolve important social problems should be based on a broad approach, thereby ensuring that all relevant interests and values are given consideration and are duly weighed. The notion that underlies this might well be termed consideration for harmony and consistency within the legal system, a notion that can reasonably be associated with the ideal of consistency. The notion of consistency is furthermore related to the concepts of predictability, due process of law and justice.

In *jurisprudence* (understood here as methods for research into the rules of law) consistency can be understood as a requirement for rationality (as in psychology or economics), for dynamic consistency (in economics and political science) or for "harmony and consequence" (in many traditional forms of analyses of the legal system). Against this background, I would like to propose in this article three types of (in)consistency that I believe can be beneficial, from a legal perspective, to bear in mind when analyzing environmental law and other natural resources law. In the following, what I call formal consistency is first *briefly* accounted for. Subsequently, I focus on consistency as a relationship between (some) legal rules and (some) consistent legal policies (which I call substantive consistency). Finally, I will test my thoughts concerning dynamic consistency. Throughout, I do not pretend to construct more than an exploratory analysis, meaning that I confront my prior knowledge about possible ways to explicate concepts of consistency with what I know or find in (Norwegian) natural resources law, and then try to reflect upon this and see what happens.

2. Formal consistency

In the legal profession it is frequently accepted that "harmony and consequence" in rules and solutions are valuable attributes.[8] These values, in my opinion, can be considered as generic terms for a number of traditional forms of formal consistency, that is, the relationship between two or more legal decisions, rights or norms. I will mention three and then acknowledge the problem of making an exhaustive list.

The first form of formal consistency is concord with the mandates of international law. From the perspective of public international law, "consistent interpretation" in this sense might be viewed as a basic legal principle.[9] Accordingly, it is not surprising that the correspondence of Norwegian law with international law is perceived as a natural legal policy goal, and under current law the basic presumption is that indeed this correspondence does exist, see Rt. 1984 p. 1175 *Sikringsdømtes ankerett (Detainee's Right of Appeal).*[10]

The second type of formal consistency entails that Norwegian law has the same solutions as the laws of other countries. It is presumed by increasingly more people that international harmonisation of the rules of law has a certain intrinsic value, among other reasons, because comprehensive harmonisation renders complicated choices of law rules superfluous. Increasingly, Norwegian jurists also study the laws of other countries, and courts of law now make reference to foreign laws in areas where this has not been common before, see for example Rt. 2008 p. 362 *Naturbetongdommen (Natural Concrete Decision)* concerning the relationship between negative easements and development plans.

A more general form of formal consistency is that rules of law or legal requirements should not directly contradict one another. If, for example, a development proscribes anything other than industry and a negative easement proscribes anything other than residences, one of them must give way to the other, and it is the easement that must do so, see Rt. 1953 p. 1360 *Kongsøre*. In this judgment there

8 E.g. Eckhoff (2005). To elaborate this is a question whether there is consistency between a harmony norm on the one hand and, on the other hand, two other norms that apparently are contradicting each other in one way or another. If you compare the two apparently contradicting norms directly, the tenor of the consistency norm will remain unclear.

9 E.g. Wennerås (2007) p. 55.

10 This is admittedly not an example drawn from environmental and natural resources law, but the general topic is pursued in e.g. Helgesen (1982) and Arnesen and Stenvik (2009).

was a "conflict" between public and private planning, and the private development was voided without compensation. More generally, one can say that the dynamic rules of property rights concerning a conflict of rights to assets reflect this type of respect for consistency. If B and S derive conflicting rights from A, then B and S cannot both acquire valid rights. On the contrary, the conflict must be solved in accordance with the rules of extinction.[11] One can also consider the principles of conflict used in solving discrepancies between rules of law as result of the same basic view: the ideal that the legal system should, to the highest extent possible, be free of inconsistencies. The rules of international private law also stem from the desire to observe this form of consistency.

In fact, it is possible to make a much longer list taking into account that many doctrinal areas of legal study seem, at least from the outside, to be very much preoccupied by formal consistency problems. Moreover, concepts of discrimination appear to be key elements in fields like women's law, labour law, EU law and refugee and asylum law. Here, one might query what makes this group of consistency more formal than other groups of consistency and what the definitional characteristics of this group of consistency are. In my view, the unifying theme is the quest to treat "like cases alike". This is not only an ethical imperative; it is also a legal value. The cynic might counter that it happens all the time that two similar cases are treated differently, in particular if the cases are resolved in different legal systems. So then what is the consistency norm? Is it anything more than the rhetorical statement that harmony is a good thing?

Be that as it may, my assessment is that these and other forms of traditional judicial consistency are important and interesting, and that it is fruitful, from a legal perspective, to further study such phenomena, also in the context of natural resources law and environmental law. However, it is my contention that what might seem like a problem of logical or formal consistency is more fruitfully discussed as a matter of weight and substantive priorities, that is to say, the sort of substantive consistency topics that will be treated in the rest of this article.

11 This is an example of conflicting rights (i.e. individual norms), not conflicting legal rules (i.e. general norms).

3. Substantive consistency

Another form of consistency that is significant in a legal context is substantive consistency, in the sense that rules of law and legal solutions should correspond with consistent legal policies. This brings us into the field of political and ethical theory, and jurists will need to learn from other fields.

At the core of substantive consistency lies the idea that social measures should be designed in accordance with Gossen's law: *The marginal utilities of goods or services (and of social measures) must be equal.*[12] Let us look at a simple example. Society's investments in safety are to be divided between two sectors, for example shipping and petroleum production. Let us assume that the investments are distributed such that the marginal utility of the investment in oil is 1, while the marginal utility of investments in ships is 2. This means that we can move a portion of the investments from petroleum to ships and lose 1, but win 2. The very redistribution of resources leads to saved human lives. There is room for these kinds of efficiency gains as long as the safety regulations are not consistent, in the sense that Gossen's law is observed: a consistent body of rules (e.g. across safety regulation, criminal law and tort law) provides incentives for the marginal utility of the safety investments to be equal in all sectors. This is a basic requirement for consistency that most public policy analysts will insist upon. Others have argued that things are not always as simple, and we thus confront the first debate on substantive consistency that we need to consider.

One issue is how environmental concerns are to be supported and emphasized across sectors, through exercise of discretion in sectoral legislation, including *ex ante* assessments, for example in conjunction with licensing hearings and in the awarding of compensation for environmental damages. I believe that the concern for cost-effective legal regulation is relevant here. The concern, as mentioned, is aimed towards an equalization of the regulations' marginal utility in all sectors, and in order to achieve this, one must require that an analysis be performed to determine the regulations' cost and utility. In terms of utility, a central factor will be to determine the value of the environmental damage that can be avoided by applying the regulations. One particular challenge here is to create consistency

12 The Norwegian Nobel Laureate Trygve Haavelmo acknowledged Gossen's contribution in the collection of essays in (applied) welfare economics and political economy by entitling it *"Variasjoner over et tema av Gossen"* ("Variations on a theme by Gossen"), Haavelmo (1972).

between *ex ante* and *ex post* regulations. The valuations in both contexts should ideally be equal, so that one obtains a common cost-effective ratio for the two control forms.

Another topic, one which raises the question of basic counterbalancing, is so-called vertical consistency: namely, the concern that whatever is decided at a superior level of governance is carried out uniformly at the lower levels. This applies, in some situations, to the relationship between the EU and Norway, or the relationship between the Norwegian Parliament on the one hand and the country's municipalities on the other. Principles of environmental law come into play here, as well, and in this instance it may also be a question of a counterbalancing against the concern for cost-effectiveness. Particular problems can arise if the superior organ adopts environmental quality norms for subordinate jurisdictions which imply inconsistent counterweighing of utility and costs. This situation will easily occur if the superior organ requires that environmental quality must be uniform with harmonized environmental quality norms. If such demands are made uniformly in all subordinate jurisdictions, one runs the risk of creating a significant material inconsistency in the form of a breach of Gossen's law. Environmental damages and the costs associated with avoiding them may be easily construed as differing greatly from one geographic area to another, and the concern for cost-effective regulation in such a situation indicates that the quality of the environment will also vary accordingly. In summary, there appears to be a fundamental opposition between the two forms of consistency in a system of multi-level control of environmental quality.

So far, I have only identified some general issues by means of a rather vague notion of (environmental) substantive consistency. An analytical approach to identifying a more stringent requirement based on the notion of substantive consistency follows from Louis Kaplow and Steven Shavell's argument, that *it will lead to inconsistencies if one stresses concerns that do not refer to the consequences for individuals.*[13] The thought is that the economic welfare theory in general, and the Pareto criteria for sound collective decision-making in particular, represent a set of ethical principles that should be used as guiding stars in the field of "public policy", including the judicial policy subgroup. If one introduces "deontic" concerns (justice, reasonableness, etc.) into these types of analyses, the result may well be, in the opinion of the authors, a decline in welfare for all individuals in

13 Kaplow and Shavell (2002); Dari Matiacci et al. (2004).

society. In their view, a legal policy analysis should therefore avoid introducing values that cannot be grounded in individual preferences. It seems to follow from Kaplow and Shavell's analysis that welfare economics should be used as *the* criterion to make public policy decisions. In practice, this would have to be implemented by accepting Cost Benefit Analysis (CBA) as the decision rule in large areas of the law. However, not everyone who understands and empathizes with their arguments thinks about CBA in this way. It could be argued that, in a democratic society, CBA should not be used as a decision rule, but rather as a means to make decision-makers more accountable by making their decisions more transparent.[14] By clarifying and systemizing costs and benefits through CBA, responsible decision-makers can be induced to reduce inconsistencies, even if CBA in general has to based on normative assumptions.

A quasi-empirical twist on this discussion, which is not new, is that research asserts that the rules of law often correspond *on a purely factual basis* with the economic welfare theory. Richard Posner has been a particularly active proponent in arguing that a great deal of law generated by (American) court decisions corresponds with economic (allocative) efficiency. He claims that this hypothesis goes a long way in explaining the content of rules of law; that is, he is of the opinion that the rules have an actual substantive consistency which comes in a precise form. The unwritten culpa rule, for example, appears to require cost-effective preventive measures. And the liability threshold levels of tolerance in laws relating to the rights of neighbours (i.e. nuisance principles) appear to entail a form of utility cost analysis in courts of law. These examples are relatively obvious, but generally speaking the form of consistency that is asserted by Posner to exist can only be uncovered through a comprehensive redefinition and reconstruction of the content of the law.[15] To the extent such efforts succeed, one might think that the problems of political legitimacy touched upon above are avoided, and that one can leave it to the courts to purify the tendencies for the law to gravitate towards economic efficiency and thus expose the true economic structure of (some parts of) the legal system. The smallest problem with this "positive" approach is that it is probably too comprehensive and broad to be considered a matter of consistency, but rather a

14 See e.g. Farber (1999) pp. 122, 203; Ogus (2006) p. 290; Revesz and Livermore (2008) p. 12; Eide (2009) p. 10.

15 It is a matter of finding a broad, synthetic "ratio decidendi" for many decisions, or potentially for entire doctrines and legal institutions. See Eng (2003) pp. 508–9.

version of a quest for coherence – which is of more questionable value. The real problem is that the "empirical" fit between law and efficiency will almost always be imperfect, and that there is no way to bridge the gap in an uncontroversial way. If, for instance, there is an 80 % correspondance to the efficiency criterion in the contract cases on whether a term is invalidated on the grounds of "unreasonableness"[16], the normative question is: So what? Political elements in legal interpretation cannot be avoided, as Posner himself now spells out clearly.[17]

This is not to say, however, that a welfare-economic approach cannot have considerable appeal as one of several legal methodologies. Let me give just one example of a contested legal issue that cries out for an improved understanding based on this kind of analysis: when a negative servitude prohibits something (e.g. a tall building) that the land use authorities have allowed (the same), there is a tendency to call this a conflict or contradiction.[18] It is clear however, that a contradiction in the formal sense cannot exist, since the planning authorities do not have the power to tell the land owner which is bound by the servitude to build the tall building. Land use planning is about prohibitions and allowances, not orders, other than those that are required to make people respect the prohibitions. Consequently, there is ample room for respecting both the servitude and development plan by simply saying that the strictest regulation applies. This is the legal solution in the American legal system, for example, and as far as I know, the legal position in the UK as well. Whether this rule should prevail or the alternative should prevail (i.e. that the servitude is invalidated because it frustrates the intentions of land use planner) is a matter of public policy and should be discussed accordingly. Despite this, the legal policy discussion of this topic in Norway has been sparse and quite formalistic, despite the fact that the issue has been unresolved since it appeared over a century ago.[19] And worse, even the issue of compensating the servitude holder in case of invalidation has not received serious public policy treatment.[20]

16 Wilhelmsen (1995).

17 Posner (2008).

18 See, for example, Rt. 1953 p. 1360 Kongsøre, Rt. 1995 p. 904 Gjensidige, Rt. 2002 p. 145 Bortelid and Rt. 2008 p. 362 Naturbetong.

19 See Rt. 1900 p. 147 and 1903 p. 417.

20 In Stavang (2009) I try to make legal sense of these and related issues pertaining to land use planning and "third party right" (i.e. private law rights other than full land ownership) and at least sketch the relevant public policy concerns.

4. Dynamic consistency

"A word is a word and a man is a man" is an old saying that still holds true. Many lawyers earn their living drawing up major commercial contracts, and it is taken as a given that these contracts – by law – are binding in their original form. If this were not the case, the promisee would feel insecure as to whether the promisor would later be tempted to renege, and this insecurity would in some cases deter the promisee from entering into the contract at all. Lofty words such as predictability, legitimate expectation and justice can be used to denote the values lawyers assign to the principle of the binding effect of promises and contracts.

But – and there is a but – from the perspective of jurisprudence, the principle that contracts are binding is not much more than that – one principle among many others. Some of these other principles point in the opposite direction. Thus, in practice, there must be room for exceptions. The most prominent Nordic legal expert on the law of obligations in the 20th century, Jan Hellner, has for example said that although the principle that contracts are binding functions as a practical rule of law in many cases, it is not particularly applicable in legal discussion: "The principle (that agreements are binding) is not applicable as an argument in legal discussion. However, it functions as a practical rule of law in the great majority of cases. As such, it can be said to be almost a tautology – it only states the obvious. Water is wet, the earth is round, and contracts are binding."[21] Nor does the principle say anything about the relationship to other principles or the fact that all contracts must be interpreted. And based on the general provision in Section 36 of the Contract Act, this can be taken even further, as stated in the first paragraph: "A contract may wholly or in part be set aside or changed to the extent its application would seem unreasonable or in conflict with good business practices. The same applies to unilaterally binding arrangements."

This provision does not state that agreements are binding in their original form. On the contrary, it states that subsequent circumstances may have considerable influence on whether and to what extent a contract is binding. If complying with an agreement in its original form proves to be too costly, the agreement ceases to apply, wholly or in part. This pragmatic approach pervades contract law: to make the best of a situation as it is.

This is an elementary principle in law. One might object, however, that there

---

21 Hellner (1986) p. 348.

is much to be gained – and this also applies to government authorities – from keeping one's word – if necessary by providing assistance in the event of the threat of legal repercussions. The objective is confidence and credibility. For social scientists, this is perhaps not primarily valuable in itself, but is something that leads to higher investment, more consumption, less unemployment and – more generally – markets that meet human requirements to a greater extent and more efficiently. By the term "keeping one's word", I am pointing to the idea of dynamic inconsistency or time inconsistency. Kydland and Prescott – who did much to develop the analysis – were primarily interested in business cycles and monetary policy, but I do not intend to refer directly to monetary policy or the strategy or legal position of the central bank.[22] Instead, I will examine their main idea – that there is much to be gained from keeping one's word – as to whether it is viable in law in a more general context.[23] My question is what guidelines and legal framework the main idea should provide for government bodies and the branches of government. I will try out the idea on the sphere of natural resources law, that is, the rules of law that apply to property, hydropower, oil, gas and environmental protection. This is a significant area in the sense that there is much to be gained from good law and much to be lost from its absence. In the following, I will explore the idea of dynamic consistency as a means by which to understand and possibly criticize specific issues in environmental and natural resources law.

My first example refers to the **legislative** branch of government. It is a long established idea that the Constitution should limit the competence of the majority (see Articles 97 and 105 of the Constitution). This can be perceived as a guarantee for positions under property law that increase investors' confidence that they will receive the expected return on their investments. My example, however, refers to something slightly different: the constraints on an owner's actions that are considered necessary for nature conservation. According to Norwegian legal tradition, owners must accept such encroachments on property without compensation. This was a source of frustration for property owners for a long period. The notion eventually emerged that property owners could respond by making their land less preservation-worthy, for example by destroying a significant geological feature or cutting down an ecologically valuable forest – **before** a preservation order had been considered. For this and other reasons, the Willoch

22 See e.g. Nordén (2002) and Qvigstad (2009).

23 In a sense, I take up a hint by Gunnar Nordén, op. cit.

government of the 1980s proposed new statutory provisions to compensate property owners affected by nature conservation decisions to a greater extent than had been customary. The idea was that conservation work could then be carried out in a more conciliatory atmosphere. In a sense, the authorities chose to honour a kind of tacit agreement between the government and property owners that there should be some balance between the parties that cannot be disturbed without financial compensation. It is this "agreement" that is binding, and thus it seems that the law implicitly acknowledges that the Kydland/Prescott analysis is relevant.

My second example refers to the **executive** branch of government. My starting point here is that municipalities and other government bodies, including the Norwegian parliament, are entitled, within certain general limits under administrative law, to make new decisions in the future notwithstanding decisions made in the past. A parliament cannot, for example, commit a future parliament to a decision concerning licensing policy. Something similar will apply to the exercise of local government authority, for example in deciding on and implementing area development plans. For major development projects, it will be of great value to private parties if they can be sure that future municipal councils will not change the area development plan on which they have based their investments. It has long been unclear to what extent prior commitment is within the authority of the municipalities. This may result in private investment that is lower than socially desirable. However, new provisions in the Planning and Building Act provide legal authority for development contracts that may ensure a greater degree of predictability. Nevertheless, there is no explicit provision regarding prior commitment of municipal executive authority, and as a result we have to rely on judicial precedents. A key decision was made in 2007 (the road project judgment): as the Supreme Court pointed out then, governments must have the authority to commit the future exercise of their authority to a certain extent in relation to a contract if this is considered necessary or desirable in order to promote the purpose of the authorizing legislation. The commitment must, however, be kept within reasonable limits and the extent to which commitments can be binding will differ across the different areas of government administration. The decision must depend on an assessment of the interest in the administration of government authority and public funds in the best interests of the people and the need to achieve the desired goals or solutions by committing the future exercise of authority. To ensure that the question of binding a current administration to future commitments has been adequately assessed, the commitment must be required to have a clear basis in the relevant contract.

It might be said that the Court has drawn up guidelines in this case that enable municipalities to make promises, and that the Planning and Building Act assumes that promises made by municipalities will normally be binding. As we can see from the wording of the Supreme Court judgment, the authority to make binding commitments is generally regulated by three factors: first, the extent to which prior commitment is desirable or necessary to promote the purpose of the Act; second, an assessment of the advantage of the exercise of discretionary authority against the need for binding commitment; and third, how clear the basis for commitment is in the relevant agreement. Again, the law seems sensitive to the Kydland/Prescott analysis.

My third example refers to the **judicial** branch of government. Passing judgment is a form of political activity in the sense that in difficult cases the judge applies discretionary judgment. A judge's personality and ethical principles *ex ante* will therefore influence his or her decisions *ex post*. This may result in reduced predictability, and as a result private parties may adapt to this uncertainty in various, perhaps undesirable ways. How can these harmful effects be reduced?[24] One possibility is to give emphasis in the application of law to objectively verifiable factors such as for example preparatory works and previous decisions (precedents). Where the wording of a law leaves substantial scope for discretion, the preparatory works and precedents can narrow this down, making judgments more predictable. But some freedom of choice will almost always remain in difficult cases. The question then arises as to which ideology should determine the effect of a judge's ethical principles. There are two schools of thought here. Some would say that judges should take account of the concrete reasonableness between the parties at the time the conflict is to be resolved. Others argue that greatest weight must be given to general, normally applicable considerations. The most decisive factor will then be the reasonableness between the type of parties contesting the case, and the relevant time will be prior to the conflict. The first of these models can be called the *ex post*-school, and the second the *ex ante*-school.

Which school is the most suitable from our perspective? The answer is clear enough that a judge's ethical principles should be reflected in general assessments

24 For analyses of judging in a dynamic (in)consistency perspective, see Anderlini et al. (2008) (theoretical) and Niblett (2009) (empirical).

of which considerations are relevant *ex ante*. This corresponds to the old rule in the Swiss code of civil law: if no answer is to be found in the act, the judge shall apply the optimal rule from a legislative perspective. Such an approach ensures that the judge is forward-looking and takes account of the long-term consequences of his or her decision. This can be interpreted as the will to "keep one's word".

I have provided three examples of how the judicial system can "keep promises". However, it would be easy to find contradictory examples to show that other considerations can be more important than confidence and credibility. Thus, I am not calling for a bright line rule of keeping one's word, but rather for the inherent trade-offs and choices in the law to be analyzed to the maximal extent possible. In addition to what I have already said about this, it may, for example, be more important that a popular majority wins at any given time than that there is an optimal climate for investment, as clearly reflected in the road project judgement of 2007 at p. 65. Here, the Norwegian Supreme Court said:

> Any doubts related to the possibility of prior commitment of the municipal authority to allocate funds derive first from the possibility that the facts may change or that new information may emerge that was not available to the municipality when the contract was concluded. When a municipality has entered into a contract for a transport sector project, demographic developments or requirements imposed on municipal services might lead to an increase in municipal expenditure on social welfare or welfare services for the elderly or on the school and day-care institutions sector that could not have been envisioned when the contract was concluded. Second, political priorities may also have changed, as a result of a change in public opinion or a change in policy following an election. Insofar as it is accepted that an administration can tie its authority to a binding commitment, it will be difficult to accomplish a change in policy. This will constitute a constraint on democracy. In view of these doubts, the courts have been reluctant to accept agreements whereby the public administration can tie its exercise of authority to a binding commitment (see NOU 2003:24 More effective building legislation, and Eckhoff and Smith, *Administrative Law*, which includes references to case law.

In my opinion, there is every reason to continue to mull over these questions. We are facing complex problems of governance where interpretation and discretion are probably essential to our efforts to achieve good results.

5. Summing up

As a tentative summary, I think one can say with certainty that there are many types (at least three) and forms of (in)consistencies, and that the legal system or legal decisions can hardly be consistent in all relations. Furthermore, it is important to remember that one can encounter stronger or weaker forms of consistency; in other words, this is a matter of differences of degree. Based on all of this, I entertain the notion that it would be fruitful to pose at least the following three questions in the research project: (1) How great a degree of consistency actually exists in selected areas? (2) How can degrees of inconsistency be explained? (3) If I can document or presume that inconsistency is partially or entirely undesirable from a social point of view, how can we remedy or prevent it (if indeed it is possible to do so at all)?

If these inferences are perceived to be too general or lofty, I offer two more specific conclusions on where the most important challenges for future research may lie. The key words are trade-offs and an empirical orientation. With regards to trade-offs, I think that an important task is to clearly identify the competing concerns that are embodied in appeals to consistency, for example when studying environmental quality standards in air or water. Here, there might be a strong drive towards formal, vertical consistency in the sense that many would like to see harmonized norms across EU/EEA member states. At the same time, it is not possible to ignore the need to fit environmental regulation to local tastes for quality improvement as well as local abatement cost.[25] In a study of the Water Directive, for instance, I would recommend that this tension between formal and substantive consistency is studied, and that the trade-offs are analyzed.

In the notion of (in)consistency trade-offs, it is implicit that there is a problem that can be solved. This begs the question of what conditions the solutions must satisfy, and this may be a hard problem when formal and substantive consistencies are in tension. It might be tempting to bury the problem by asserting that formal consistency is just a means by which to solve problems of dynamic (in)consistencies, but I do not see how this assertion can be substantiated. The

25 This is, of course, part of the broad debate on "federalism", that is, centralization versus decentralization in an international system of multi-level governance; see Esty and Gerardin (2001) for a collection of short contributions to the debate and Revesz (1992, 1996 and 2001) for thorough discussions of federalism in environmental law.

more promising way forward, I think, is a pragmatic approach with a focus on consequences and an empirical orientation.[26] Moreover, there seems to be a potential for CBA as a means by which to reduce inconsistencies. To many, it may seem that CBA is not what legal scholars ought do be doing. CBA may, however, be meta-studied as a tool to reduce inconsistencies. Thus, a specific legal research question might be to what extent regulatory and environmental impacts assessments that have to be carried out according to law, are regulated by a set of rules that minimizes undesirable inconsistencies.

In conclusion, I find that (in)consistency concepts can have a variety of (rather) precise meanings, and that it will be interesting to try to understand and to criticize (environmental and natural resources) law from the perspectives of the concepts discussed in this article. I hope this can also be an inspiration for others.

Literature

Anderlini, Luca, Leonardo Fello and Allessandro Riboni. 2008. Statute Law or Case Law? *CESifo Working Paper* No. 2358 July, http://papers.ssrn.com/sol3/papers.cfm?abstract_id=1187642, pp. 1–48.

Arnesen, Finn and Are Stenvik. 2009. *Internasjonalisering og juridisk metode – særlig om EØS-rettens betydning i norsk rett,* Oslo.

Blandhol, Sverre. 2005. *Nordisk rettspragmatisme: Savigny, Ørsted og Schweigaard om vitenskap og metode,* Oslo.

Coase, Ronald H. 1988. *The Firm, the Market, and the Law,* Chicago and London.

Dari Matiacci, Guiseppe, Gödel, Kaplow and Shavell. 2004. Consistency and Completeness in Social Decisionmaking, *Chicago-Kent Law Review,* Vol. 79, No. 2, pp. 497–520.

Eckhoff, Torstein. 2005. *Rettskildelære,* 5. ed. by Jan Erik Helgesen, Oslo.

26 An outline of a pragmatic approach to environmental law is found in Farber (1999), and legal pragmatism more generally put forth in Posner (2003). In various works, Sverre Blandhol has documented a longstanding Nordic tradition for legal pragmatism; see, for example, Blandhol (2005). Remarks on the relation between a pragmatic approach and an economic approach to law have been made by many scholars, for example Kolstad (2008).

Eide, Erling. Inconsistency in law, team theory, and cost-benefit analysis, *Unublished outline of paper submitted for presentation at the 2009 EALE conference in Rome.*

Eng, Svein. 2003. *Analysis of Dis/agreement – with particular reference to Law and Legal Theory,* Dordrecht.

Engel, Christoph. 2006. Inconsistency in the Law: In Search of a Balanced Norm, In: Christoph Engel and Lorraine Daston (eds.), *Is there Value in inconsistency?,* Baden-Baden pp. 223–281. (also available at: http://papers.ssrn.com/sol3/papers.cfm?abstract_id=628387)

Englard, Izhak. 1990. Victor Mataja's Liability for Damages from an Economic Viewpoint: A Centennial to an Ignored Economic Analysis of Tort, **10** *International Review of Law and Economics*, pp. 173–191.

Esty, Daniel C. and Damien Gerardin (eds.). 2001. *Regulatory Competition and Economic Integration – Comparative Perspectives,* Oxford and New York.

Farber, Daniel. 1999. *Eco-Pragmatism. Making Sensible Environmental Decisions in an Uncertain World,* Chicago and London.

Fennel, Lee Anne. 2009. Willpower and Legal Policy, *Annual Review of Law & Social Science*, (forthcoming, Vol. 5, December 2009, available at http://papers.ssrn.com/sol3/papers.cfm?abstract_id=1428523).

Festinger, Leon. 1957. *A Theory of Cognitive Dissonance,* Illinois and New York.

Haavelmo, Trygve. 1972. *Variasjoner over et tema av Gossen,* Memorandum fra Sosialøkonomisk Institutt, Universitetet i Oslo, Oslo.

Helgesen, Jan Erik. 1982. *Teorier om "Folkerettens stilling i norsk rett"*, Oslo.

Hellner, Jan. 1986. Pacta sunt servanda, In: Bratholm et al. (eds.), *Samfunn Rett Rettferdighet. Festskrift til Torstein Eckhoffs 70-årsdag,* TANO, pp. 335–349.

Hsee, Christopher K. and Jiao Zhang. 2004. Internal and Substantive Inconsistencies In Decision-Making, In: D. Koehler and N. Harvey (eds.), Blackwell Handbook of Judgement and Decision Making, Oxford (references in this article is to the relvant page in the draft available at http://papers.ssrn.com/sol3/papers.cfm?abstract_id=929939

Jolls, Christine, Cass Sunstein and Richard Thaler. 2002. A Behavioral Approach to Law and economics. In: Ellickson, Rose and Ackerman (eds.) *Perspectives on Property Law,* Third Edition pp. 221–230.

Kahneman, D. 1994. New challenges to the rationality assumption, **150** *Journal of Institutional and Theoretical Economics,* pp. 18–36.

Kaplow, Louis and Steven Shavell. 2002. *Fairness versus Welfare*, Cambridge and London.

Kolstad, Olav. 2008. Rettsøkonomi i juridisk argumentasjon, *TfR*, pp. 393–440.

Kungl. Vetenskapsakademien, Finn Kydland and Edward Prescott's Contribution to Dynamic Macroeconomics: The Time Consistency of Economic Policy and the Driving Forces Behind Business Cycles, Advanced information on the Bank of Sweden Prize in Economic Sciences in Memory of Alfred Nobel 11 October 2004, http://nobelprize.org/nobel_prizes/economics/laureates/2004/adv.html, pp. 1–31 at pp. 2 and 5.

Kydland, Finn E. and Edward C. Prescott. 1977. Rules Rather than Discretion: The Inconsistency of Optimal Plans, **85** *The Journal of Political Economy*, pp. 473–492.

Natural Resources Research Group. 2007. *Consistency in Environmental Law*, (project proposal of 2007 available at: http://www.jus.uio.no/forskning/grupper/naturressurs/Prosjekter/Milj%C3%B8%202015/Consistency%20in%20Environmental%20Law%20Revised.pdf)

Niblett, Anthony. 2009. Inconsistent Contract Enforcement, http://papers.ssrn.com/sol3/papers.cfm?abstract_id=1434685, pp. 1–35.

Nordén, Gunnar. 2002. Norges Banks rettslige stilling: En sytemorientert analyse med implikasjoner på nivået for juridisk metode, *TfR*, pp. 710–775.

Ogus, Anthony. 2006. *Costs and Cautionary Tales. Economic Insights for the Law*, Oxford and Portland.

Perez, Oren and Gunther Teubner (eds.). 2006. *Paradoxes and Inconsistencies in the Law*.

Posner, Richard A. 2003. *Law, Pragmatism and Democracy*, Cambridge and London.

Posner, Richard A. 2008. *How Judges Think*, Cambridge and London.

Revesz, Richard L. 1992. Rehabilitating Interstate Competition: Rethinking the "Race to the Bottom" Rationale for Federal Environmental Regulation, **67** *New York University Law Review*, pp. 1210–1254.

Revesz, Richard L. 1996. Federalism and Interstate Environmental Externalities, **144** *University of Pennsylvania Law Review*, pp. 2341–2416.

Revesz, Richard L. 2001. Federalism and Environmental Regulation: A Public Choice Analysis, **115** *Harvard Law Review*, pp. 555–641.

Revesz, Richard L. and Michael A. Livermore. 2008. *Retaking Rationality – How Cost-Benefit Analysis Can Better Protect the Environment and Our Health*, New York.

Schelling, Thomas C. 1960. *The Strategy of Conflict,* Cambridge, MA.

Stavang, Endre. 2009. Reguleringsplan og tredjemanns rett, *unpublished manuscript,* pp. 3–95.

Thaler, Richard H. and Cass R. Sunstein. 2008. *Nudge. Improving Decisions About Health, Wealth and Happiness,* New Haven 2008/London 2009.

Qvigstad, Jan F. 2009. On Keeping Promises, In: Rune Slagstad (ed.), *On Keeping Promises. A collection of articles based on three lectures given at a seminar arranged by Norges Bank and the Norwegian Academy of Science and Letters on 11 November 2008,* Norges Bank Occational Papers No. 39, Oslo.

Wennerås, Pål. 2004. Permit Defences in Environmental Liability Regimes – Subsidizing Environmental Damage in the EC? *The Yearbook of European Environmental Law Vol. 4*, pp. 149–180.

Wennerås, Pål. 2005. A Progressive Interpretation of the Environmental Liability Directive, *JEEPL*, pp. 257–267.

Wennerås, Pål. 2007. *The Enforcement of EC Environmental Law*, Oxford and New York.

Wennerås, Pål. 2008. Towards and Ever Greening Union? Competence in the Field of the Environment and Beyond, **45** *Common Market Law Review,* pp. 1645–1685.

Wilhelmsen, Trine-Lise. 1995. Avtaleloven § 36 og økonomisk effektivitet, *TfR,* pp. 1–246.

Transport Liability Regimes and Economic Efficiency

Trine-Lise Wilhelmsen

1. Introduction

The purpose of this paper is to discuss different transport liability regimes in the context of economic efficiency. Transport liability regimes refer to provisions defining the carrier's liability in case of damage to the carried goods under different kinds of transport. Economic efficiency in relation to legal rules is defined through theories in law and economics. The core of this topic is to what extent legal rules result in maximum value for society, or if the regulation can be changed to increase value. In the latter situation, the existing rules will lead to waste of resources.

The context of efficiency is a tribute to Erling Eide, who was the first scholar to develop this field at the Faculty of Law. His work includes legal and economic analysis of tort law. A tort law topic is therefore in line with some of his research. The reason for choosing transport liability regimes as a topic is that these regimes are currently under discussion both in the EU and internationally. Transport liability for damage to cargo is traditionally regulated by international conventions providing rules for contracts of carriage of goods by sea, road, railroad and air, respectively. The regulations are mandatory, and can therefore not be departed from in countries that have ratified the conventions. All the Nordic countries have ratified the current main international conventions and their liability regimes.

However, a new convention for transport wholly or partly by sea ("maritime plus"), was signed inter alia by Norway and Denmark in Rotterdam 23. September 2009 (Rotterdam Rules).[1] The Rotterdam Rules is not signed by Sweden or Finland.

Parallel to the international work on the Rotterdam Rules there has been a development within the EU towards a defined transport policy. As a part of this process, a working group has made a draft of a separate transport liability regime (ISIC). These rules are not directed at carriage by sea, but at transport in general, regardless of the mode of transport.[2]

The fate of the ISIC draft is yet undecided. The Rotterdam Rules are signed by 21 states,[3] but not ratified by any state, and the question of enforcement is thus uncertain.[4] The future regulation of transport liability is therefore unclear. In regard to both the Rotterdam Rules and the ISIC, efficiency is a defined goal.[5] An evaluation of the liability regimes in these rules and other transport liability models in the context of efficiency can therefore provide some relevant arguments for choosing which rules should be adapted. This is particularly of relevance for the Nordic countries where the different attitude to the Rotterdam Rules may threaten the traditional Nordic cooperation in the field of maritime law.

Due to the limitation of pages, the article cannot go into a detailed analysis of the question at hand. The goal is limited to providing an overview of the transport liability regulation, to outlining the main models of transport liability for damage to goods and to providing some efficiency considerations that may be of relevance.[6] Only ordinary liability rules will be discussed, and not the particular liability rules for bill of lading.

---

1 United Nations A/RES/63/122, United Nations Convention on Contracts for the International Carriage of Goods Wholly or Partly by Sea, 2 February 2009, cf. http://www.comitemaritime.org/draft/pdf/Resolution.pdf. Cf. also CMI Yearbook 2004 p. 132 ff. On the signing ceremony, cf. http://www.rotterdamrules2009.com/cms/

2 Integrated Services in the Intermodal Chain (ISIC). Final Report Task B: Intermodal liability and documentation. Southampton 2005.

3 <http://treaties.un.org/Pages/ViewDetails.aspx?src=TREATY&mtdsg_no=XI-D-8&chapter=11&lang=en#EndDec>

4 Ratification by 20 states is necessary to obtain enforcement, Rotterdam Rules art. 94.1.

5 Rotterdam Rules, The General Assembly, p. 1, fifth paragraph, ISIC, Final Report Task B: Intermodal liability and documentation, Introduction to the ISIC project, second paragraph.

6 A more detailed presentation both of the legal regulation and the efficiency considerations presented here is found in Wilhelmsen, *Rett i havn*, Oslo 2006. This presentation includes a previous draft of the Rotterdam Rules, but not the ISIC draft.

2. Overview of the transport liability regulation

2.1 Unimodal and multimodal transport. The parties to the contract

In order to outline the rules regulating transport liability, it is necessary to distinguish between unimodal and multimodal transport. Unimodal transport is a transport carried out by one mode of carriage, i.e. carriage by ship, road, railroad or air.[7] If the transport is organized by a combination of separate means of carriage, for instance land road to a port and ship between two ports, this is called multimodal transport.[8] Unimodal transports have traditionally been regulated by international conventions that are incorporated into Norwegian legislation, cf. 2.2 below. Multimodal transports, on the other hand, are today regulated through international or Nordic standard agreements, cf. 2.3 below.

The unimodal and multimodal rules are operating with different categories of parties to the contract of carriage.[9] For the sake of simplicity, the person promising to provide the carriage is in this article named the carrier, whereas the buyer of the transport service is called the shipper.

2.2 International and national regulation of unimodal transport liability

Carriage by sea, road, railroad and airplane is regulated by international conventions that are incorporated into Norwegian legislation. **Carriage by sea** is regulated *internationally* by the Hague-Rules,[10] which is ratified by most shipping nations.[11] The Hague Rules were amended to the so-called Hague-Visby Rules in 1968.[12] The Hague-Visby Rules were criticized as favouring the traditional ship-

7 Wilhelmsen p. 22 and note 15, Vestergaaard Pedersen, *Transportret*, Copenhagen 2008, p. 52.

8 Wilhelmsen p. 23 and note 16, Vestergaaard Pedersen p. 52, COM (97) 243 final pt. 15.

9 Wilhelmsen, pp. 57–59, Vestergaaard Pedersen p. 48 ff.

10 International Convention for the Unification of Certain Rules of Law relating to Bills of Lading, Brussels 1924.

11 Falkanger and Bull, *Innføring i sjørett*, Oslo 2004, p. 239; Lüddeke and Johnson, *The Hamburg Rules*, London 1995, pp. 51–52.

12 Protocol to Amend the International Convention for the Unification of Certain Rules of Law Relating to Bills of Lading, Brussels 1968; Falkanger and Bull pp. 239–240.

ping nationalities, and a new convention named the Hamburg Rules was therefore enacted in 1978.[13] The aim was that the Hamburg Rules should follow the Hague-Visby rules, but neither Norway nor the other Nordic countries have ratified this convention.[14] The Hague and the Hague-Visby rules are still the dominant international regimes for carriage by sea.

In *Norway*, the maritime transport liability regime for damage to goods is included in the Maritime Code (MC) chapter 13.[15] As a starting point these rules conform to the Hague-Visby Rules 1968. The Hamburg Rules from 1978 are, as mentioned, not ratified by the Nordic countries, but the Nordic legislators have chosen solutions that are as similar to the Hamburg Rules as possible without having to revoke the Hague-Visby rules. Further, special solutions are chosen for national transport since this is outside the scope of the conventions.[16] The regulation is mandatory in favour of the shipper, cf. MC § 254 first and second subparagraph.

International **transport by road** is regulated by the CMR-convention 1956.[17] The CMR-convention is ratified by a majority of the European countries, including Norway, and is incorporated in Norwegian law in *veifraktloven*.[18] The regulation is mandatory, cf. § 5. Transport liability is regulated in chapter IV.

International **transport by railway** is regulated by the COTIF-convention[19] Annex B named CIM,[20] which was amended in 1999.[21] The conventions are directly incorporated in Norway.[22] The convention does not apply to national railway transport. This kind of transport is regulated by the CN-conditions[23]

13 United Nations Convention on the Carriage of Goods by Sea, Hamburg 1978.

14 Falkanger and Bull pp. 240–242.

15 *Lov om sjøfarten av 1994 nr. 39 (MC).*

16 Falkanger and Bull p. 242.

17 Convention on the Contract for the International Carriage of Goods by Road (CMR), Geneva, 1956.

18 *Lov om vegfraktavtaler av 1974 nr. 68 (veifraktloven).*

19 Convention concerning International Carriage by Rail (COTIF), Bern 1980.

20 International Convention concerning the Carriage of Goods by Rail (CIM), Bern 1970.

21 Protocol of 3 June 1999 for the Modification of the Convention concerning International Carriage by Rail (COTIF) of 9 May 1980, Vilnius 1999, Vestergaard Pedersen p. 129.

22 *Lov om overenskomst om internasjonal jernbanetrafikk av 2004 nr. 82 (COTIF-loven).*

23 *Generelle Transportvilkår for CargoNet Konsern, 6. utg. 1. januar 2010 (CN-vilkårene).*

with an Annex.[24] The liability rules in both instruments are very similar to the regulation in CIM/*veifraktloven*.[25]

Transport by air is regulated internationally by the Montreal Convention[26], containing liability rules in chapter III. The liability rules are incorporated in Norway in *luftfartsloven*[27] chapter X, D.

2.3 International and national regulation of multimodal transport liability

The international attempts at harmonization have been less successful for multimodal transports. Several attempts, hereunder two conventions, have failed.[28] Nor is there any Norwegian legislation that regulates multimodal transports.[29]

The lack of international mandatory harmonization and national mandatory legislation has resulted in several international rules or standard agreements on multimodal transport. The main international regulation is the UNCTAD/ICC Rules for multimodal transports.[30] The liability regime here is based on one of the multimodal convention drafts.[31] The same approach is used by the international freight forwarder sector in their standard agreement named the FBL rules.[32] A Nordic alternative to this regulation is *Nordisk Speditørforbunds alminnelige bestemmelser NSAB 2000*, which also contain liability rules in case the freight forwarder acts as carrier, but these liability rules are based on the CMR/CIM

24 *Vedlegg til "Generelle transportvilkår for CargoNet AS", Tilleggsbestemmelser for transport i egne tog (Systemtog) i norsk trafikk (CN-vedlegg).*

25 *CIM Title III, CN-vilkårene art. 8.*

26 Convention for the Unification of Certain Rules for International Carriage by Air, Montreal 1999.

27 *Lov om luftfart av 1993 nr. 101 (luftfartsloven).*

28 Wilhelmsen p. 28. The two conventions are Transport Combiné de Marchandises (TCM) 1971 and United Nations Convention on International Multimodal Transport of Goods, Geneva, 1980.

29 Bull, *Innføring i veifraktrett*, Oslo 2000, p. 124; Falkanger and Bull pp. 313–315.

30 UNCTAD/ICC Rules for Multimodal Transport Documents (UNCTAD/ICC), 1992. The rules do not have status as legislation and must be incorporated in the individual contract, cf. Ramberg, *The law of freight forwarding and the 1992 FIATA Multimodal Transport Bill of Lading*, Zurich 1993 p. 33.

31 TCM 1971, cf. further Wilhelmsen pp. 28–30 and pp. 158–159.

32 FIATAs (negotiable) combined transport bill of lading (FBL), developed by The International Federation of Freight Forwarders Associations, cf. Ramberg p. 24 ff., Wilhelmsen pp. 28–29.

regulation. The last alternatives are developed by BIMCO[33] to be used in the shipping sector. The relevant regulation is here provided in Combiconbill (1995)[34], which is based on the Hague-Visby Rules, and Multidoc 95,[35] which is based on the UNCTAD/ICC Rules.

The international development on multimodal transports contains however as mentioned two new steps. The first is the Rotterdam Rules, which contrary to the previous conventions on maritime transport, regulates carriage wholly or partly by sea.[36] The multimodal approach is therefore more limited than the standard contracts because part of the transport must be performed by sea. The liability regime in these rules are contained in ch. 5 and based on the Hague-Visby rules. The second step is the ISIC draft, which applies to multimodal transports in general.[37] The regulation is basically mandatory, but the parties can agree to opt out of the regime.[38] The liability rules are contained in part 3. The rules here are stricter than the other regimes, but fairly close to the carriage by air regulation.

3. Models for transport liability

The purpose here is to outline three issues in the different transport liability regimes that are relevant for the evaluation in regard to efficiency, namely the basis for the carrier's liability, the extent of losses covered and the so-called network principle.

3.1 Basis for liability

Even though there are several different transport regimes, the regulation of the basis for transport liability may be divided into four main models moving from stricter to more lenient regimes. The first and strictest liability for the carrier is

33 The Baltic and International Maritime Council.

34 Combined Transport Bill of Lading, cf. further Wilhelmsen pp. 29–30

35 Multimodal Transport Bill of Lading of 1995, (Multidoc), cf. further Wilhelmsen pp. 29–30.

36 Rotterdam Convention art. 5 (1) cf. art. 1.1.

37 ISIC art. 2 cf. art. 1.1(a).

38 ISIC art. 2.

the so-called control liability. The clearest example of this model is the ISIC draft. The point of departure in this regime is that the carrier is liable for total or partial loss of the goods or damage to the goods regardless of fault.[39] However, the carrier is not liable for such damage or loss "to the extent that it was caused by circumstances beyond the control of the" carrier.[40]

The second and somewhat less strict regime is no-fault liability combined with a longer list of exclusions. This approach is used in the unimodal regimes for road and railroad, and in NSAB. The exclusions for liability contain a specified list of circumstances that the carrier is not liable for, and thereafter a more general exclusion for damage that the carrier could not prevent.[41] The following clause in NSAB § 16 provides a typical example of the list of exclusions.

> There is no liability if loss, depreciation, damage or delay is caused by:
> a) fault or neglect of the customer,
> b) handling, loading, stowage or unloading of the goods by the customer or anyone acting on his behalf,
> c) the inherent nature of the goods to be easily damaged, e.g. by breakage, leakage, spontaneous combustion, rotting, rust, fermentation, evaporation or being susceptible to cold, heat or moisture,
> d) lack of or insufficient packing,
> e) faulty or insufficient address or marking of the goods,
> f) faulty or insufficient information about the goods,
> g) circumstances which the freight forwarder could not avoid and the consequences of which he was unable to prevent.

A third model is liability for negligence with reversed burden of proof. This approach is used in the Maritime Code § 275 first subparagraph for national transport, and in some of the international multimodal regimes.[42]

---

39 ISIC art. 8.1.

40 ISIC art. 8.4. *Lov om luftfart av 1993 nr. 101 (luftfartsloven)* § 10-19 has a very similar regulation, but the exclusions are somewhat more elaborated.

41 *Veifraktloven* § 27 cf § 28 and § 29, CIM art. 23, *CN-vilkårene* art. 8.2 cf. 8.4 and 8.5, NSAB § 15 and § 16.

42 UNCTAD/ICC 5.1, FBL clause 6.2, Multiwaybill clause 10 (b), but all contain special exclusions for carriage by sea, cf. Ramberg pp. 42–43.

The last and most lenient model for the carrier is negligence with reversed burden of proof combined with a list of exclusions. This is the traditional model in maritime transport, but the list of exclusions varies. The simplest list contains exclusions for navigational error and fire only.[43] A more extended list is found in the Hague-Visby Rules and also in some of the multimodal regimes.[44] Art. 17 of the Rotterdam Rules provides the latest international version of this approach:

Article 17 Basis of liability

1. The carrier is liable for loss of or damage to the goods, as well as for delay in delivery, if the claimant proves that the loss, damage, or delay, or the event or circumstance that caused or contributed to it took place during the period of the carrier's responsibility as defined in chapter 4.
2. The carrier is relieved of all or part of its liability pursuant to paragraph 1 of this article if it proves that the cause or one of the causes of the loss, damage, or delay is not attributable to its fault or to the fault of any person referred to in article 18.
3. The carrier is also relieved of all or part of its liability pursuant to paragraph 1 of this article if, alternatively to proving the absence of fault as provided in paragraph 2 of this article, it proves that one or more of the following events or circumstances caused or contributed to the loss, damage, or delay:
   - (a) Act of God;
   - (b) Perils, dangers, and accidents of the sea or other navigable waters;
   - (c) War, hostilities, armed conflict, piracy, terrorism, riots, and civil commotions;
   - (d) Quarantine restrictions; interference by or impediments created by governments, public authorities, rulers, or people including detention, arrest, or seizure not attributable to the carrier or any person referred to in article 18;
   - (e) Strikes, lockouts, stoppages, or restraints of labour;
   - (f) Fire on the ship;
   - (g) Latent defects not discoverable by due diligence;
   - (h) Act or omission of the shipper, the documentary shipper, the controlling party, or any other person for whose acts the shipper or the documentary shipper is liable pursuant to article 33 or 34;

43 MC § 275 cf. § 276 for international transport by sea, UNCTAD/ICC 5.4 and FBL clause 6.6 for carriage by sea.

44 Hague-Visby Rules art. IV 2, Combiconwaybill clause 9 (1) cf. 9 (3) (a) to (h) and 9 (5), Multiwaybill clause 11 for carriage by sea.

(i) Loading, handling, stowing, or unloading of the goods performed pursuant to an agreement in accordance with article 13, paragraph 2, unless the carrier or a performing party performs such activity on behalf of the shipper, the documentary shipper or the consignee;
(j) Wastage in bulk or weight or any other loss or damage arising from inherent defect, quality, or vice of the goods;
(k) Insufficiency or defective condition of packing or marking not performed by or on behalf of the carrier;
(l) Saving or attempting to save life at sea;
(m) Reasonable measures to save or attempt to save property at sea;
(n) Reasonable measures to avoid or attempt to avoid damage to the environment; or
(o) Acts of the carrier in pursuance of the powers conferred by articles 15 and 16.

3.2 The amount of loss covered

A characteristic feature of the transport liability regimes is that the liability for damage and loss is limited. The limitation amounts however, differ between the different regimes. The lowest limitation amounts are found in the maritime regimes and some of the multimodal regimes, with 667 SDR per package and 2 SDR per kg/gross weight.[45] The amounts are raised somewhat in the Rotterdam Rules art. 59 to 875 SDR per package and 3 SDR per kg. A median level of 8,33 SDR per kg is used in international transport by road,[46] whereas the amounts used for national transport in Norway and also in several international instruments are 17 SDR pr. kg.[47]

3.3 Incorporating the mandatory regulation – the network principle

As mentioned, the international and Norwegian regimes for unimodal transports are mandatory as a main rule. The extent to which a multimodal regime may

45 MC § 280 first subparagraph, Hague-Visby art. IV 5 a, UNCTAD/ICC 6.1, Multiwaybill clause 12 (a). It is raised in the Hamburg Rules to 835 units per package or 2.5 units per kg, cf. art. 6 no. 1 (a).
46 *Veifraktloven* § 32 third subparagraph.
47 MC § 280 second subparagraph, *veifraktloven* § 32 second subparagraph, *luftfartsloven* § 10-22 fourth subparagraph, CIM art. 30 § 2, ISIC art. 9.1.

depart from the liability rules in the mandatory unimodal regimes if the damage occurs while the goods are on a mode of transport regulated by mandatory rules is discussed.[48] In order to avoid a conflict of regulations, this issue is solved by incorporating the mandatory rules into the multimodal regulation through a network clause.[49] The extent of the incorporation of the mandatory rules varies, but the result is a double liability regime whereby "the ordinary" liability regime in the regulation is combined with the mandatory regulation. The core of the network principle is that (i) damage occurring while the goods were carried on a mode of transport regulated by a mandatory regime is regulated by this regime and (ii) damage caused at an unknown time/place and damage occurring outside the scope of the mandatory regime is covered by the "ordinary liability regime".

4. Efficiency considerations

4.1 Efficiency and policy considerations

One goal of the Rotterdam Rules is to obtain uniform rules in order to "enhance legal certainty, improve efficiency and commercial predictability".[50] The ISIC draft is a part of the EU transport policy, where the goal is to "improve the quality, efficiency and transparency of intermodal transport chains".[51] In the EU transport policy, however, efficiency is not only defined as a goal per se, but also as a tool for inducing sustainable transport. The core of this argument seems to be that efficient liability rules are necessary in order to encourage shippers to shift from the more polluting road transport to a less polluting combination of transport modes.[52]

48 Cf. further Wilhelmsen ch. 7.5.3.

49 Cf. Rotterdam Rules art. 26 and Wilhelmsen ch. 7.2.3, 7.3.3 and 7.4.3.

50 Rotterdam Rules, The General Assembly, p. 1 fifth paragraph.

51 ISIC, Introduction to the ISIC project, second paragraph. Cf. further Eftestøl Wilhelmsson, Sustainable mobility – Mot en grønn Europeisk transportrett? In JFT no. 3–4/2009 pp. 228–229 and COM (97) 243 final nr. 6, 41, 81 and 82.

52 Cf. Further Eftestøl Wilhelmsson, EU Intermodal transport and carrier liability – content and context, in SIMPLY 2007, p. 137 ff., Eftestøl Wilhelmsson, Sustainable mobility – Mot en grønn Europeisk transportrett? In JFT no. 3–4/2009 p. 225 ff, COM (97) 243.

> In the European discussion on intermodality, carrier's liability is seen as just one of several obstacles to the main goal of increasing intermodal freight transport within the EU, making the European Transport Chain more efficient and sustainable.[53] A main issue here is to encourage a shift from road transport to multi-modal transport to counter the environmental and social costs entailed by road transport.[54] The objective is to develop a framework for an optimal integration of different modes so as to enable an efficient and cost-effective use of the transport system through door-to-door services while favouring competition between transport operators.[55] In order to achieve this goal, measures have to be taken to avoid "friction costs" in regard to infrastructure, points of transport between modes, and mode based information transmission systems. The last issue includes legal friction costs due to the use of different liability conventions and national legislation for each mode of transport.[56] The uncertainty in relation to the issue of carrier liability during multimodal transports was therefore considered an obstacle to an efficient European transport chain,[57] which again is considered necessary to reduce the harmful effects, inter alia pollution, which increased transport activity generates. This argumentation presumes that efficiency considerations may have a double effect: efficient legislation result in maximum value to society, and may also result in decreased pollution through a shift from road transport to multi-modal transports. It is however, outside the scope of this analysis to consider the link between efficiency considerations and environmental concerns further.

As further goals ISIC mentions uniformity, avoidance of legal complications and facilitation of claims settlements.[58] The relationship between uniformity, legal clarity, commercial predictability and efficiency is not explained.

Uniformity is obtained through mandatory rules.[59] In the absence of regulation, the parties will have to negotiate individual contracts or use standard contracts. In terms of law and economics, negotiation costs are transaction costs that

53 Cf. Eftestøl Wilhelmsson, EU Intermodal transport and carrier liability – content and context, in: SIMPLY 2007, p. 139.

54 Wilhelmsson l.c. p. 141, COM (97) 243 final no. 3.

55 Wilhelmsson l.c. p. 141, COM (97) 243 final no. 16.

56 Wilhelmsson l.c.p. 141-142, COM (97) 243 final no. 26–44.

57 Wilhelmsson l.c. p. 141.

58 ISIC p. 11 no. 10, p. 9 no. 3 and p. 11 no. 9.

59 Op.cit. p. 11 no. 10.

have to be included in the price of the transport.[60] The same holds for legal costs connected to the interpretation of the regulation and the settlements.[61] In terms of efficiency, therefore, these goals may be expressed as a goal to reduce transaction costs.

Efficiency considerations may however also be tied more directly to different liability models. Law and economic theory analyses damage and liability with different approaches. One approach is to analyse the efficient division of risk and liability in a market with free competition under different presumptions in relation to liability costs, risk costs, transactions costs and attitude towards risk.[62] Another approach is Calabresi's normative theory stating that tort law rules should aim at minimizing the total costs of measures to prevent damage, damage costs and administrative costs.[63] In Norwegian law this theory is analysed i.a. by Erling Eide.[64] As prevention of damage normally is a rationale for liability rules, this approach is chosen here. This model combines efficiency considerations and legal policy considerations, and therefore also says something about the functionality of the transport liability regimes in regard to prevention as a goal for liability rules.

In the following, the damage and liability model is presented in 4.2 and 4.3. This model is thereafter applied on the liability regimes together with a discussion on transaction costs.

4.2 Damage and liability – the basic model

The approach in this model is to define how different rules influence the optimal level of care in order to minimize the sum of costs for preventive measures and damage. The main presumptions in the theory are that the liable party or injurer is

---

60 Eide, *Rettsøkonomiske analyser av forslaget til ny sjøtransportkonvensjon*, seminar contribution, 20–21 February 2003, http://folk.uio.no/erikro/WWW/cog/cog.html (Eide 2003) p. 10.

61 Eide and Stavang, *Rettsøkonomi*, Oslo 2008, pp. 129–130.

62 Eide 2003.

63 Calabresi, *The Cost of Accidents*, 1970, Eide, Rettsøkonomi – en introduksjon, in: JV 1992 193–224 Eide 1992 p. 213, Eide and Stavang, *Rettsøkonomi for privatrett og miljørett*, Oslo 2001, p. 103, Eide and Stavang 2008, pp. 237–238.

64 The model is described in detail in Eide 1992 p. 213–215, Stavang, Økonomisk analyse av erstatningsrett, in *Rettsøkonomi, Institutt for Privatrett Stensilserie B* no. 22, Oslo 1999, p. 3 ff., Eide and Stavang 2001 p. 101 ff, Eide and Stavang 2008 p. 236 ff., and Shavell, *Economic Analysis of Accident Law*, 1987, p. 5 ff.

acting rationally by seeking to minimize his own costs in relation to damage, that he has full information about the tort rules, and that the rules are enforced.[65]

The theory demonstrates that no liability is never optimal, that no-fault liability will induce the injurer to choose a level of care that minimizes the sum of prevention costs and expected damage, and that liability for negligence will induce the injurer to choose the level of care necessary to avoid liability so that he is only liable for loss prevention costs.[66]

The model further analyses the significance of the victim's potential for preventive measures and the interaction between the negligence on the part of the injurer and the victim.[67] The result here is that lack of liability for the injurer is not optimal because the injurer will not take care. But no-fault liability is not optimal either, because in this case the victim will not take any preventive measures. The efficient solution is therefore no-fault liability with exclusion for the situation where the victim's loss prevention is not optimal because in this case both parties will take preventive measures.

4.3 The efficient basis for liability in contractual relationships

The basic model presumes that there is no contractual relationship between the injurer and the victim. In the event of a contractual relationship, for instance between a carrier and a shipper, the model must be supplemented with the shipper's willingness to pay for the carrier's services. The shipper's willingness to pay will depend on how he assesses the risk involved in the transport.[68] The injurer's/carrier's inducement to prevent damage will therefore depend both on the risk of damage and the possibility to sell the service for a better price.[69]

The model builds on a presumption that the carrier maximizes his own profit. It is further presumed that he acts in a market with perfect competition, which means that the price of the service provided is equal to the total costs necessary to produce the service, including the costs connected to liability against

65 Stavang 1999 p. 5, Eide and Stavang 2001 pp. 101–102 and Eide and Stavang 2008 p. 236.

66 Eide and Stavang 2008 pp. 238–240, Shavell p. 8.

67 Shavell p. 9 ff., Stavang 1999 pp. 26–28, Eide and Stavang 2001 p. 126 ff., Eide and Stavang 2008 p. 262 ff.

68 The model is based on Shavell p. 47 ff.

69 Shavell p. 47 and pp. 51–52.

the customers/shippers.[70] A third presumption is that the risk of damage depends on negligence or non-negligence. With these presumptions, the following table showing level of care, cost of care, percentage of probability of an accident and expected accident losses may be used for the discussion:[71]

Level of care	Cost of care	Accident probability	Expected accident losses
None	0	9 %	9
Care	2	3 %	3

The carrier's costs in producing one unit of transport = 10. This amount does not include costs in relation to care or liability against the customers. Based on these figures, the optimal level of care may be discussed depending on the shipper's information about the risk.

In the first case the shipper has **full information about the risk of damage**. If the carrier does not face liability for damage, he will not have any costs connected to care or expected accident losses.[72] In this case, a carrier C-1 may choose to sell one unit of transport for 10, which is the production cost. A shipper who has full information about the risk inherent in the transport, however, will know that the carriage will in fact cost him 10+9=19 due to the accident costs. Another carrier C-2 chose to take care. The cost per unit of transport will be raised by 2 to 12. At the same time, the shipper's risk will be reduced to 3. The shipper's total cost will therefore be 15. A cost-minimizing shipper with full information about the risk of damage will select C-2 with total costs of 15 instead of C-1 with total costs 19. The result is that the less careful C-1 will lose his customers to the more careful C-2 even if no liability is imposed.

If the carrier is facing strict liability, he will be liable for cost of care and expected accident costs. As 2+3 is less than 9, he will choose care. If we presume that the norm for negligence follows the optimal care in the ordinary tort law model, the result is the same for liability for negligence. The result is therefore that the carrier will choose care regardless of liability for damage.[73]

70 Shavell p. 47.

71 Taken from Shavell p. 49.

72 Shavell p. 52.

73 Shavell p. 52–53. In the same direction but with another approach Eide 2003 pp. 5–6.

In the second case the cargo owner **does not have sufficient information about the probability of damage** to calculate the correct price for the service from different service providers.[74] Under this presumption, liability for the carrier will mean that he will not take care because he cannot expect the shipper to be willing to pay the extra cost when he is not informed about the probability of damage. Furthermore, the level of care taken by shippers will not be optimal in the absence of liability. Customers will take too little care if they underestimate the risk and too much care if they overestimate it. In addition, purchases will not be optimal in the absence of liability. If he overestimates the risk, the total costs (price + accident costs) will be too high, and he will buy less than the optimal amount. On the other hand, if he underestimates the risk, the costs are too low, and he will buy too much.

In case of liability for negligence the carrier will take optimal care in relation to the evaluation of negligence. However, if the shipper wrongly estimates the risk of damage presuming care, he will take more or less than optimal care and buy more or less than the optimal amount.[75] Furthermore, a negligence rule corresponding to the optimal level of care presumes that the judge has sufficient knowledge to evaluate the carrier's activity. If this proves difficult, the evaluation of negligence may well lead to too much or too little care.[76]

In case of no-fault liability with exclusion for the shipper's negligence, the situation will be that both the carrier and the cargo owner will choose an optimal level of care. In addition, it does not matter whether the shipper wrongly calculates the risk when the carrier is fully liable. The market price in this case will reflect the correct risk of damage, and the shipper will decide how much transport to buy based on the market price alone.[77]

4.4 Efficiency and the legal regulation

4.4.1 Basis for liability

The model demonstrates that if transport is provided in a market with perfect competition and full information, the optimal level of care is not influenced by the liability rules. In this case it does not matter whether liability is based on

74 Shavell pp. 53–54.

75 Shavell pp. 53–54.

76 Shavell p. 56.

77 Shavell p. 54.

negligence with a shifted burden of proof with or without exclusions, or on no-fault liability with or without exclusions.

This implies that if the shipper is professional with extensive activity and sufficient transport volume to establish his own statistics over probability of accidents and accident losses, liability for the carrier is not necessary to obtain optimal level of care for the carrier and optimal level of purchase from the shipper. This result is particularly interesting in relation to the list of exclusions in the Rotterdam Rules and previous international maritime regimes, which under these circumstances do not result in any loss of efficiency. At the same time, a rule of liability for negligence will result in transaction costs in relation to the settlements, which must be calculated into the price of the transport.[78] A rule of liability for negligence combined with an extensive list of exclusions is likely to create more legal complications and thus higher transaction costs. In relation to this group of shippers it seems to be more efficient to transfer the whole risk to the shipper rather than make a division similar to the Rotterdam Rules. But also no-fault liability seems to provide an efficient solution as a fully informed shipper would be willing to include liability costs in the price. In order to avoid transaction costs however, exclusions should be avoided. In terms of transaction costs, no-fault liability is also better than liability for negligence. The most efficient regime in this context is therefore the ISIC Draft for multimodal transports.

In relation to shippers with less activity and limited knowledge of the probability of damage, on the other hand, a rule of liability will be required to obtain an optimal level of care and an optimal amount of purchase of the service. The most optimal solution in this case is no-fault liability. The regime closest to this solution is the ISIC Draft. No-fault liability is also the starting point in the international and national unimodal regimes for road and railway, and in NSAB, but here the efficiency is reduced by a more or less extensive list of exclusions. The list of exclusions in the Rotterdam Rules and the previous international maritime regimes, on the other hand, is not in conformity with economic efficiency in this situation except to the extent that they regulate the acts of the shipper, cf. below. The negligence rule which is the starting point in these regimes will be optimal only if the courts manage to define negligence near the point of optimal care in the model.

78 Wilhelmsen p. 337, Eide 2003 pp. 6–7.

4.4.2 Negligence from the cargo owner

It follows from the traditional tort law model that no-fault liability is not efficient unless it is combined with an exception from liability if the victim is negligent, cf. 4.2 above. Negligence by the shipper is not directly regulated in the international or national maritime regulation. However, as this regulation is based on negligence from the carrier with a shifted burden of proof, the carrier will be free from liability if he demonstrates that the loss is not due to negligence on his part, but rather to the acts or omissions on the part of the shipper. Further, several of the exclusions from liability in these regimes concern circumstances tied to the shipper.

Transport liability regimes based on no-fault liability will also normally contain exclusions for risk factors where acts or omissions on the part of the cargo owner normally will be significant.[79] Examples are exclusions for "fault or neglect of the customer" and "handling, loading, stowage or unloading of the goods by the customer".[80] The ISIC Draft does not contain exclusions tied directly to the acts of the shipper, but contains an exclusion for circumstances outside the carrier's control which presumably will lead to the same result. In relation to this issue, the legal regulations seem to correspond with efficiency considerations.

4.4.3 The losses to be indemnified

The starting point in the tort law models is that the element of damage costs contains all costs related to the damage suffered by the victim. Optimal level of care therefore presumes that the injurer is liable for the whole loss.[81] This is also true when there is a contractual relationship between the injurer and the victim unless the purchaser has full information and no liability is necessary to create efficiency. If the purchaser does not have full information, an efficient regime presumes that the market price shall reflect the correct risk for damage. This is only obtained if the seller is liable for the whole loss. This is also true if the potential loss is high.[82]

A characteristic feature in relation to the transport liability regimes, on the

79 Wilhelmsen p. 339.

80 NSAB 2000 § 16 letter a) and b), referred above in chapter 3.1, cf. also *veifraktloven § 29, CN-vilkårene 8.4.*

81 Shavell pp. 127–128.

82 Shavell p. 129.

other hand, is that the liability is limited. As mentioned in chapter 3.2, the limitation amounts vary in different regimes, from lowest in the international maritime conventions to highest in the EU draft and Norwegian inland transport. This is not in conformity with the efficiency considerations applied here.

4.4.4 The need for mandatory regulation

It follows from 4.3 that the most efficient legal regime will depend upon the shipper's information about the risk. It is also clear that attitudes towards risk and the evaluation of risks differ between different persons, depending on how the risk of damage is calculated and the possibilities for financial coverage, for instance through insurance. One shipper may prefer to combine low freight costs and limited carrier liability with high risk for damage and high insurance costs, whereas another might prefer to buy less insurance and pay higher freight costs with more carrier liability. This implies that the regulation should not be mandatory.[83] The unimodal transport regimes have traditionally been mandatory, and this is also the chosen solution for the Rotterdam Rules. In addition to inefficiency due to lack of freedom to chose an individual level of risk, the mandatory approach means that any regime will have to include the other mandatory rules through a network principle to avoid collision of conventions, thus creating a very complex regulation of liability. This will again lead to lack of clarity and predictability and added transactions costs. The ISIC Draft on the other hand is an opt out regulation, opening for individual preferences in regard to risk for damage. The ISIC Draft therefore seems to be the most efficient solution in this respect. This draft further presumes that there will be no conflict of conventions and therefore no network clause is necessary.[84]

83 Wilhelmsen pp. 315–319, in particular p. 316. Cf. also Eide 2003 pp. 8 and 10, with a different approach.

84 Cf. ISIC pp. 12–13. This is not problematic in regard to regimes that are mandatory in favour of the shipper only, because the ISIC draft contains better solutions for the shippers. CMR, however, is mandatory also in favour of the carrier, but here ISIC presumes that the ISIC draft will prevail.

5. Conclusion

In regard to the efficiency considerations discussed here, it seems that the ISIC Draft contains the most efficient solution by combining a no-fault liability with few exclusions and a possibility to opt out. Transaction costs in the form of negotiation costs are avoided through uniformity if the parties use the regime, optimal level of care is secured through no-fault liability, and transaction costs are again reduced due to few exclusions. For shippers it may be efficient to opt out if the amount saved by carrying their own risk is higher than the transaction costs connected to negotiate an individual contract.

The Rotterdam Rules, on the other hand, may create uniformity, but apparently at the cost of efficiency in regard to loss prevention and also in regard to transaction costs due to an extremely complicated liability regulation. In terms of the efficiency considerations discussed here, it is difficult to see that anything will be gained in regard to legal clarity, commercial predictability and efficient level of care by adopting this liability regime, as compared with the existing international or national transport liability regimes.[85]

If an efficient liability rule is necessary to obtain a shift from road transport to more environmentally friendly transport, that is railway or ship, this provides an added argument in favour of the ISIC Draft. However, this link between efficiency and sustainability is not further analysed here.

85 This view on transactions costs is in line with general criticism of the Rotterdam Rules, in particular from the shipper side, cf. http://www.comitemaritime.org/draft/views.html

Economic Substance and Tax Avoidance

Frederik Zimmer

1. Introduction

Tax avoidance issues emerge when there is a certain degree of contradiction between the economic substance of a transaction and its legal form. Most legal studies on tax avoidance discuss the conditions for assessing the taxable income of a transaction not according to its legal form but according to its economic substance, i.e. the conditions for applying a tax avoidance norm.[1]

There has been much less focus on how the taxation should be carried once it has been decided that a tax avoidance norm applies, in particular on what economic substance the taxation should be based.[2] In many, perhaps most, cases this is rather obvious but, as will be shown, that is not always the case. A related issue, which will also be considered, is the possible consequences an application of a tax avoidance norm may have for other income tax questions which may arise either simultaneously or later. Further, the possible consequences for the application of other taxes – the inheritance tax in particular – will be dealt with briefly. It is generally assumed that taxation based on the tax avoidance norm does not have any private law implications. That assumption will not be focused upon.

This article deals with these issues under Norwegian tax law. Because the tax avoidance norm in Norway is based on case law, the main source is the Supreme

1 See for instance for Norway Magnus Aarbakke, *Omgåelse av skatteregler som rettsanvendelsesproblem, Lov og Rett* 1970 p. 1; Bettina Banoun, *Omgåelse av skattereglene,* 2003; Frederik Zimmer, Norway's Antiavoidance Norm, in *Tax Notes International,* September 14, 2009, p. 921.

2 See, however, Banoun op. cit. p. 337 in particular.

Court's judgments in tax avoidance cases. This article mainly focuses on judgments from the last 10–15 years. However, a couple of situations are regulated by the tax statute.[3] This rule will only briefly be touched upon.

I am fully aware that an article like this one cannot be regarded as a proper study in law and economics – the scientific field to which Erling Eide has made so many important contributions. Nevertheless, I hope that he – and other readers – will find it worth reading. It certainly has something to do, at the very least, with the relationship between (tax) law and economics.

2. Which economic substance, if any?

The slogan "substance prevails over form" implies that when deviating from the legal form, the tax assessment should be based on the economic substance of the transaction in question. However, that slogan is not necessarily part of Norwegian law, and therefore it cannot be taken for granted that tax authorities, when finding the tax avoidance norm applicable, are obliged to describe the transaction in private law terms on the basis of its economic substance (hereafter referred to as recharacterization) and carry out the tax assessment on that basis. Possible alternative approaches entail more or less radical interpretations of the statute text or simply that the favourable tax effects sought by the taxpayer are not accepted. However, the interpretational approach is often not available under accepted interpretation methods.[4] Furthermore, in my opinion, the latter approach is unsatisfactory because it is not based on an ambition of consistency; it implies that the tax authorities do not endeavour to explain what, in their opinion, the taxpayer has done "in reality". This leaves the recharacterization approach as the one to be preferred generally. The main purpose of the following is to discuss the extent to which the outcome of Supreme Court cases during recent years can be explained as resulting from this approach.

In most cases the economic substance is certainly easy to find and, provided a

3 General Tax Act (hereinafter GTA) of 26 March 1999 no. 14, sec. 14–90.

4 The relationship between statute interpretation and application of the anti-avoidance norm during tax assessment is not clear in all respects but will not be discussed here. It is generally agreed that the tax avoidance norm provides legal basis for deviating from the legal form to a greater extent than statute interpretation would do; see references in footnote 1.

tax avoidance situation exists, there is in fact no alternative to basing the taxation on that substance. For instance, in cases where an asset is transferred first to the taxpayer's children or a tax exempt institution controlled by him before being sold to a third party as part of an overall plan (step transactions), the economic substance is obviously a direct sale from the taxpayer to the third party.[5] Similarly, if a sale of shares within a group of companies is not accepted, the economic substance derives from the fact that no sale of shares has taken place.[6] The same applies to so-called wash sales[7] and redemption of shares immediately followed by the signing up for the new shares in the same company by the same shareholder.[8] If the taxpayer has a sales option for an asset at about the same price as the price for which it was acquired by the taxpayer, the other party may be found to be the owner of the asset for tax purposes and, if so, this of course will be the economic substance on which the taxation will be based.[9]

However, the case is not always so straightforward. In the judgment in Rt. 1995 p. 638 *Skau and Gundersen*, there seems to have been some confusion as to which economic substance was or should be the basis of the tax assessment, once tax avoidance was established. Mr. Skau and Mr. Gundersen owned the shares of Møbelsenteret AS (hereinafter M AS). In 1987 they embarked on a series of transactions, the purpose of which was to establish a group structure and demerge the company. First, they established a new company, SG Holding, with themselves as shareholders. In 1988 they transferred their shares in M AS to SG Hold-

---

5 See *Norsk Retstidende* (hereinafter Rt.) 1978 p. 60 *Smestad*, Rt. 1982 p. 789 *Torkildsen*, Rt. 2006 p. 1062 *A*.

6 See Rt. 2002 p. 456 *Hydro Canada* and Rt. 2006 p. 1232 *Telenor*; in both cases, however, no tax avoidance was found to exist. However, in Rt. 2002 p. 798 *Nordea*, the Supreme Court found, in a related situation (sale of shares in a subsidiary to another subsidiary followed by a merger of the subsidiary and the sub subsidiary), unconvincingly in my opinion, that no realization of shares had taken place without resorting to the tax avoidance norm.

7 Sale of assets, typically shares, followed by an acquisition of same or similar assets, with the purpose of acquiring a right to deduct losses without actually giving up ownership of the asset, see for instance Rt. 1925 p. 472 *Kallevig* and Rt. 1928 p. 495 *Finne*. In such cases, the same result may be reached by liberal statute interpretation.

8 Rt. 1998 p. 1225 *Troll Salmon*, Rt. 2001 p. 170 *Espeland*. Also in these cases, the interpretation approach seems viable.

9 Rt. 1996 p. 1256 *Libæk*, Rt. 1998 p. *Scott*. In both cases, the Supreme Court, with some reservations, concluded that there was no tax avoidance; however, depreciations were disallowed because the taxpayer did not bear the risk for the reduction in value of the asset.

ing in the amount of approximately NOK 3.5 million. Under rules in force at that time, the sale did not trigger any capital gains tax. SG Holding financed the acquisition by taking up a bank loan and forwarded the money to Skau and Gundersen respectively, also in 1988, as consideration for the acquisition of the shares in M AS. SG Holding was able to repay the bank loans by means of group contributions from M AS during the following years.[10]

The tax assessment board found the tax avoidance norm applicable and based the tax assessment on the view that the payment of NOK 3.5 million was taxable as dividends distributed from M AS to Skau and Gundersen in 1988 since they could not have been considered as having sold the shares in M AS because they still controlled them, now via SG Holding.[11] The case was appealed to the claims assessment board which upheld the assessment but seems to have based its result on another view of the economic substance, namely that SG Holding should be examined more closely, and the group contributions from M AS consequently should be regarded as being distributed directly to Mr. Skau and Mr. Gundersen.

The Supreme Court, however, found that the tax avoidance norm was not applicable. In reaching this result, the Court obviously adhered to the view of the

10 Both M AS and SG Holding were demerged, resulting in Mr. Skau and Mr. Gundersen being sole shareholders in a holding company. As this is not essential for the present analysis, the text is simplified in this respect.

11 See Rt. 1995 p. 638 at p. 639: *"Ligningsmyndighetene fant ... at overdragelse av aksjene til et holdingselskap som skattyterne helt ut kontrollerte hadde liten realitet, og at det måtte være riktig å skjære igjennom slik at betalingen ble ansett som utdeling av utbytte fra Møbelsenteret AS."* My translation: "The tax authorities found that the sale of the shares to the holding company had little economic substance and that the payment should be considered as a dividend from M AS."

Essentially, in this respect this case is similar to Rt. 1994. 912 *Hovda*. In that case, Hovda owned all the shares in two companies, SMV and SMI. SMI sold a real estate and decided to use the proceeds to buy Hovda's shares in SMV for NOK 800,000. Also in this case the capital gain was tax free under rules applicable at that time. The tax authorities recharacterized the transaction to a distribution of profits from SMI to Hovda, based on the view that the sale of the shares had scant economic substance because Hovda still controlled them via SMI. The Supreme Court upheld the taxation.

The difference between this case and *Skau and Gundersen* is essentially that the buying company SMI in *Hovda* had the funds to pay for the shares whereas SG Holding in *Skau and Gundersen* did not but had to borrow them, in practice from the company which had them (via repaying the bank loans with money received as group contributions). In my view, and as I will argue, this difference is not essential and should not influence the way in which the transaction is recharacterized.

claims assessment board but found that SG Holding did not warrant investigation. The Supreme Court must have tacitly rejected the recharacterization on the basis of which the tax assessment board had reached its result. This seems clear also from the Court's further reasoning. Finding no tax avoidance, the Court did not have to deal directly with the taxpayer's objections, one of which was that the shareholders could not be taxed in 1988 (the year of the sale of the shares in M AS to SG Holding) because the group contributions were granted only in later years. This objection obviously echoed the claims assessment board's recharacterization but insisted that such a recharacterization could not lead to the result that the whole amount was taxable in 1988. This objection would seem unconvincing, however, if the Supreme Court had recharacterized the facts of the case in the same way the tax assessment board did, namely that the taxation was based on the view that the sale of the shares lacked economic substance and that, therefore, there was a cost-free transfer of money to the shareholders that same year. Instead, the Supreme Court, in finding that there was no tax avoidance, argued that the *group contributions* should be taxed in the hands of the receiving company and could not be taxed as dividends in the hands of the shareholders. It is interesting to note that the discrepancy between the two ways of recharacterizing the transaction does not seem to have been clarified during the deliberations in the Court.[12]

Also in Rt. 2000 p. 1865 *Nygård* there seems to have been some confusion as to the economic substance of the transaction. In addition, this case illustrates the question of whether it is at all necessary, under the tax avoidance norm, to establish a recharacterized transaction as the basis for levying the tax.

A sole proprietorship was transformed into at partnership (in which the partners had pro rata responsibility for the debts) in which the taxpayer – the former sole proprietor – owned 95 % and his wholly owned joint stock company 5 %. The transfer was supposed to lead to much higher depreciable amounts on the assets in the hands of the partnership, which were profitable because of asymmetries in the tax rules. The tax authorities accepted the creation of the partnership and the transfer of the business to it but did not accept the increase in value

12 Even if the Court of Appeal seems to have based its view on the view of the tax assessment board, see *Dommer, uttalelser m.v. i skattesaker og skattespørsmål (Utv.)* 1993 p. 1371.

Skau and Gundersen is unconvincing for several reasons; see Banoun op. cit. p. 216. See also under section 3 below.

of goodwill and other assets. Thus, it seems that the tax authorities were not interested in establishing a recharacterized transaction based on the economic substance but instead resorted to the tax avoidance rule to introduce a radically restrictive application of the rule on determining the depreciable amount on acquired assets.

The Supreme Court accepted the tax assessment but seems to have based its decision on the view that the assets had not been transferred at all to the partnership. The Court wrote that from a tax law point of view it was reasonable to consider the case as one in which no change of ownership had in fact taken place.[13] But the Supreme Court nevertheless accepted the taxation which was, as explained, based on another basis.[14] Again, the difference in approach was not made clear.

Rt. 2006 p. 1573 *Dillerud* again leaves the impression that the Supreme Court was not preoccupied with establishing the recharacterized transaction.[15] Mr. Dillerud owned 33 % of a partnership in which his wife also owned 33 % and his sister-in-law the remaining 34 %. The profits for the tax year in question had been apportioned and distributed among the participants accordingly. However, it was found later that Mr. Dillerud had worked 16 days for the partnership without claiming a salary. The Supreme Court upheld the tax assessment of Mr. Dillerud of an imputed salary income for that work. As this resulted in increased costs for the partnership, the profits of the partnership and the taxable incomes of the wife and sister-in-law were reduced accordingly. These two partners, therefore, had received a larger amount from the company than what turned out to be the taxable amount, but the Supreme Court made no attempt to explain which recharacterized transaction could explain that result. The only possible explanation I can see is that Mr.

13 Rt. 2000 at p. 1871: "... *fra en skatterettslig synsvinkel er det nærliggende å se det slik at det ikke har funnet sted noe eierskifte i forhold til regnskapsvirksomheten.*"

14 Because partnerships are not taxable entities the practical difference of the two approaches was not great. Taxation of the partnership – as carried out by the tax authorities – implied that 5 % of the profits should be taxed in the hands for the newly established joint stock company, whereas 95 % of the profits should be taxed in the hands of the former sole proprietor. Based on the view emerging from the reasoning of the Supreme Court, all 100 % of the profits should be taxed in the hands of the sole proprietor.

15 Admittedly, this is not a proper tax avoidance case but rather an arm's length case, decided under GTA sec. 13-1, which is the Norwegian arm's length rule. However, as far as economic substance is concerned, it is nevertheless of interest.

Dillerud had granted a gift – or at least a payment without any consideration – to the two partners (which was not taxable in their hands). This is not an unreasonable assumption but the fact that such a disposition had to be constructed in order to reach consistent results could perhaps be invoked as an argument against constructing an imputed salary in the first place.

These cases may leave the impression that there is no requirement for applying the tax avoidance norm that a recharacterized transaction based on the economic substance of the transaction is established. However, none of the cases is decisive. Thus, in none of them does the Supreme Court deal with the recharacterization issue as such, and it is striking that, in both *Skau and Gundersen* and *Nygård,* the fact that two possible recharacterizations was possible does not seem to have been made clear during the proceedings.

Application of tax laws, as all laws, should seek consistency, and a tax assessment would lack consistency if a recharacterized transaction is not established by the tax authorities.[16] A requirement for establishment of a recharacterized transaction will contribute to sound and exact legal reasoning within tax administrations and courts; the cases discussed above show that the argument of the Supreme Court was not altogether clear because a proper recharacterization had not taken place. In addition, giving up the search for a consistent recharacterized transaction may result in the anti-avoidance norm being made even more unclear than necessary. Lastly, there seems to be little need for applying the anti-avoidance norm to cases where a recharacterized transaction cannot be established.

For these reasons, it is concluded that the tax authorities, in tax avoidance cases, should be obliged to consider which transaction should prevail for tax

16 In a much older, and well-known, tax avoidance case, Rt. 1971 p. 246 *Kielland,* the Supreme Court was concerned that the tax assessment was not consistent with the way the tax authorities had recharacterized the transaction. Mr. Kielland had transferred shares to a holding company, establishing a debt claim on that company. The transfer did not trigger capital gains tax, and dividends received by the holding company were tax free according the rules applicable at that time. The tax authorities, however, recharacterized the transaction to the effect that Mr. Kielland was still the owner of the shares. The effect of this should have been that Mr. Kielland was taxed currently for dividends on the shares and that he was liable to net wealth tax on the shares (but not on the debt claim). However, such taxation was only carried out in years in which instalments on the debt claim were paid and not in other years. The Supreme Court did not discuss further the lack of logic of this approach but found that the recharacterization could at least explain the tax assessment which had taken place even if further tax assessment perhaps could have been carried out.

purposes – the transaction according to its legal form or a recharacterized transaction based on its economic substance.

3. Simultaneous collateral income tax effects

The recharacterized transaction may imply other income tax effects. For instance, in cases concerning cross ownership of shares in order to avoid the so-called partition rules,[17] the fact that the Supreme Court found this amounted to tax avoidance must imply that no taxation of capital gains at the establishing of the cross ownership could be carried out.[18]

An important question is whether *all* such consequences shall be pursued.[19] In a *dictum* in Rt. 1997 p. 1580 *Zenith,* the Supreme Court seems to presuppose that this is not always needed or necessary. In this case, all shares in a company, which owned assets consisting almost exclusively of cash and provisions to which large latent tax obligations were attached, were sold. While realizing that the sale of shares does not normally affect the tax position of the company, the sale in this case was clearly tax motivated and tax authorities therefore regarded the sale of shares in reality as a sale of the tax provisions. As such, the transfer of tax provisions is not allowed; the provisions were taxed in the hands of the company in the year of the sale of the shares. However, the tax authorities assumed that this should have no impact on the tax treatment of the shareholder in terms of the sale of the shares.

Thus, it can be said that the approach of the tax authorities was in one way inconsistent: the legal form of sale of all shares were recharacterized on a company

---

17 According to those rules, which applied from 1992 through 2004, the so-called "top tax" and employee social security contributions should be levied also on company income, provided that at least 2/3 of the shareholders (or those entitled to dividends) were active in the company. By selling 34 % of the shares to a non-active person these rules could be circumvented.

18 See Rt. 1998 p. 1764 *Wisth & Finnøy,* Rt. 1998 p. 1771 *Essem* and Rt. 2007 p. 209 *Hex.* At least in the last-mentioned case the mutual sale of shares at the establishing of the cross ownership seems to have amounted to a taxable realization of shares. However, none of the judgments mention this issue.

19 GTA sec. 14-90, which establishes a limited tax avoidance rule for change of ownership in companies and mergers/demergers concerning the carrying forward of losses and the postponement of taxation of capital gains, restricts the effects of the rules to the losses or the capital gains in question. Thus, the sale of shares, the merger, etc. are not as such affected by the application of the rule.

level to mean that the company had transferred the provisions. At the same time, at shareholder level, the legal form of a sale of shares was upheld. Though this was not a necessary part of the reasoning of the Supreme Court (no tax avoidance was found) the Court seems to have accepted this approach, writing that there was nothing to prevent the limiting of the recharacterization to the effects on the tax provision of the company while at the same time carrying out the taxation of the capital gain on the shares according to the legal form under the ordinary rules; this was considered as seemingly inconsistent – implying that it was not inconsistent in reality – and a necessary effect of bringing the tax avoidance norm to work.[20] However, later in its reasoning, the Court referred to the fact that the tax authorities had to rely on its own interpretation of the rules in order to avoid double taxation[21] and saw this as an argument in favour of being careful in using the tax avoidance norm since that could create disturbances in a finely tuned set of rules, which would be unfortunate in view of the need for predictability in the field of taxation.[22]

This reasoning begs comment. Firstly, one may ask whether the approach of the tax authorities was in fact inconsistent. One alternative approach might have been to recharacterize the sale of shares as a transfer of the tax positions only, and thus not tax any capital gain on shareholder level. However, this could in turn create

---

20 In Norwegian: *"Jeg bemerker at det ikke kan være noe til hinder for på denne måte å begrense en gjennomskjæring til aksjeoverdragelsens virkninger for skattekredittene i et selskap og for øvrig behandle selskapet og aksjeoverdragelsen etter vanlige skatterettslige regler. En slik tilsynelatende inkonsekvens vil ofte være en nødvendig følge av at det foretas gjennomskjæring."*

The taxpayer contended that this approach would lead to double taxation in that the same income would be taxed both at company and shareholder level. However, according to the special capital gain computation rules which applied at the time, the tax liability of the company was taken into consideration when computing the capital gains on the shares at shareholder level. Thus, no double taxation would occur. However, in order to reach that result the tax authorities had to deviate somewhat from an interpretation of the rules established by the Minstry of Finance. In addition, the capital gain on the shares in this case was not taxable in Norway because the seller was a resident of the Netherlands and the tax treaty did not allow Norway to tax that gain. However, the parties agreed that this special feature of the case should not have any impact on the rationale.

21 As explained in the preceding footnote.

22 In Norwegian: *"Den fremgangsmåte som ligningsmyndighetene her har benyttet, illustrerer problemer som generelt knytter seg til en gjennomskjæring på ulovfestet grunnlag. En slik gjennomskjæring vil ofte medføre forstyrrelser i et finmasket regelverk. Og særlig vil jeg peke på de betydelig vansker borgerne får med å forutse de skattemessige virkninger av ulike privatrettslige disposisjoner. Dette er viktige hensyn på skatterettens område, ..."*

other problems, in particular that the capital gain on the shares might exceed the tax provisions, and there would probably be no legal basis for carrying over the seller's cost price of the shares to the buyer in order to realize that gain on a later sale.[23] Another approach could be to regard the sale of shares as a sale of parts in a partnership. However, that would be difficult because of the long practice of not using the anti-avoidance norm to pierce the corporate veil as such. In addition, the applicable share capital gains rules (abolished in 1992) did in fact take the company's tax positions into consideration in a way somewhat similar to the rules concerning capital gains on parts in partnerships. Therefore, the approach actually taken was perhaps not so inconsistent after all; in fact, the Supreme Court itself describes it as "seemingly" inconsistent. More generally, the decision may be understood to be based on a view that the recharacterization should apply only to the taxpayer in question and not to other taxpayers (here, the company and not the shareholders). This view has some support in other cases as well.[24]

Secondly, one may question the implication of the Supreme Court's statement that a consistent approach could create disorder in the finely tuned rules. One should think that, on the contrary, a consistent approach would be more predictable than a non-consistent approach. However, as illustrated below, a consistent approach may in some cases result in unreasonably heavy taxation and may for that reason be non-recommendable.

Thirdly, the general observation of the Court concerning the exercise of caution when applying the tax avoidance norm has only to a very limited extent been reflected in later cases. For instance, Rt. 2008 p. 1520 *Conoco* – in which the Supreme Court admittedly found no tax avoidance – concerned the allocation of a debt claim to a mother company (which was subject to the petroleum tax) or its subsidiary (which was not). The taxpayer argued that allocating the claim to the subsidiary, as the tax authorities had done, would have several private and company law consequences and would create some problems. However, such arguments were bluntly rejected by the Supreme Court, which stated that possible difficulties resulting from a recharacterization could of course not be taken into regard when deciding the tax avoidance ques-

23 In this particular case, such carry-over of the tax base would result in the gain being taxable in Norway after all because the buyer of the shares was a resident of Norway.

24 The *Øverby* case discussed below.

tion.[25] Besides being difficult to harmonize with the Supreme Court's view in *Zenith* it is, more generally speaking, highly questionable as to whether it is correct to disregard such effects when deciding which legal alternative should prevail.

One of the main possible inconsistencies which may occur is double taxation. This issue was touched upon in *Skau and Gundersen.* As described above, the Supreme Court reasoned that the provision of group distributions from M AS to SG Holding was the tax-triggering event. This probably explains why the Court stated that a taxation of the shareholders under the tax avoidance norm must have consequences for the tax assessment of SG Holding which in fact had been taxed for the group contributions.[26] However, one may ask whether taxation both of the shareholders (for money paid to them) and the receiving company (for the group contribution) amounts to an unacceptable double taxation. In my opinion, the answer is no. The taxation of SG Holding for the received group contributions is levelled out by the deduction for the same contributions granted to M AS. Therefore, the companies seen together had not incurred any taxation because of the contribution. The situation is not different from a case in which the necessary group contributions had been provided from M AS to SG Holding *before* the money had been paid to the shareholders. The latter creates no double taxation. Thus, the Supreme Court was wrong in assuming that a recharacterization must have had consequences for tax assessment of the company.

Whereas the most common collateral income tax effect is a possible double taxation (in which case it should be relieved), other unfavourable effects may also be triggered. In *Dillerud,* the recharacterization resulted in very severe tax effects; in fact, this was to some extent the purpose of the tax authorities in the first place. The effect of allocating a salary for 16 days work to Mr. Dillerud was that he and his wife were entitled to more than two-thirds of the income from the company which, in turn, triggered the top tax and employee social security contribution.[27]

---

25 In Norwegian: *"Eventuelle vanskar på desse punkta som følgje av gjennomskjæring, kan naturligvis ikkje ha innverknad på vurdering av om det skal skje gjennomskjæring."*

26 In Norwegian: *"Men dette (dvs. skattlegging av aksjonærene) måtte i tilfelle få konsekvenser for ligningen av holdingselskapene."*

27 Whereas the initial allocation of salary to Mr. Dillerud amounted to NOK 200,000, this allocation in turn triggered a so-called personal income – which is the basis for calculating the top tax and social security contribution – of no less than NOK 1,155,942. In addition, because he had not informed the tax office of his salary-free work for the partnership, a 30 % penalty tax was added!

As already indicated, tax authorities obviously refrain from extending the recharacterization to another, although related, taxpayer. An illustrative example is Rt. 1999 p. 1347 *Øverby.* In that case, the tax assessment of shareholders who had acquired claims on their company from the bank at a low price was based on the view that the bank had relinquished the debts on the condition that a certain amount was paid to it from the shareholders of the debtor company.[28] Based on this view, the company should in principle have been denied the right to carry forward its losses.[29] However, it appears from the premises of the decision of the District Court that the recharacterization of the transaction on shareholder level was not carried through on company level; thus, the company was allowed to carry forward its losses.[30]

The most far-reaching case concerning collateral simultaneous effects – admittedly in a somewhat different direction – is Rt. 1999 p. 946 *ABB.* The facts of this case are essentially similar to *Zenith* but the transaction lacked reality to such an extent that the Supreme Court found that it amounted to tax avoidance. The follow-up question was whether the seller of the shares (the mother company) was liable for the calculated company taxes of the subsidiary under a statute rule holding shareholders liable for the company's taxes when the company has been liquidated without its taxes having been paid.[31] The majority of the Court (four of five judges) found that the recharacterization of the transaction implied that the identity of the company was altered to such an extent that it could have been taxed as if it had been liquidated according to company law. Therefore, the basic requirement under the liability rule that the company had been dissolved[32] was met. In my opinion, this case stretches the effects of the recharacterization too far. It was not only a question of consistent application of the recharacterized transaction in relation to other income tax rules, but also a very free interpretation of the wording of the statute rule in question concerning the liability to pay the taxes, which is almost a private law effect.[33]

---

28 This recharacterization had the effect that later payment from the company to the shareholders as partial payment on the loan (which would have been tax-free) was considered as taxable dividends. However, the Supreme Court did not accept that recharacterization.

29 GTA sec. 14-6.

30 See Utv. 1999 p. 864 at p. 865.

31 General Tax Act 1911 sec. 32, now Tax Payment Act of 17 June 2005 no. 67 sec. 16–13.

32 In Norwegian: *"oppløst".*

33 Banoun, who discusses this case at length op. cit. at p. 162 et seq., argues that the result of the case, rather than its premises, could be defended if the recharacterization of the initial transaction is also carried through on the level of the selling shareholder, who in fact was the primary beneficiary of the transaction.

A seemingly unsolved issue arises in relation to tax rules which require a disposition to be "legal" for the taxpayer to benefit from a certain favourable tax rule. For instance, in order to benefit from the so-called shielding allowance in dividends the distribution has to be legal.[34] If, as for instance in *Hovda* and in *Skau and Gundersen,* a sale of shares is disregarded and the consideration received by the seller is therefore recharacterized as dividends, the question arises as to whether this "distribution" is "legal" under the shielding allowance rules. The "distribution" has typically not been decided under the procedural rules for dividends, and the "distribution" may in addition exceed the company law limitations for dividend distributions. However, when regarded as a sale of shares, the transaction may be perfectly legal under company and private law rules. The question is whether the legality requirement can be applied to the recharacterized transaction (dividends) or whether it should be applied to the transaction according to its legal form (sale of shares). Even though *ABB* may seem to lend some support to the first mentioned approach, that decision should, as indicated above, be narrowly interpreted and should therefore not be followed by analogy. Applying the legality requirement to the recharacterized transaction may lead to unreasonable results not least because it may be impossible for the taxpayer to fulfil the private law requirements for two types of transactions at the same time.[35] Thus, the best arguments seem to be in favour of applying the legality requirement to the formal transaction only. This is supported by the fact that the rationale of the legality requirement is weak.[36]

---

34 In Norwegian: *"lovlig"*, see GTA sec. 10–12. The shielding allowance is calculated as a percentage of the taxpayer's cost price of the shares and should reflect a risk-free return on the investment. The policy idea is to tax dividends within those limits in a similar way as interest income (no economic double taxation) in order to create a certain degree of neutrality between loan and equity investments.

35 The issue was discussed neither in *Hovda* nor in *Skau and Gundersen,* probably because there was no relief in the tax effect at shareholder level at the time in question (during the 1980s); the legality requirement was at that time attached to a right to a deduction within certain limits on company level. But taxation of the company was not part of the court cases.

36 See for instance Zimmer, Har vi bruk for lovlighetsvilkåret? in *Skatterett* 2008 p. 1.

4. Subsequent collateral income tax effects

In many cases, there will be no question of subsequent income tax effects of the recharacterization. For instance, if the right to carry-forward of losses is rejected then that loss is lost forever. The same applies to the rejection of postponement of capital gains.[37]

In other cases it is clear that the recharacterized transaction shall not apply to future income taxation because the tax effects are derived from the private law position – which is not affected by the recharacterization for tax purposes. This is, for instance, the case when a sale of shares has been disregarded because the seller still controls them. Thus, in a case like *Skau and Gundersen,* for instance, it must be clear that a future sale of the shares is done by the buyer of the shares (in case SG Holding) and not by its shareholders even if the sale of the shares was disregarded under the tax avoidance rule.

Cases are not always so straightforward, however. Assume for instance, as the tax authorities did in *Conoco,* that an item of income should be allocated to the mother company and not the subsidiary which would follow from the legal form. Nevertheless, the income is received by the subsidiary. What happens if and when the subsidiary distributes this income to the mother company as dividends? If the mother company is taxed for the dividends it may be claimed to be a double taxation because that company has already been taxed for the income that is distributed. However, it can be argued that such double taxation is in line with the general double taxation of company profits: if the legal form had been followed, the subsidiary would have been taxed for the income, and the distribution would have been taxable in the hands of the mother company.[38]

Whenever a deduction for capital losses is rejected under sales within a group of companies, an important question is whether the loss can instead be deducted at a later stage. The rationale for not accepting a loss deduction at the time of the intra-group sale is that the seller still controls the sold shares through its ownership of the buying company. Therefore, it may be argued that the loss should be

37 As mentioned above, these two effects are regulated – for companies – in GTA sec. 14–90.

38 Under the current exemption system, corporate shareholders, as a main rule, are exempt from tax on share income (dividends and capital gains on shares), GTA sec. 2–38. However, 3 % of the income is taxable as is income from shares in companies resident in low tax states and from portfolio investments in companies resident in states outside the EEA area.

deductible when such control disappears, typically when the shares are sold out of the group. There seems to be no legal basis to justify keeping such a possible "latent deductible loss" as a separate legal item. The question is rather whether the loss can be added to the cost price of the shares and therefore be reflected in the gain/loss calculated when the shares are sold out of the group. In a related situation – in cases of writing share capital down combined with a simultaneous subscription for new share capital by the same shareholders – tax authorities and the Supreme Court assume that the loss on the shares which was written down cannot be deducted but should be added to the cost price of the new shares.[39] The same view seems to be held by tax authorities in cases of intra-group sale of shares. However, in these cases an additional question is whether the loss should be added to the seller's shares in the acquiring company or to the acquiring company's shares in the acquired company. Tax practice seems to favour the first mentioned solution.[40] The logic of that solution may be questioned because it seems to imply that the loss can be deducted only when the shares in the acquiring company are sold and not when the acquired company is sold out of the group, even if the loss was attached to the shares of the acquired company.[41] However, an argument in favour of that practice is that the deductible loss will be allocated to the same company which sold the shares at a loss in the first place.

5. Effects on other taxes (inheritance tax, wealth tax)

As for wealth tax effects it must be clear that these are derived from the private law relations and not from the recharacterized relation. For instance, if sale of shares is disregarded for income tax purposes the sale shall nevertheless be taken into consideration when deciding the allocation of assets to taxpayers for wealth tax purposes. In cross ownership cases, for instance, in which the mutual sale of

39 Rt. 1998 p. 1425 *Troll Salmon* and Rt. 2001 p. 170 *Espeland.*

40 See Rt. 2002 p. 456 *Hydro Canada* where it emerges from the minority vote that the tax authorities had accepted that the loss on the sold shares (in the Canadian subsidiary) should be added to the seller's (Norsk Hydro's) cost price on the shares of the acquiring company (the Danish subsidiary). The same emerges from the premises of the appeals court case in Utv. 2009 p. 245 *Ementor.*

41 Thus, in *Hydro Canada,* a sale by the Danish subsidiary of the shares in a Canadian sub-subsidiary would not trigger the right to deduct the loss in question; a sale by Norsk Hydro of the shares in the Danish subsidiary would be required.

shares was disregarded for income tax purposes,[42] the sold shares should nevertheless be regarded as owned by the buyer of the shares for wealth tax purposes.

The relation to the inheritance tax has been raised primarily in step transaction cases in which children have been the intermediate link. Even if the transaction is recharacterized to mean a sale directly from the parent to the third person, the fact remains that the money has ended up with the children. This will, of course, trigger inheritance tax. But should the inheritance tax be calculated based on the private law transaction (which means that the *asset* in question is received) or based on the recharacterized transaction (which means that the parent has received consideration for the sale of the asset and passed the money on to the children)? Because assets are often valued for inheritance purposes significantly below their market price, this question is important.[43] The tax administration's view is that the inheritance tax treatment should not be affected by the recharacterization for income tax purposes, which means that the children must be considered as having received the asset in question.[44] This view should be endorsed, since the inheritance tax effects should be derived from the private law positions.

A follow-up question derives from the fact that the children have received all the money whereas the parent in question nevertheless will have to pay the income tax on the capital gain. Therefore, based on the recharacterized transaction it could be argued that the children should be considered as having received the consideration, less the tax on the capital gain. However, the fact remains that they have received the whole consideration and there is no reason why they should not pay inheritance tax on that, even though the parent's income after tax is lower. However, in practice a deduction has been allowed if the children pay an amount to the parent to cover the income tax on the capital gain.[45]

6. Concluding remarks

This brief study shows that the use of the tax avoidance norm usually means that the tax assessment is based on a recharacterized transaction which reflects the

42 See *Wisth & Finnøy*, *Essem* and *Hex* (see references in footnote 18).

43 This is most important for non-listed shares; see Inheritance Tax Act of 19. June 1964 no. 14 sec. 11 A.

44 See Ministry of Finance in Utv. 2004 p. 535.

45 See preceding footnote.

economic reality of the transaction. It is argued that the tax assessment in tax avoidance situations should always be based on a recharacterized transaction, except where (liberal) statute interpretation is possible.

Further, possible double taxation resulting from the recharacterization should be avoided. However, the study shows that what may sometimes appear to be double taxation does not always amount to that in reality. As a main rule, other income tax consequences – simultaneous or subsequent – should primarily be pursued, at least for the same taxpayer. On the other hand, the recharacterization for income tax purposes should, in general, not be used for wealth tax or inheritance tax purposes.

Bibliography, Erling Eide

compiled by Hilde Westbye

1968

KRONIKK Yrkesetikk og samfunnskritikk ved universitetene. IN: Aftenposten. 18.06 1968. p. 4.

1969

Bør vi ta den økonomiske langtidsplanlegging alvorlig? IN:Tenkegruppe 99: Fremtiden utfordrer politikerne. Fridtjof Frank Gundersen (ed.) 1969.

En metode for konstruksjon av aggregerte korttids produktfunksjoner illustrert med data for den norske tankflåte. Oslo, 1969. (Memorandum (Universitetet i Oslo. Sosialøkonomisk institutt); no. 1969-5-6).

Verdier og fakta i sosialøkonomien. IN: Sosialøkonomen 3 (1969) pp. 32–36.

1970

A note on residuals management decisions. Oslo, 1970. (Memorandum (Universitetet i Oslo. Sosialøkonomisk institutt); no. 1970-12-1).

Er det perspektiv over perspektivanalysene? IN: Minervas Kvartalsskrift 2 (1970) pp. 145–151.

1971

A note on residuals management decisions. IN: Sosialøkonomen (1971) pp. 20–23.

Vår teknologiske fremtid – kan den utforskes? IN: Bergens Privatbanks Kvartalsskrift 4 (1971) pp. 235–249.

1972

EF og miljøvernet. IN: Morgenbladet. 23.05 1972. p. 3.

Liberalkonservativt miljøvern i EF. IN: Morgenbladet. 02.06 1972. p. 3.

Miljøvern, kapitalisme og EF. IN: Morgenbladet. 01.07 1972. p. 2.

Natur- og miljøvern som argument for EF. IN: Norsk natur 3 (1972) pp. XXIX–XXXII.

Økonomisk vekst og "livsstandard". IN: Norges Industri 21 (1972) pp. 22–23.

1973

En kritisk kommentar til Kolstads artikkel – "Planlegging og ledelse i fremtidssamfunnets bedrifter". IN: Norges Industri 19 (1973) pp. 21–23.

Hvordan skal statens oljeinntekter anvendes. IN: Norges Industri 7 (1973) pp. 23–24.

Virkninger av statens oljeinntekter på norsk økonomi. IN: Sosialøkonomen 10 (1973) pp. 12–21.

1974

Do new factories embody potential best practice technology? Oslo, 1974. (Memorandum (Universitetet i Oslo. Sosialøkonomisk institutt); no. 1974-5-7).

Den seiglivede kapitalismen IN: Kapitalismen: en diskusjon om teori og praksis. 1974, pp. 51–56.

Den seiglivete kapitalismen. IN: Norges Industri 2 (1974) p. 19.

Det kapitalistiske system i praksis IN: Kapitalismen: en diskusjon om teori og praksis. 1974, pp. 25–39.

Hvilke virkninger vil oljeinntektene få for vår nasjonale økonomi? IN: Bergens Privatbanks Kvartalsskrift 2 (1974) pp. 103–119.

1975

Prinsippielt om virkningen av petroleumsinntekene på vår økonomi. NTH. Seminar om "Olje og miljø". Trondheim, 1975.

Målsetninger og virkemidler i miljøvernpolitkken. IN: Minervas Kvartalsskrift 1 (1975) pp. 7–23.

1976

Do new factories embody potential best practice technology? IN: Empirical Economics 2 (1976) pp. 119–127.

Anmeldelse: Nasjonalregnskap, modeller og analyse. En artikkelsamling til Odd Aukrusts 60-årsdag (Oslo, 1975). IN: Sosialøkonomen 8 (1976) pp. 30–31.

Konstruktøren alene utformer ikke morgendagens skip. IN: Ajour 2 (1976) pp. 51–52.

1978

Engineering production and cost functions for tankers – Doctoral thesis. Universitetet i Oslo, 1979. Oslo, 1978.

Takk til NRK. IN: Aftenposten Morgen. 08.05 1978. p. 2.

1979

Engineering production and cost functions for tankers. Amsterdam, 1979.

The concept of production factors in ship design. IN: Advances in marine technology: proceedings: papers presented at the International Symposium on Advances in Marine Technology held in June 1979 at the Norwegian Institute of Technology. Stian Erichsen et al. (eds.). Trondheim, 1979, pp. 91–110.

1980

Aktuelle spørsmål i norsk oljepolitikk i lys av økonomisk teori. IN: Sosialøkonomen 3 (1980) pp. 12–18.

Om slektskapet mellom spillteori og teori for kollektive beslutninger. Oslo, 1980. (Memorandum (Universitetet i Oslo. Sosialøkonomisk institutt); no. 1980-4-30).

1981

Kritikk av noen forutsetninger i Kriminalmeldingen. IN: Lov og rett 6 (1981) pp. 312–323.

Petroleumsøkonomiske notater. Oslo, 1981. (Marius / Sjørettsfondet; no. 66).

Anmeldelse: Economic models of criminal behavior, Heineke J.M. (ed.)(Amsterdam, 1978). IN: Economic Journal 362 (1981) pp. 584–585.

Anmeldelse: Ekonomi och rättssystem, Lars Werin (Stockholm, 1979). IN: Tidsskrift for rettsvitenskap 5 (1981) pp. 752–754.

1982

Kapitaliseringsrente ved personskadeerstatning. IN: Lov og rett 1 (1982) pp. 30–42.

Anmeldelse: Studies in shipping economics : in honour of professor Arnljot Strømme Svendsen, Einar Hope (ed.) (Oslo, 1981). IN: Statsøkonomisk tidsskrift (1982) pp. 149–151.

1983

Organisasjonene – gruppemakt mot fellesskap. IN: Norges industri 15 (1983) pp. 14–16.

Realbeskatning og nominalismen i norsk rett. IN: Sosialøkonomen 6 (1983) pp. 5–6, 10.

De høye festeavgiftene. IN: Aftenposten Morgen. 05.10 1983. p. 20.

Odd Eidem og dødsstraffen. IN: Aftenposten Morgen. 20.07 1983. p. 6.

1984

Hva er det offentliges oppgaver i fremtiden, og hvordan skal de finansieres? IN: Sosialøkonomen 11 (1984) pp. 48–49.

Renter og verdisikring av pengekrav. IN: Tidsskrift for rettsvitenskap 5 (1984) pp. 477–533.

Anmeldelse: Marknadens villkor, Göran Skogh (Lund, 1982). IN: Tidsskrift for rettsvitenskap 3 (1984) pp. 318–319.

Anmeldelse: Økonomer om samfundet. Fra Adam Smith til Milton Friedman, Henrik Preben Perregaard (Copenhagen, 1982). IN: Lov og rett 1 (1984) pp. 60–61.

1985

Myndighetenes holdning til prisveiledning. IN: Aftenposten Morgen. 12.07 1985. p. 10.

Kvalitetskrav, konkurransepolitikk og forbrukerpolitikk. IN: Fakta om norske husholdningers bruk av tid og penger. Oslo, 1985, pp. 22–29.

1986

Anmeldelse: Skatt og skade, Nils Nygaard (Bergen, 1985). IN: Tidsskrift for rettsvitenskap 5 (1986) pp. 708–712.
Fusjonskontroll i Norge? IN: Kvartalsskrift / Bergen bank 2 (1986) pp. 54–60.

1987

Ekspropriasjonserstatning i en inflasjonstid – valg av kapitaliseringsrente. IN: Lov og rett 3 (1987) pp. 165–177.

1988

Gode grunner for resultatdeling. IN: Kvartalsskrift / Bergen bank 3 (1988) pp. 65–70.
Skatteøkning koster flesk. IN: Dagens Næringsliv Morgen. 14.10 1988. p. 6.

1990

Veiledning i besvarelse av oppgaver i sosialøkonomi. Co-author: Vidar Ringstad. Oslo, 1990. (Stensilserie (Universitetet i Oslo. Institutt for privatrett) / Serie B; no. 7).
Anmeldelse: Ekonomiordbok : Engelsk-svensk fackordbok för ekonomifunktionen; Svensk-engelsk fackordbok för ekonomifunktionen, N F Edström, L A Samuelson, O K Böök(Lund, 1988). IN: Tidsskrift for rettsvitenskap 1/2 (1990) p. 198.
Økonomiske tiltak. Logikk som opium. IN: Aftenposten Morgen. 22.11 1990. p. 13.

1991

A criminometric study using panel data and latent variables. Co-authors: Jørgen Aasness og Terje Skjerpen. Oslo, 1992. (Discussion paper (Statistisk sentralbyrå); no. 74).

Regnefeil øker krisen? IN: Dagens Næringsliv Morgen. 14.12 1991. p. 47.

1992

Rettsøkonomi – en introduksjon. IN: Jussens venner 4 (1992) pp. 193–224.

Misvisende om renter. IN: Dagens Næringsliv Morgen. 13.03 1992. p. 27.

Regnefeil ga bankkrise? IN: Dagens Næringsliv Morgen. 16.01 1992. p. 7.

Regnefeil øker faktisk bankkrisen – Medforfattere: John G.S. Meldgaard og Thorleif Engelsen. IN: Dagens Næringsliv Morgen. 10.02 1992. p. 2.

Regnefeilen og banktapene. IN: Dagens Næringsliv Morgen. 25.02 1992. p. 2.

1993

A criminometric study using panel data and latent variables. Co-authors: Jørgen Aasness og Terje Skjerpen. Oslo, 1993. (Rapport (Forskning om økonomisk kriminalitet (program)); no. 3).

Criminometrics, latent variables, and panel data IN: Statistical modelling and latent variables. K. Haagen, D.J. Bartholomew, M. Deistler (eds.). Co-authors: Jørgen Aasness og Terje Skjerpen. Amsterdam, 1993.

1994

Criminometrics, latent variables, panel data, and different types of crime. Co-authors: Jørgen Aasness og Terje Skjerpen. Oslo, 1994. (Discussion papers (Statistisk sentralbyrå. Forskningsavdelingen); no. 124).

Economics of crime : deterrence and the rational offender. In cooperation with Jørgen Aasness og Terje Skjerpen. Amsterdam, 1994. (Contributions to economic analysis; no. 227).

Kriminaløkonomi. Stavanger, 1994.

Fakultært forskerutdanningsseminar i rettsvitenskap 4/1994 : rettsøkonomi, Voksenåsen 8. til 9. desember 1994. Erling Eide and Endre Stavang (ed). Oslo, 1994.

Veiledning i besvarelse av oppgaver i sosialøkonomi. Co-author: Vidar Ringstad.

Oslo, 1994. (Stensilserie (Universitetet i Oslo. Institutt for privatrett) / Serie B; no. 14).

1995

Accident liability with weighting of probabilities. Oslo, 1995. (Stensilserie (Universitetet i Oslo. Institutt for privatrett) / C. Working paper law and economics; no. 2).

Kapitaliseringsrenten – ny episode. IN: Lov og rett 5/6 (1995) pp. 351–358.

RDEU models of crime. Oslo, 1995. (Stensilserie (Universitetet i Oslo. Institutt for privatrett) / C. Working paper law and economics; no. 1).

Valg av investeringsobjekt for erstatningsbeløp. IN: Lov og rett 1 (1995) pp. 58–64.

Anmeldelse: Økonomi for jurister, Trond Eklund, Knut Knutsen, Aage Sending (Oslo, 1994). IN: Lov og rett 2 (1995) pp. 146–147.

1996

Law and economics of the environment. Erling Eide and Roger J. van den Bergh (ed). Oslo, 1996.

Economics of criminal behavior- survey and bibliography. Oslo, 1996. (Stensilserie (Universitetet i Oslo. Institutt for privatrett) / C. Working paper law and economics; no. 5).

Hvorfor anta at lovbrytere er rasjonelle? IN: Lov og rett 9 (1996) pp. 579–588.

Rettsøkonomi for offentlig rett. Oslo, 1996. (Stensilserie (Universitetet i Oslo. Institutt for privatrett) / Serie B; no. 20).

Rettsøkonomi, rasjonell adferd og reelle hensyn. IN: Veien mot rettsstudiet. Oslo, 1996.

Anmeldelse: Legal realism and economics as behaviour : a Scandinavian look at economic analysis of law, A.C. Stray Ryssdal (Oslo, 1995). IN: Lov og rett 7 (1996) pp. 464–467.

Minnepris i økonomi. Aftenposten overdriver forskjell IN: Aftenposten Morgen. 15.10 1996. p. 15.

1997

The Economics of Crime: Main Problems and Some Solutions. IN: Nordic Journal of Political Economy 1 (1997) pp. 65–77.

Rettsøkonomi for offentlig rett. 2. ed. Oslo, 1997.

1998

Løsninger på miljøproblemer: Reguleringer, avgifter og erstatningsrett. IN: Markeder, ressurser og fordeling: artikler i anvendt økonomi. Asbjørn Rødseth og Christian Riis (eds.). Oslo, 1998, pp. 81–102.

Fordeler og ulemper ved åpenhet i forvaltningen. IN: Åpne dører: venneskrift til Astrid Gjertsen på 70-års-dagen 14. september 1998. Georg Apenes et al. (eds.). Fredrikstad, 1998, pp. 85–89.

KRONIKK. Riksadvokatens forskningsproblem. IN: Aftenposten Morgen. 05.03 1998. p. 23.

1999

Rettsøkonomi. Co-author: Endre Stavang. Oslo, 1999. (Stensilserie (Universitetet i Oslo. Institutt for privatrett) / Serie B; no. 22).

Rettsøkonomi for offentlig rett. 3. ed. Oslo, 1999.

Rettsøkonomi, Del 4, Økonomisk analyse av tingsrett. Oslo, 1999. (Stensilserie (Universitetet i Oslo. Institutt for privatrett) / Serie B; no. 24).

Hvordan virker sanksjoner? IN: Konkurranse 3 (1999) pp. 10–12.

Kriminaløkonomi – De ukjente studier av almenprevensjon. IN: Tidsskrift for rettsvitenskap 1/2 (1999) pp. 77–119.

Intellektuell abdikasjon. IN: Aftenposten Morgen. 18.06 1999. p. 14.

Ubegrunnet om Kosovo fra UiO. IN: Aftenposten Morgen. 30.05 1999. p. 9.

Narkotikakrigens høye pris. IN: Dagsavisen. 25.02 1999. p. 2.

2000

Economics of Criminal Behavior. IN: Encyclopedia of Law & Economics. (5. vol). Cheltenham, 2000, pp. 345–389.

Law & economics in Norway. IN: Encyclopedia of Law & Economics. (1. vol). Cheltenham, 2000, pp. 309–312.

Oversikt over litteratur om svart arbeid og skatteunndragelser. Oslo, 2000. (Rapport (Frischsenteret); no. 6/2000).

KORT SAGT. Homofile og kirken. IN: Aftenposten Morgen. 27.03 2000. p. 17.

2001

Rank dependent expected utility models of tax evasion. Torino, 2001. (Working paper, International Centre for Economic Research; no. 27/2001).

Rettsøkonomi : analyse for privatrett og miljørett. Co-author: Endre Stavang. Oslo, 2001.

2002

Engineering Production Functions for Tankers. IN: Microeconometrics of Production: Norwegian Contributions. Oslo, 2002, pp. 230–248.

Optimal provision of public goods with rank dependent expected utility. Oslo, 2002. (Memorandum (Universitetet i Oslo. Økonomisk institutt); no. 3/2003).

Politikernes – ikke politikkens – tilbaketrekning. IN: Nytt norsk tidsskrift 2 (2002) pp. 213–215.

Rettsøkonomi – status med eksempler. IN: Økonomisk forum 1 (2002) pp. 22–29.

Rettsøkonomi for offentlig rett. 4. ed. Oslo, 2002.

Rettsøkonomiens lysende fortid og utfordrende fremtid. Refleksjoner omkring en encyclopedi. IN: Rettsteori og rettsliv – Festskrift til Carsten Smith til 70-årsdagen 13. juli 2002. Oslo, 2002.

Sterk reduksjon til forskningen. IN: Aftenposten Morgen. 11.05 2002. p. 9.

2003

Optimal provision of public goods with rank dependent expected utility. IN: Public Finance/Finances Publiques 3–4 (2003) pp. 296–311.

En enkel dynamisk modell for skatteunndragelse med normer og rasjonell adferd. Oslo, 2003. (Rapport (Frischsenteret); no. 1/2003).

Streng straf mindsker kriminaliteten. IN: Politiken. 02.06 2003. p. 5.

2004

Recent developments in Economics of Crime. Berkeley, 2004. (German Working Papers in Law and Economics; no. 8).

Inflasjonskompensasjon i festeavtaler. HR-2004-00218A. IN: Nytt i privatretten : nyhetsbrev for informasjon på det privatrettslige område 2 (2004) pp. 10–11.

Anmeldelse: Economic Behavior and Legal Institutions: An Introductory Survey, Lars Werin (New Jersey, 2003). IN: The Scandinavian Journal of Economics 4 (2004) pp. 823–825.

Misforståelser om kriminalitetens kostnader. IN: Morgenbladet. 09.07-15.07 2004. p. 21.

2005

Rettsøkonomi 1. Co-author: Endre Stavang. Oslo, 2005.

Anmeldelse: Konkurrence mellem retssystemer: Delaware-effekten i et europæisk selskabsretligt perspektiv, Hanne Søndergaard Birkmose (Copenhagen, 2004). IN: Tidsskrift for rettsvitenskap 1/2 (2005) pp. 188–192.

Anmeldelse: Økonomiske incitamenter og markeder: i offentlig organisation og regulering, Kirsten Bregn (ed.) (Copenhagen, 2003). IN: Tidsskrift for rettsvitenskap 1/2 (2005) pp. 194–198.

Homofil krusning på opprørt hav. IN: Aftenposten Morgen. 28.08 2005. p. 5.

Høyres prinsipper i bispesaken. IN: Aftenposten Aften. 25.02 2005. p. 27.

2006

Economics of crime. Co-authors: Paul H. Rubin og Joanna M. Shepherd. Boston, 2006.

2007

Accident Liability with Rank dependence. IN: Kritische Vierteljahresschrift für Gesetzgebung und Rechtswissenschaft 1/2 (2007) pp. 160–171.

Rettsøkonomiske analyser av tingsrett og beslektede emner. Co-author: Endre Stavang. Oslo, 2007. (Stensilserie (Universitetet i Oslo. Institutt for privatrett) / Serie B; no. 40).

Retting eller omlevering – hva er mest forbrukervennlig? IN: Lov og rett nr. 5 (2007) pp. 283–300.

Straff virker – på andre. IN: Aftenposten Morgen. 06.02 2007. p. 3.

Kunst for oljepengene! IN: Morgenbladet. 23.02–01.03 2007. p. 21.

2008

Rettsøkonomi. Co-author: Endre Stavang. Oslo, 2008.

Kapitaliseringsrenten som juristskapt virkelighet. IN: Nytt i privatretten : nyhetsbrev for informasjon på det privatrettslige område 2 (2008) p. 15.

Omsorg fra rettslige foreldre. IN: Aftenposten Morgen. 29.02 2008. p. 4.

Holdninger er kraftig endret. IN: Aftenposten Morgen. 18.02 2008. p. 3.

2009

Revelation of tax evasion by random audits report on main project, part 1. Co-authors: Harald Goldstein, Paul Gunnar Larssen og Jack-Willy Olsen. Oslo, 2009. (Rapport (Frischsenteret); no. 1/2009).

Is the consumer directive advantageous for the consumers? IN: European Journal of Law and Economics 3 (2009) pp. 289–307.

Notat om plikt til å utarbeide tilstandsrapport. IN: NOU 2009:6 Tilstandsrapport ved salg av bolig. 2009, pp. 172–184.

Lovarbeid i svensk rett. Nya ersättningsbestämmelser i expropriationslagen m.m. : slutbetänkande. SOU 2008:99. IN: Nytt i privatretten : nyhetsbrev for informasjon på det privatrettslige område 1 (2009) p. 19.

Anmeldelse: Konkurranserett : en strategisk og rettsøkonomisk tilnærming, Peder Østbye (Bergen, 2008). IN: Tidsskrift for rettsvitenskap 1 (2009) pp. 162–164.

Snåsamann mot kolikksmerter. IN: Aftenposten Morgen. 30.01 2009. p. 5.

Kolikkbarn og regneferdigheter. IN: Aftenposten Morgen. 11.02 2009.

2010

Revelation of tax evasion by random audits report on main project, part 2. Co-authors: Anders Berset, Harald Goldstein, Paul Gunnar Larssen and Jack-Willy Olsen. Oslo, 2010. (Rapport (Frischsenteret); no. 1/2010).

Contributors

Bettina Banoun is a partner in the Oslo-based law firm Wiersholm and a specialist in tax law, litigation, company law and EEA law. She has a Ph.D. in tax law from the University of Oslo and is the author of several articles regarding tax law.

Roger Bowles is Professor of Economics at the University of York and Director of the Centre for Criminal Justice Economics and Psychology. His principal area of interest is the application of economics to crime and the criminal justice system. He is currently managing two major projects, namely Mainstreaming Methodology for Estimating the Costs of Crime and a Prevention Cohort Study.

Hans Chr. Bugge is Professor of Environmental Law at the Department of Public and International Law, University of Oslo. He holds a doctorate in regional planning from the University of Paris II (Doctorat de spécialité) and is dr.juris from Oslo University having written a thesis on responsibility for pollution in Norwegian law. He has written several books and a number of articles in the field of environmental law and sustainable development.

Robert Cooter, a pioneer in the field of law and economics, has a Ph.D. in economics from Harvard and is Professor of Law at Berkeley Law School. He is one of the founders of the American Law and Economics Association and served from 1994 to 1995 as its president. Cooter has published widely on private law, constitutional law and economics, and law and economic development.

Jon Elster is Robert K. Merton Professor of Social Sciences at Columbia University (Political Science) and Professor at Collège de France. His research interests include the theory of rational choice, the theory of distributive justice and the history of social thought (Marx and de Tocqueville).

Henrik Lando is Professor of Law and Economics at Copenhagen Business School. His interests fall within the field of economic analysis of law, mainly contract, tort and criminal law, and rules of evidence; his background in the field of economics is in contract and incentive theory and in the theory of the firm. His main area of research currently lies in contract law and economics, and in contract practices of firms.

Kalle Määttä is a Professor of Legal Economics at the University of Joensuu in Finland. His expertise is in the areas of environmental and energy taxes, environmental policy and economics, and value added tax. His research interests are energy policy, criminal economics and legal economics.

Gunnar Nordén is a Research Fellow at the University of Oslo and a J.S.D. candidate at the Yale Law School. His main research interests lie in the intersection of law and economics and legal theory.

Anthony Ogus is Emeritus Professor, University of Manchester and Erasmus Professor of Fundamentals of Private Law, University of Rotterdam (part-time). He has published widely in the field of economic analysis of law, especially on the theory of regulation.

Leif Petter Olaussen is Associate Professor at the University of Oslo and has worked on a broad variety of topics within the field of Criminology and Sociology of Law, both on empirical topics and on the ontology and epistemology of criminological and sociology of law research.

Anders Ryssdal is a partner in the Oslo-based law firm Wiersholm and has more than 20 years of experience in litigation, arbitration, antitrust/competition and general corporate law. He holds an LL.M degree from Harvard Law School, a dr. juris degree (in law and economics) from the University of Oslo and has a substantial legal authorship.

Erik Røsæg is Professor of law at the University of Oslo (the Scandinavian Institute of Maritime Law). His main research areas are maritime law and third party interests in private law (including bankruptcy).

Hans-Bernd Schäfer is a pioneer in the field of law and economics in Germany and Europe. He is Professor at Bucerius Law School in Hamburg and was the director of the Institute of Law & Economics at Hamburg University and the director of the European Master Programme in Law & Economics for many years. His main areas of expertise are economic analysis of law and development economics.

Beate Sjåfjell is an Associate Professor at the University of Oslo (Department of Private Law), with a doctorate in EU company and securities law, in a sustainable development perspective. Her field of interest covers European company and financial market law, law and economics, general EU law, environmental law, human rights and labour law. She is the project leader for the research project "Sustainable Companies" (2010–2012).

Endre Stavang is Associate Professor at the University of Oslo (Department of Private Law) with property law as his main area of expertise.

Trine-Lise Wilhelmsen is Professor at the University of Oslo (Scandinavian Institute of Maritime Law) with maritime law and insurance law as her main fields.

Frederik Zimmer is Professor at the University of Oslo (Department of Public and International Law) with tax law as his main area of expertise.